FAITH IN THE NEIGHBORHOOD

UNDERSTANDING AMERICA'S RELIGIOUS DIVERSITY

VOLUME TWO

# Praying

FAITH IN THE NEIGHBORHOOD
UNDERSTANDING AMERICA'S RELIGIOUS DIVERSITY

VOLUME TWO

# Praying

LUCINDA MOSHER

Seabury Books
*An imprint of Church Publishing, Inc.*
*New York, New York*

*For Barrie*



A catalog record for this book is available from the Library of Congress.

ISBN: 1-59627-016-0

Printed in the United States of America.

*Church Publishing, Incorporated*
*445 Fifth Avenue*
*New York, New York 10016*
*www.churchpublishing.org*

# Table of Contents

# Acknowledgments

CYNTHIA SHATTUCK, my editor, thought up the idea of the *Faith in the Neighborhood* series, and decided that the second volume should be about rituals of faith. Without her brainstorm, her belief that I could execute it, and her subsequent firm guidance, there would have been no Book One—thus, certainly, no Book Two. And so, as with Book One, the first round of thanks is for her—and for everyone at Church Publishing who allowed this series to be.

The Trinity Grants Program at Trinity Church–St. Paul's Chapel (New York City), by virtue of its generous underwriting of the Neighbor-Faith Project (an educational initiative for Episcopal parishes which I conducted during 2003–2005, in collaboration with The Interfaith Center of New York), provided research support for Books One and Two of the *Faith in the Neighborhood* series. To both agencies and their officers, and to the Trinity Church Vestry, goes my deep appreciation—not just for the financial backing, but for enthusiasm and creative input as well.

The Rev. Daniel Appleyard, Dr. Claude Jacobs, and all who make the Worldviews Seminar happen each summer in Dearborn, Michigan, and allow me the privilege of being its instructor, have in no small way informed this series and this book. So, obviously, have the numerous people who participated in research conversations, and the leaders of the many religious institutions which have allowed (even encouraged) my many visits—and I dare not try to list them all for fear I would omit one or several of them! Research assistants for this volume include Millicent Browne, Alice Fisher, and Mark Furlow. To all of these people and to my patient team of conversation-transcribers go many thanks. Dr. Kusumita Priscilla Pedersen, Millicent Browne, and Deborah Davis read early drafts. This book is stronger for their many helpful suggestions.

I am grateful to the schools, colleges, universities, seminaries, and churches that have, during the past decade and a half, given me opportunities to teach about the world's religions, America's religious diversity, and a Christian theology of the neighbor. Each venue and each crop of students has helped me refine my ability to assess what it would be helpful for an empathetic visitor to know, and how to articulate this vast and complex material more clearly. I am grateful to the authors and producers of audio-visual aids whose works I have digested, whose ideas and ways of explaining things have so become a part of the way I teach. Where I have made good use of them, I do so with great respect and a deep sense of indebtedness. On the other hand, the responsibility for any factual or conceptual errors rests with me.

Finally, even more so than with Book One, there are no adequate words for the depth of gratitude due my partner in everything, who read drafts of this book more times than anyone, whose support for this project remains constant, very skilled, and unconditional: my husband, Barrie Mosher.

*Lucinda Mosher*
*Transfiguration 2005*

# Preface

"RELIGION" IS HARD to define, say religious studies specialists. There is no broadly agreed upon definition of the term, they'll tell us, but "we recognize it when we see it." And what do we see? We see rituals and practices—outward expressions of a tradition's beliefs and doctrines. These are key elements by which, as Byron Earhart puts it, a group of people seeks to "establish, maintain, and celebrate a meaningful world."[1]

We drive past our neighbors' places of worship, and we wonder: What do they do in that building? We have a chance to peer inside, and we wonder: Why do they bow before that statue? Why do they wave a stick of incense? When they go through those motions, what are they saying? What does it mean? We notice that a corner of our neighbors' living room seems to be set aside for devotional acts, and we wonder: Do they do something special every day? Do they call it "praying"? What rituals do our neighbors' faith demand of them? Even when those neighbors are quite literally right next door, we may be curious but far too polite to come right out and ask!

When we do ask questions about whether and how our neighbors of other religions "pray," we are actually asking as well about their cosmology: we are asking whether they believe in God, and if so, what they believe *about* God. We are asking whether they believe that the spiritual realm is simple or complex. If we find that they do not believe in God, we may wonder: At what, then, is their ritual directed, and why? In every case, we are asking how the exchange between the earthly, human realm and the realm of transcendence works. When we ask questions about our neighbors' devotional lives, we are also asking about how their religion conceives of the passage of time, how ritual and practice punctuate the day, the week, or the month, and when to wish them Happy New Year. We are also asking about how they assign extraordinary meaning to ordinary elements such as fire and water.

In this second volume of the series *Faith in the Neighborhood,* we will get acquainted with the "devotional habits" of some of our neighbors: the core rituals and practices of some of the religions in the American neighborhood. As we learn about our neighbors' rituals of faith, we will learn whether they call it worship or veneration, praying or practice, ceremony or service or observance. We will find out what is done at home, and what requires a congregation or a temple or a shrine. Thus we will move from the intimate and personal to the corporate and public. We will learn whether there is a requirement to go on pilgrimage—to leave the neighborhood purposefully in order to return with one's spiritual batteries recharged—and if so, where our neighbors go and what they do while they are away. As we learn about our neighbors' devotional habits, we will find out how the most basic of elements are put to extraordinary use, how the five senses are engaged, what each religion-community calls its dedicated worship spaces and ritual leaders, and what we are likely to find inside.

As anyone who has ever tried to teach a course called "Christianity 101" to a classroom of fifty college students can tell you, no matter what Christian custom you name, and no matter how you describe its meaning, someone will raise a hand to protest, "But in my church, we don't do it that way"; or, "But in my church, we don't call it that"; or, "But in my church, that's not what it means." This is not surprising. Think of baptism and communion, Christianity's most basic rites. Each are performed and explained in more than one way. Likewise, as anyone involved in the Christian ecumenical movement will attest, and as many of us know from our daily interactions in our own neighborhoods, the intra-Christian conversation is complex, sometimes heated, and often confusing.

We need to keep this in mind as we hear about Hindu, Buddhist, Jewish, or Muslim ways of doing things—and more. The descriptions and interpretations of rituals and customs in this short book are representative: everything described here has indeed been found in a living religion-community somewhere in the United States. However, the descriptions and interpretations given here are not comprehensive. Whichever religion we are describing, somewhere in America there is a family, a congregation, a community who does things or talks about things a little (or even a lot) differently from what the neighbors who speak in this book tell us here.

So, don't be surprised if your neighbor says, "We don't do it that way at all!" Rather, enjoy the opportunity to say, "Well then, please tell me how you *do* pray (or practice or celebrate), and please help me understand why."

## Method and Approach

*Faith in the Neighborhood* is for Christians who, having begun to notice the religious complexity of their neighborhoods, are ready to dig below the surface to understand their neighbors as they understand themselves. They are ready to become, as Martin Forward puts it, "theologically and religiously multilingual." This is a Christian endeavor because, as Jesus teaches, love of neighbor goes hand in hand with loving God, and we know as well that we are not to bear false witness against our neighbor. Surely the more we know about our neighbor's concepts, categories, and vocabulary, the better we can bear truthful witness regarding our neighbor's religious beliefs and practices.

Most college textbooks on the world's religions tell the story of one religion at a time. This can be helpful, but in real life our many religions intertwine (or collide) in the factory, the office suite, the boardroom, the classroom, the shopping mall, the sidewalk, the street fair, the city park, and the potluck supper. *Faith in the Neighborhood* is for the reader who is not satisfied with working through a menu of religions, but instead prefers to listen to the voices of America's many religions as they glide in and out of the narrative—just as they do in our daily lives. That is why this series proceeds thematically, with each volume devoted to a different topic. So Volume One is about belonging: the rites and behaviors through which people commit themselves to a religion. Volume Two is about public and private worship and practice, thus our religions' "clocks and calendars." Volume Three is about death, grieving, and health; Volume Four, faith and family life; Volume Five, religious knowledge and instruction; and Volume Six, works of charity and social activism.

Each book in the series engages more than a dozen of America's religions. In a series such as this, it is difficult to do justice to the wide variety and nuance within each religion. We all have a tendency to speak or write of "the Buddhist community in Los Angeles," or "the Jewish community in Texas," or "America's Hindu community." These blanket terms are convenient, but they blur the fact that they cover quite a swath of diversity. Almost every religion in this series is better understood as a mosaic. Viewed at a distance, a mosaic is a coherent picture; from close up, the viewer is very much aware of the many individual pieces of glass or stone that make up that picture. Each piece has distinct edges, and some are distinct in color and texture as well, yet their relationship to each other is obvious. So it is with America's many Buddhisms, or Judaisms, and so on.

As our conversation proceeds, there will be times when all dozen-plus religions will respond to the matter at hand; but other times, not. Sometimes one branch or school of thought will be given the floor; at other times, another. In the end, a range of voices will have had a chance to speak. By taking this approach, we acknowledge that we cannot help but make comparisons, but we are careful not to insist that each religion fit every category or provide an answer to every question.

*Faith in the Neighborhood* makes broad use of insights shared by scholars such as Diana Eck, Catherine Albanese, Ninian Smart, Byron Earhart, and Mary Pat Fisher, who have reported on America's complex and changing religious landscape or provided us with methods and resources for understanding other people's religions. When the series speaks of "America," it is following the example of Albanese and Eck—both of whom use the term as short-hand for "within the U.S.A.," all the while acknowledging that there is more to "America" than a single country.

These books are based on interreligious conversations in many parts of the United States. Some have been lively multireligious discussion circles. Others have been small-group conversations between Christians and followers of one other religion (a Jewish-Christian dialogue, for instance). Still others have been one-on-one interviews. All quotations come from real conversations, but names have been omitted in most instances—both to enhance the flow of the text and to allow the speakers their privacy. Throughout, an effort has been made to balance "ordinary adherents" with "highly trained religious leaders," women with men, and older adults with young people. A short series such as this can only hint at the range of attitudes and understandings. There cannot help but be branches or denominations unrepresented in the conversation pool; there cannot help but be perspectives unreported. Indeed, there are dozens of religions in the American multi-faith landscape that are not even mentioned! Yet that is part of the point: the discussion never ends.

## Series Resources

Learning about other people's religions means learning new words from many languages. While each term is defined the first time it is introduced, a glossary at the back of each volume will remind you of definitions. If you need to get your bearings, or to review, a very basic outline of each religion is included before the glossary, along with suggestions for further reading.

## CHAPTER ONE

# To Whom? For What?

A MAN POURS MILK over a statue. A young woman sits solemnly behind a large book, swooshing over it occasionally with a yak-hair whisk. A man sits before a small portrait, puts a dot of red powder between his eyes, then marks a U on his forehead with yellow paste. These are our neighbors, each participating in a ritual of his or her faith. Unless we take time to understand *why* our neighbors of other religions perform their devotional habits, unless we have some accurate sense of *what* or *whom* these acts are directed toward, our neighbors' rituals of faith can seem to us as odd or as trivial as the rituals of a professional baseball player as he prepares to take his turn at bat.

A young girl is watching her mother prepare dinner—perhaps you have heard this story. Mom rubs seasoning on the roast, slices off each end, puts it in a pan, and pops it in the oven. "I know why you rub the seasoning on the roast," the child says, "but why do you slice off the ends?" "That's what my mother always did," comes the reply. "I don't know why she always did that, but her roasts were delicious, so I do it the way she did. Let's ask her." Grandma replies that she was just imitating Great-Grandma, who (it turns out) sliced off the ends so the roast would fit in the only pan she had.

When it comes to rituals of faith, many devout persons in America's multireligious neighborhood are trying to maintain the practices of those who came before them, adapting them to the American context if necessary. Undoubtedly, some just imitate Great-Grandma and leave it at that. But many others have gone searching for the answer to the question, "Why do we do what we do?" America's multireligious context itself has encouraged them to become very clear about what their devotional habits mean, and how to do them well. These are the neighbors we will meet in this book. They know quite plainly to whom or toward what their rituals of faith are directed. They have worked hard to learn how to explain this to other Americans, and they would like you to understand the object their devotion. This is why we are beginning our exploration of our neighbors' rituals of faith with a theology lesson.

The Christian religion teaches that God is in essence absolutely One, absolutely relational, and definitely personal. That, in a nutshell, is what Christians mean by saying that God is Triune (One-in-Three; Three-in-One) and that in Christ Jesus we have *Emmanu-el:* God With Us. But a nutshell is hardly adequate for holding the mystery of the doctrines of Trinity and Incarnation. For centuries, Christians have explained the details to each other—sometimes in scholarly books, sometimes in poetry, sometimes in art. "God-talk" varies, sometimes sharply, from one branch of Christianity to another. It varies within the same branch or denomination for a host of reasons.

If God-talk is complex and varied among Christians themselves, then it should not surprise us that adherents of other religions in the neighborhood will offer complex and varied explanations of whatever is ultimate for them. We might also expect that the ability of our neighbors to explain their religion's teachings will vary according to such factors as depth of training, command of English, which branch of their religion they belong to, and the seriousness with which they hold to a specific position. Conversation about how the "Whom" or the "What" toward which our neighbors direct their prayers and other rituals of faith is tricky terrain, but it is worth traveling if we really want to understand how our neighbors demarcate sacred space and time with ritual and practice.

As we begin, it is also important to remember that many definitions of "religion" presume that religion is inherently *theis-*

*tic*—that is, that a notion of God (or Gods) has to be involved. However, the working definition of "religion" used here insists that a religion can be *non-theistic:* that a religion can be a religion even if it does *not* operate from a notion of "God," at least as an ultimate creator. We must keep this in mind as we explore whether, when, or how people worship, and as we think about how they describe the focus of their practice, or how they name and explain the object of their devotion.

## There is But One God...

Having said all that, when it comes down to it, the vast majority of religions *do* operate from a presumption that there is an Ultimate—a single Source. While most Americans, regardless of their religion, are happy to employ the English word "God" when referring to it, each theistic religion has its own theology—its own way of describing God and God's relationship to the physical and spiritual realms. God may have many names, and the spiritual realm may be quite complex. Yet God is God.

*Judaism*

"As a Jew," a young rabbi offers, "I think about God as Transcendent Being—as a connecting force for all humanity in the world. No matter what's going on, it's always on a much smaller scale than God." For Jews, God is YHWH (or, YHVH). This holiest name is the transliteration of four Hebrew consonants: *Yod-Heh-Vav-Heh.* It is also shorthand for the Hebrew statement *Ehyeh asher ehyeh*—"I am that I am"; "I will be what I will be." This is the answer Moses received when he asked for the identity of the voice speaking to him from the burning bush.[2] YHWH is often called the Tetragrammaton (the four-letter name). "It symbolizes the essential infinity and eternity of the One Who Was, Is, and Will Be," one instructor explains. It is also unpronounceable. Jewish mystics say, "Go ahead. Try to pronounce it. You'll find that it is

יהוה

pure breath. God is Being Itself, and has in-breathed all of creation." Yes, you can insert vowels and pronounce it as *Yahweh* if you must, but most Jews think the divine name is too holy and intimate to be spoken. Instead, when they see YHWH in writing, they substitute *Adonai* (Lord) or *Ha-Shem* (the Name). For some Jews, it is too holy to write, except in certain circumstances; and, by extension, it is unseemly to write even its English equivalent. So, they write "G–d" instead.

The range of Jewish notions of God is quite broad. "For me, God is Creator, Law-giver, Loving Father," says a Conservative political scientist. "There are Jews who are non-theistic, however. They may even call themselves atheistic. For them, ritual is more about filial rather than divine obligation." The Humanistic Judaism movement, for example, offers a place for people who want to identify somehow as Jews, who find meaning in the rhythm of the Jewish calendar and in some of Judaism's rituals, but not in "God-talk." The Reconstructionist movement also makes room for atheists and agnostics as well as theists.

On the other hand, says Rabbi Jack Bemporad, "Reform Judaism holds the rather classical view that God creates the world and, perhaps, in some form or other, guides the world, but is distinct from the world—and I don't mean logically distinct, but ontologically distinct in the sense that creation is an independent entity that has an integrity in its own right."

"I think my rather fundamentalist, very observant Orthodox upbringing managed to instill in me a child-like innocence in my feeling about God," a Talmud scholar explains. "Intellectual skepticism does rear its head periodically, but those very early, basic, simple understandings about God stay with me even as I've gotten older and my theology has gotten more complicated and conflicted. Now, as a parent of small children," she continues, "I realize that when you are trying to convey a message about what you believe to a child, you've got to strip it down to its essentials; and so I do call upon the fact that, if you woke me up in the middle of the night and asked me, I would say, 'Yes, I do believe in a personal God.' That's important to my children. I also want to combine the more particular Jewish notion of

God and the more universal concept of God, and convey that to them as well. We have lots of discussions about that."

"In some ways," says a Conservative rabbi in New York, "I have a personal relationship with God, and I need to take care of that relationship. And, since, according to Genesis, we're all created in God's image, there's a relationship between human beings, and that relationship is based on God's presence. This underlies my whole outlook on life. I have to believe that people are basically good, because the image of God is part of everybody."

"In my brand of Judaism," says a Michigan writer, "God does not have a 'personal' feeling. I conceive of God as the power that drives the universe—part of which we can see. I believe that God has, at certain points, intervened in history, and may have some kind of relationship with the Jewish people that may not be quite the same as the relationship with other people—but that is hard to know." Because Hebrew is a gendered language, "even rocks and rubber tires are bound to appear either 'male' or 'female.'" He makes poetic translations of Jewish texts for liturgical use at his Conservative synagogue, and, he says, "I presume that God transcends our typical human understanding of male and female, so that implying that God is masculine in an English translation may well be misleading."

"I try to think about each image of God," says one young woman. "No matter how much I might not really like some of them, the challenge is to think about how I can relate to them positively, instead of just throwing that language out. I think that speaking of God only in gender-neutral terms or non-hierarchical terms puts a limit on God. It's saying that it's impossible for God to be manifest in that way, just because I don't like it. Just as using only male language about God has been limiting, so, too, is doing the opposite."

### *Islam*

"If there is one big misconception Americans have about Islam and Muslims that I would like an opportunity to set straight," says a Shi'ah university student, "it is that we pray to something else besides God! I always get that question: 'Who do you pray to?' I pray to God, I say. 'Well then, what's Allah?' I'm like, 'Allah is the Arabic word for God.' People just don't understand it. I think it's because in movies, if there is a scene with Arabs in it, they throw in the word 'Allah' to spice it up a bit and make it look authentic. It does so much harm. I think people need to get their language straight. It's offensive when somebody thinks I don't believe in God, or that I am praying to some other deity. It's disturbing."

Literally, *Allah* means "The God" (*al-Lah*, from the Arabic *ilah:* "god" or "deity"), and Arabic-speaking Jews and Christians also use this word to say "God." When visiting a mosque, look for *Allah* in Arabic script (which runs, visually, from right to left)—perhaps as a wall-hanging, or perhaps imbedded in the architectural details.

For Muslims, God is *Wahid*—absolutely One. *Tawhid*—all of the implications of God's Oneness—is, therefore, a core Islamic concept. God is totally *other* than humans (or any creature), Muslims stress. But, as the Qur'an teaches, God is also as close as your jugular vein. "God is the One who created me and continues to provide for me," adds an Alabama astrophysicist. "God is compassionate, just, caring, and always available. He can be tough sometimes, but I am convinced that those times are ways of educating or training us, or even challenging us to help us grow even more. Knowing that God is just helps me cope with certain difficulties in my life. It means he does not do anything that is not fair." God is demanding, but God is just. God may be wrathful, but the Qur'an's references to God's compassion and mercy outnumber its references to God's wrathfulness at a ratio of five to one.

"Muslims are taught that we are never truly separated from God," a Muslim chaplain explains. "Our illusory constructions about ourselves veil us from a Reality that has never stopped being present. We originated in the presence of God and we will end in the presence of God. In the meantime, we have this bumpy period—life—which is kind of a test. The question is, Can we recollect the Divine Presence in the various challenging situations in which we find ourselves, and can we act in accordance? We are bound to fail a lot, but that's okay. It's understood from the beginning that failure is going to happen. What's important is that we persevere in this learning experience."

Islam teaches that God has spoken through a series of prophets. According to Islamic understanding, Muhammad is the Seal of the Prophets (the last one God will ever send). Like several before him, he is a prophet who received a "book," and that makes him a Messenger of God. The Qur'an (Islam's holy book) is believed to be God's very words. That the Angel Gabriel assisted in transmitting this revelation to Muhammad points to the fact that Islam teaches of a cosmological hierarchy. Angels were created before humans, but rank below them in certain respects; *jinn* or spirits (who have been created out of fire, but share some qualities with humans) rank even lower.

When the Islamic call to prayer asserts *Allahu akbar,* says scholar and peace activist Rabia Harris, "it has *enormous* implications which are lost in translation! *Allahu akbar* doesn't mean 'God is great' or 'God is greatest'; it means, 'God is *greater.*' That 'greater'—*akbar*—is where the phrase becomes spiritually active. Because if we say it to ourselves, and grasp what we've actually said, then wherever we are now, God is greater than that. Whatever is depressing us, whatever is exalting us, whatever we are patting ourselves on the back about, whatever we are feeling defeated about. No matter what's going on, God is greater. And that *moves* you."

"*Allahu akbar* is a useful recollection when it comes to race relations, gender issues, or any sort of power struggle," Harris suggests. "*Allah akbar* says that you may feel like you're being tromped on now, but God is greater than this moment and the time will change. It's also a warning that power is always a test, never a gift. If you've been put in a power position, you had better remember that the moment of accounting is waiting for you. No matter how great you think you are, God is greater. It keeps us honest, if we listen to it."

According to a well-known *hadith* (authenticated report), the Prophet Muhammad said that "God (great and glorious is He) has ninety-nine Names, one hundred minus one; because He is One, He loves odd numbers, and whoever believes in what the Names mean and acts accordingly will enter the Garden [that is, Paradise]." As one graduate student explains, "God's ninety-nine Names include every attribute, every polar opposite. God is the Honorer, and the One Who Brings Down; the

One Who Creates, and the One Who Destroys. You get this very wide vision of who Allah is, which encompasses the personal and the impersonal. More than anything, that has influenced how I see God." The Beautiful Names are drawn from the Qur'an, and include descriptions like the Compassionate, the Merciful, the Just, and the Patient. Human beings may reflect any of the divine attributes, but only God possesses them all at once and always; and of all human beings, say Muslims, the Prophet reflected more of them at once than anyone else.

While it is safe to say that all Muslims are aware of the notion of the Ninety-Nine Beautiful Names of God, the range of emphasis placed on it by various Muslim groups and individuals is quite wide. And, Muslim mystics are likely to say that the number ninety-nine is too low. "It is just a convenient way of coalescing the Qur'anic references to the divine," says one. "God has 1001 names," says another. "God's names are infinite," says a third.

*Bahá'í Faith*

The Bahá'í Faith stresses three principles: the Oneness of God, the Oneness of humanity, and the Oneness of religion. "There is a oneness to God, there is a unity to the divine essence," a New Yorker explains, "but also an incomprehensibility, an unknowability. We are dependent creation; God is independent. So we can know *of* God through the Manifestation of God." By the term "Manifestation of God" Bahá'ís mean *prophets.* Bahá'ís believe in "progressive revelation"—the notion that the one-and-only God has been revealed through Abraham, Moses, Zarathustra, the Buddha, Jesus, Krishna, and Muhammad, and has spoken through Bahá'u'lláh. "They all had the same essence," explains a Bahá'í athlete. "They all served the same purpose throughout history." For Bahá'ís, Bahá'u'lláh is "the Manifestation of God for the current age."

"Another term that Bahá'ís sometimes use for the Manifestation of God," says a middle-school teacher, "is 'The Dawning-Place of Understanding.' For Bahá'ís, this is where knowledge of God begins. We know of God because we could see Jesus and know what he said and did, and what Muhammad said and did, and what Bahá'u'lláh said and did."

"Bahá'u'lláh, our founder, taught us that God is immanent and invites intimacy, yet is utterly transcendent," says a graduate student. "It is a paradoxical concept," he continues. "Bahá'ís believe that God is this unknowable essence. But at the same time, we are told that through prayer and devotion we can show forth God's attributes. So that is how we should model our life—showing forth the attributes of God, reflecting his light. The way we do that is following his teaching." Even the Bahá'í way of talking about intimacy with God can be paradoxical, says a classmate, "because a lot of Bahá'í writings talk about becoming intoxicated with the wine of the love of God—yet we don't drink! So how is it that I can become intoxicated, but I don't know what it's like to be intoxicated?"

Bahá'ís avoid anthropomorphism when describing God. Instead, like Muslims, Bahá'ís describe God in terms like the All-Knowing, the All-Glorious, the All-Wise. Among these many Names of God, *al-Abha* (All Glorious) is called the "Greatest Name." It figures in the invocation *Yá Bahá'u'l-Abhá* ("O Glory of Glories" or "O Glory of the All-Glorious"), which in calligraphic form becomes a Bahá'í symbol.

*Zoroastrianism*

"God is 'Essence'—Being itself," says one Zoroastrian educator. Zoroastrians, followers of the Prophet Zarathustra, have come to America both from Iran, where this ancient religion originated, and from India, where they are called Parsis, and where they have thrived for hundreds of years. Zoroastrians call God Ahura Mazda (Wise Lord). Ahura Mazda is the First, the Eternal, the Omniscient, the Creator, Maintainer, and Promoter of the Universe, the Only that is to be worshiped. All that comes from Ahura Mazda is good, Zoroastrians stress; so evil has some other source. To say this is not being "dualistic," it is being logical! "If God be perfect in goodness and wisdom," argued an ancient Zoroastrian theologian, "then ignorance and evil cannot come from Him. It they could come from Him, God would not be perfect; and if He were not perfect, He should not be praised as God and perfectly good."[3]

Beyond this, as one attorney points out, "there is a big difference, both in belief and practice, between those of us who follow the *Gathas,* which are believed to be Zarathustra's own words, and those who follow the later traditions and texts." One of these big differences between the *Gathas*-only reform movement and other Zoroastrians is the way in which they talk about the spiritual realm as a whole. Similar to the way in which Christians speak of "angels, archangels, and all the company of heaven," traditional Zoroastrians speak of the six *Amesha Spentas* (Bountiful Immortals), each sitting on its own golden throne surrounding the throne of God. "It is important not to gloss over the *Amesha Spentas,*" says one community leader. "They are central to Zoroastrian theology and Zoroastrian ethics." Their names are Discerning Mind, Righteousness, Benevolence, Good Power, Perfection, and Immortality—divine attributes which are to be emulated by humanity in order to bring about the perfection of creation, which is the ultimate goal.

In striving toward that goal, a New Jersey educator explains, human beings are confronted by Twin Spirits: Spenta Mainyu and Angra Mainyu—the good force and the destructive force. Humanity has complete freedom of choice, but Zarathustra urges us to choose the good. Assistance comes from angelic beings (the *Yazatas*) and one's guardian spirit (one's *Fravashi*). Spenta Mainyu and Angra Mainyu are in constant battle, but ultimately, good will triumph by Ahura Mazda's power.

The *Gathas*-only reformers pay little heed to any of this cosmological complexity—and some of them even reject it explicitly. They prefer to emphasize the absoluteness, and the simultaneous transcendence and nearness, of Ahura Mazda—who has endowed humanity with free will. For some of them, *spenta mainyu* and *angra mainyu* are attitudes rather than entities: *angra mainyu* tolerates evil; *spenta mainyu* bears full responsibility for choices made, and strives to choose good explicitly.

In Zoroastrian iconography we find the *Fravahar* (sometimes spelled *Faravahar* or *Farohar*)—an ancient figure which looks like a bearded man astride widespread wings; his "saddle" is an unbroken ring, and below that extend tail-feathers and two long threads, each with a curl at the end. Some say that the literal meaning of this figure's name is "forward-pulling force"; others say it comes from the verb "to choose." Some say it depicts the guardian spirit God provides for each person. Others see it as a primer: the rows of feathers, the curls by the tail, and every other detail of the figure symbolizes an element of Zoroastrian teaching—particularly, the role played by Good Thoughts, Good Words, and Good Deeds in the soul's journey toward union with Ahura Mazda.[4]

"As I understand what God is, according to our Zoroastrian religion," says a New Jersey chemist, "God is a force—a creative force, such a force as wants things to be perfect. God wants his creation to be perfect, and human beings are essentially the agents that are expected to lead from creation to perfection. The relationship between God and humanity in Zoroastrianism is more like the human being as a co-worker with God. The relationship is not so much father to son, or master to slave or anything like that. It is more like the relationship between friends." A law of consequences is at work, most Zoroastrians will assert. The traditionalists may believe that the soul is rewarded or refined in the afterlife, but Zoroastrians who rely on the *Gathas* alone may not agree. The *Gathas,* they will point out, are not explicit about whether a law of consequences operates in this life or the next—or both.

### *Sikhism*

The Sikh religion dates from the late 1400s, and Sikhs have been in the United States since the 1800s. Observant men (and some women) are readily distinguishable by their turbans. Sikhs stress the Unity of God, the Supreme Reality. Look at the flag outside a Sikh house of worship. The symbol you will see is actually the words *Ik Ongkar* (the Only One), which is one of Sikhism's names for God. Sikhs also call God *Waheguru* (the Almighty), or simply *Nam* (the Name). But, as one office-worker stresses, "Sikhism says *God* is *God,* regardless of the name you use. The fact that other religions call God by different names is acceptable to us." "We worship the same God as you," insists a Sikh technology consultant as he talks about diversity with the Parents Association of an Episcopal day school.

The Sikh understanding of God is summarized in the *Mool Mantra,* the opening lines of the Sikh scripture. The *Mool Mantra* is recited in Punjabi. Its first words are *Ik Ongkar,* and its meaning is something like: "There is but One God, the Truth, the Creator; without fear, without anger, the Timeless Being, unborn, self-existent, realized by the Guru's grace."

"God is a light that lives inside of everything," a New Mexico office administrator asserts. "The way the Gurus have taught about the Creator is that it is both manifest and unmanifest, both formless and form, both beyond our comprehension and something that lives inside of ourselves. God is a collective, creative energy that runs through the entire creation, and is also holding the entire creation, and is manifest in the entire creation that is inside of me, and that consciousness has no fear and no anger. The Divine moves by its own impulse, by its own purity, by its own projection. So it's something that is within me, and is way bigger than me. It's within everything, and holding everything. It's playful, and it's something you can experience as a human being. You can touch that Creator, that divine light inside of yourself."

### *Hinduism*

Ask a Baptist and an Orthodox Christian and an Episcopalian about saints—who they are and how they are venerated—and you'll get contrasting answers. Ask a Methodist and a Roman Catholic about devotion to Mary the Mother of Jesus, and again, each response will be authentically Christian, yet different. Ask what it means to insist that God is Triune, and how the three Persons of the Trinity relate to each other, and yet again, there may be significant differences in the way a Presbyterian and an Orthodox Christian responds. Christians share core vocabulary and concepts, but they have contrasting ways of explaining the nature of "angels and archangels and all the company of heaven." We will be a more empathetic visitor to the Hindu worldview if we remember this when we ask about the Hindu understanding of the Ultimate.

"In the American context," says one educator, "many Hindus quite readily say, 'We worship God.' The Hindu will use the word "G–o–d," but the word doesn't come from our scripture. So when you ask us about who God is and where God is, you need to be careful not to impose your connotations of the word on us." What is a more authentically Hindu word?

Most often, Hindus will speak of Brahman.[5] Brahman is Ultimate Reality, the Supreme, the Primal Soul. It is a common term, but not the only possibility. "I prefer Bhagavan," one woman asserts. "Bhagavan means that which includes the limitless six elements: wealth, knowledge, overlordship, valor, dispassionateness, and fame. When I say these elements are limitless, it means that you can't put a boundary around them. If Bhagavan can't be boundaried, then obviously, 'God' cannot have a form."

In Hindu understanding, God is formless, but "forms of the divine" play a major role in devotional practice. "I am a devotee of Krishna," one neighbor says; "I am a devotee of Kali," says another. Images of the divine play a major role in connecting the individual to the Almighty. There is no contradiction here, your Hindu neighbor may explain. Brahman is both impersonal and personal, and from the perspective of most Hindus, human beings have little choice but to relate to God personally. Over the centuries, Hindus have developed various ways of naming Brahman's personal aspect. This is as it should be, they may tell you, because, according to the *Rig Veda* (Hinduism's oldest scriptures), "Truth is one; the wise call It by various names."[6] They may point to an often quoted passage from the *Upanishads* (a later scripture collection), which goes something like this: "How many Gods in Hinduism? 330 million gods. How many Gods in Hinduism? 330 gods. How many Gods in Hinduism? Thirty-three gods. How many Gods in Hinduism? Three gods. How many Gods in Hinduism? One!" The point is, there may be a mind-boggling number of *devas* (celestial powers), but there is only one Lord.

It is very common among American Hindus to assert that *all* of India's 330 million deities are manifestations of the one Brahman. There is but One God, and these many deities God are like the many colors one sees when a single beam of white light passes through a prism. One may worship God by whichever deity one prefers. "We worship God," says the administrator of a large South Indian-style temple. Gesturing at the many deity-images it houses, he continues, "All of these are human constructs. If they help you reach God, use them. But God is God."

"That is what the average Hindu will tell you," says Long Islander Rathi Raja, Executive Director of Young Indian Culture Group. "I'll be honest with you. There are heavy intellectual books on Hindu theology. But when it comes to the essential stuff, I think that the average Hindu is very casual about other Hindus' ways of belief and practice. There is little judgmentalism."

The willingness to see all deities as manifestations of the one Supreme has been called "universalism" or "inclusivism" by some, and is closely linked to Hinduism's ancient *advaita* (non-dualist) school of thought—the notion that God and the human soul are of the same essence, that they are essentially one. It is widespread among American Hindus for several reasons. One reason is that Swami Vivekananda, who came to Chicago and spoke at the first Parliament of the World's Religions (1885), was a non-dualist. "What he taught was nothing new, really," Raja explains. "But he made this ancient scriptural tradition understandable by a white, Christian audience. He gave it a voice."

Another important reason is that American Hindus often have subordinated their theological differences in order to have a critical mass for establishing and supporting a temple. This has meant that a single temple may be home to imagery and rituals that would never be found sharing a temple in India. "That is changing, though," observes Deepak Sarma, assistant professor of religious studies at Case Western Reserve University. "Now there are so many Hindus here. Before, you had people binding together because they were Hindus. Now you have people binding together because they are Vaishnavas. There is more difference now, because there is more diversity among American Hindus."

This brings us to Hinduism's three well known theological systems. For some Hindus, Brahman-as-Personal is Vishnu; for others, Shiva; and for still others, Devi (also called the Parashakti, the Eternal Mother, or, simply, the Goddess). Each system or stream has its distinctive beliefs about the divine and worship practices, and among Hindus in America we do find some strong adherents of each.

People who see Vishnu as Ultimate are called Vaishnavites (or, adherents of Vaishnava Vedanta). They believe that the world has experienced a series of *avatars* (manifestations) of Vishnu, including Rama and Krishna. In their devotional life, they may gravitate to a particular *avatar.* For many of them—even most, perhaps—this is Krishna. "The narrative of Krishna is one that evokes God for me most easily," one young professional explains. "Krishna, for me, is an instrument to direct me toward Vishnu. For me, Krishna is far more personal than Rama. Somehow, I identify more with him. So, in the morning, I will worship Vishnu via Krishna. Then I think about Ganesh, who is really a sub-deity. And I worship him because he, after all, is the Remover of Obstacles, and I want things to go smoothly. But, ultimately, God for me is Vishnu. The deities and subdeities might rely on God to function. But they are not manifestations—they are not avatars, as it were—of Vishnu. I think that Vishnu is to the many Hindu gods as the Christian God is to the many saints and angels. I really do see it that way."

However, some people in the Vaishnava stream have comparatively little to say about Vishnu. Ask one educator who is at the apex of the divine hierarchy, for example, and he says "Krishna," without hesitation. Krishna is compelling for many reasons. Look in the *Bhagavad-Gita,* suggests the abbot of a New York ashram. The *Bhagavad-Gita* (the Song of God) is a portion of the Hindu epic, the *Mahabharata.* At one point in the story, Arjuna (a human being with divine origins) is on the battlefield of a huge fratricidal war. Krishna is with him, and, the abbot explains, "Krishna—the supreme personality of Godhead—takes the position of the chariot-driver of his devotee, Arjuna! Right there, this is a very wonderful, very attractive understanding of who God is and how he relates with us. God took the position of a servant! He was the chariot-driver of his devotee." But, not only does Krishna take the role of servant, he also takes the role of a firm (yet kindly) instructor on the meaning of material existence and the human being's role as part of it.

Adherents of Hinduism's second major theological system are called Shaivites, people for whom Shiva is Ultimate. America's Shaivites include the founders of the periodical *Hinduism Today.* Based in Hawai'i, this community is the hub of a network of followers of Satguru Sivaya Subramuniyaswami. Shaivites think of Shiva's *functions* as personalities: Brahma is Shiva-as-Creator; Vishnu is Shiva-as-Preserver; Rudra, as Destroyer; Maheshvara, as Veiler; and Sadashiva, as Revealer. As Nataraj (Lord of the Dance) Shiva animates the cosmos from within. Shaivites have special regard for Shiva's sons: Ganesha (also called Ganapati, and who is regarded as something of an archangel) and Karttikeya (who may go by other names, such as Skanda or Kumara).

Adherents of the third major Hindu theological system are called Shaktas, and for them, Brahman-as-Personal is feminine. Some Hindu sacred literature describes the deities as sacred couples. Thus Vishnu and Lakshmi may be seen as two forms of the One: counterparts, as are fire and heat, or perfume and its scent. Brahma and Saraswati are likewise a sacred couple, as are Shiva and Parvati (and Parvati also goes by the names of Kali and Ambika). However, for Shaktas, the One is Devi, the Goddess, often called the Eternal Mother. Some approach her as Kali or Durga (fierce forms), or as Parvati or Ambika (gentle forms)—and not necessarily as half of a sacred pair. "I don't think of any of the gods as lesser or more," says one woman. "I worship Lakshmi individually, not as a partner of Vishnu."

One midwestern physician has built a temple dedicated to the Parashakti, the Ultimate-as-Feminine, in response to a vision he had of her while deep in meditation. The Devi Mandir in California's Bay Area is home-base for a community of devotees of the Divine Mother under the guidance of their guru, whom they call Shree Maa (the Respected Holy Mother).

For the outsider, things get complicated because a single Hindu deity may bear many labels, either because of regional preferences, or because it is traditional to call it by a different name depending on what relationship it is engaged in or what attitude it is assuming. Think of it this way, says a Hindu automotive engineer in Detroit. "You have a gentleman who is the father to someone. He is a son, also. He is also a brother and a community person. So, various people know him in different ways. He is called a husband or a father or a mechanic, depending on the task he is performing, but he himself is the same. God is the same, but you may know him through which way you see it. That's the way I see it."

Also, the same deity-name may show up in more than one theological system, but function quite differently from one to the next. For example, in one system Vishnu names a *function* of the Ultimate; in another Vishnu *is* the Ultimate. For many Hindus, Ganesha is important, treasured, but is merely a helper of God. For some, he *is* God. "He is so powerful," one man asserts. Some even speak of Ganesha as tantamount to AUM—the primal sound with which all creation begins. When it comes to the Trimurti, the classical depiction of God as creator, sustainer, and destroyer simultaneously, Shaivites may name those three aspects of Ultimate Reality as Brahma, Vishnu, and Rudra; universalists may speak of Brahma, Vishnu, and Shiva; and ardent Vaishnavites may not even mention it.

For a great many American Hindus, the world itself is a manifestation of God: there is no difference between the essence of God and the essence of creation. "So in the Hindu view, and this goes for people who range from the very academic to the man on the street who has a simple relationship with a deity," asserts Rathi Raja, "everything is God." A Hindu businesswoman in upstate New York agrees. "What I believe is that God is in everybody," she says. "That's what it means when we say *namaste:* 'The divine in me greets the divine in you.' There is no such separate thing that is God. God comes in the form of everybody."

"You know, actually," the businesswoman continues, "there is a nice Indian story about how a beggar went from house to house. He kept asking, and people kept saying, 'We don't have; we don't have; we don't have anything to give.' Then he went to a poor family's house. They didn't have enough food for themselves. But they said to the beggar, 'You are welcome to share what we have. We have very little, but what we have, we share it with you.' And he replied, 'Oh, you have more than enough!'

They sat down together to eat, and they kept taking out the food from the pot; it was never getting empty—because the beggar was God!"

The technical term for this notion is *advaita* ("not two," or "non-dualism"). On the other hand, however, some Hindus are indeed dualists. Deepak Sarma, an adherent of the Madhva Dvaita Vedanta school of thought, offers himself as an example. "In my world," Professor Sarma explains, "the motto is 'All things are different.' All things are different from one another, and the most difference is between God and the individual self. This is the exact opposite of the non-dualist position's claim that ultimately, God and the individual self are the same, and that the difference we perceive is an illusion. The dualist is a realist. Things exist; they are different. People are different. Selves are different. They are certainly different from God. The individual selves, the deities, and God are in an interesting hierarchy—with God at the top. That is how I see the relationship. For the non-dualist, God is really the same as all material things. In my world, God is totally different."

"The *dvaita* versus *advaita* distinction is not so much about God," Rathi Raja points out. "It is about the nature of the human relationship to God. From an *advaita* point of view, the journey through life is the journey to knowledge that the individual and God are one; in *dvaita,* the journey is to knowledge that the individual and God are different. But regardless, Bhagavan *per se* is complete, infinite Being, with no boundaries."

The various classical Hindu schools of thought regarding the relationship between Brahman and the material world do not line up neatly with the three major theological streams. Professor Sarma is a Vaishnavite dualist, but there are also strong Vaishnavites who are non-dualists. However, Hindus who are inclusive theologically are most likely to be non-dualists as well. All of this adds to the diversity of Hinduism in America. Just as other religions have their denominations, so it is with Hinduism in America.

Nevertheless, the trend toward ecumenism is persistent. Just as Protestants in small-town America have often consolidated into one "community church" or "federated church" rather than trying to maintain separate-but-tiny Presbyterian, Methodist, and Congregationalist institutions, so life in America has encouraged Hindus to work ecumenically. In America, it is not unusual to walk into a temple that accommodates both Shaivites and Vaishnavites. Often this has been a financial decision, with the desire to have a place for public worship and community activities trumping theological differences. "The idea of having two altars is not to divide the temple, but to provide for differences of worship," Rathi Raja insists.

"There are parts of India where people have gotten very hung up, and have said, 'I'm a devotee of Shiva, and I will not mix with a devotee of Vishnu.' There was a time when Vaishnavites and Shaivites would not intermarry. But this really belongs in a different generation," Raja continues. "If we focus on the division, it gets into our brain that there is only this division. That is not so. There will still be people who are strong Shaivites or strong Vaishnavites; but there will also be a very large number of Hindus who will come into the temple and say, 'You know what? I'm not going to take any chances. I'm going to pray to everybody. I'm going to cover my bases.' I don't mean to trivialize this. I do it myself. We have to be focused on the American context. To be honest, now most people don't care. We intermarry. We have both shrines in our home. It is not a big deal."

### *Afro-Caribbean Religions*

So far, we have been sparing in our use of "monotheism," and have avoided using terms like "pantheism" and "polytheism." Why? The reasons have to do with accuracy and neighborliness. In the case of pantheism, there is more than one definition in common use, so that using the term may generate confusion rather than clarity; with regard to polytheism, it is too often used dismissively rather than respectfully, and as our discussion of Hinduism should have shown, inaccurately. Better to presume that most systems of belief and practice have some sense of the Ultimate Source of All, and that most will have some way of accounting for a spiritual realm that is complex—just as the physical world is complex. This brings us to America's African religions.

African traditional religion has come to the United States directly, brought by recent immigrants from various African countries, but it also found its way here as one of the legacies of slavery. In this category are the Afro-Caribbean religions. Each of these religions acknowledge a plurality of divine actors on the cosmic stage, but it is fair to say that each embraces a strong notion of God Almighty, who is both transcendent and near-at-hand; called by various names, but nevertheless, one. American teachers from several sub-Saharan countries have insisted that God as worshiped by traditional Africans is *God*—not (as one of them put it) "some purely transcendent high god or merely the god of one particular people."

Some American streams of Afro-Caribbean spirituality draw on Yoruba culture of West Africa for their vocabulary of the divine. The Yoruba term used most often for God is Olodumare (Entity), a name which implies that God is "that-which-nothing-preceded." God is First Cause: the omnipresent, immutable, reliable, source of all wisdom. Another common Yoruba term for God Almighty is Olorun (Sky-Resident), which points to divine transcendence, distance, separateness. Yoruba names for God may also be strung together as a compound name (for example, Olofin-Olodumare), emphasizing that they indicate aspects of the divine rather than many different deities.

Why so many names for God? Because, says a Ghanaian proverb, "One person's hand is not sufficient to cover the face of God." That is, no single name will express God's nature and character in full. As one Lùkùmì priest insists, "These are all praise-names for God Almighty, the Creator of the Universe. But this is a BIG universe, so we deal with it in layers."

Mention of Lùkùmì (the religion of friends) brings us to Afro-Cuban religion. It has long been called Santería (literally, "saint-worship") in reference to the way in which Afro-Cubans redefined traditional Roman Catholic saint imagery for use in veneration of West African *orisha* (spirits). Thus St. George was paired with Ogun (Lord of Iron), St. Lazarus with Babalu Aye (Father of the World—the *orisha* of diseases and infirmities), and St. Barbara with Shango (Ruler of Lightning). One Lùkùmì priest in Brooklyn says it provided a veneer—a way of worshiping "under cover," to avoid harassment. The cover is no longer so necessary, he says, nor is the name Santería. He'd rather his religion be called Lùkùmì.

Most adherents insist that their veneration of ancestors and *orisha* is not *worship,* but recognition that the life-energy of the One and Only Supreme God is manifested through many channels. Others may say, as does one prominent Nigerian-American, that the *orisha* are aspects of Olodumare himself.

"You'll also hear of *orisha* in Haiti and here in New York City," says Dowoti Désir, a *manbo asogwe* (Vodou priest). "When we die, our spirit is still accessible. The *orisha* are like tributaries that converge into this great river, this great force, the *grande bwa* or the *poto mitan*—this big tree that is God, God's energy, and God's force."

Adherents of Vodou are more likely to speak of the *lwa* than *orisha.* "In Vodou, we're part of a continuum," Désir continues. "Our cosmological world is an ellipse. We depict this as *Dambala*—the Great Serpent with its tail in its mouth, the circle of life and death. It includes a realm where we exist as mortals, and then another realm of ancestors, and the *lwa.*" *Lwa* are spiritual entities with which one may have a relationship. Each has its sacred colors, days, numbers, foods, ritual objects, and more. Service to a *lwa* can include wearing its preferred colors, making offerings of its preferred foods, and so on. There is also the world of the invisible below. Presiding over it all is Bon Dieu (in Kreyòl, Bondjé), who is also called Gran Met (Great Master).

In both Lùkùmì and Vodou, the spiritual realm is described as very populous, and Désir says she found this quite appealing. "It took me a long time to acknowledge that Vodou is monotheistic," which, she says, is rather ironic, since her journey first to Lùkùmì and then to Vodou was at least in part a flight from monotheism. "But yes," she continues, "in Vodou, there's acknowledgment of one Supreme Being. Bon Dieu maintains an abstract relationship. He/She maintains some distance from which she/he can observe what we are doing without having to get involved in the muckiness of our day-to-day existence, and we acknowledge that distance. In our day-to-day interactions with each other, we understand we are not God. We know that God is embodied in us, but we are not God. So Bon Dieu has intermediaries for us to work with." This may explain, Désir thinks, why Vodou is "more kinetic, more performance-oriented, much more ritualized" than other religions.

*Native American Religions*

America's First Peoples each have their own tribal (or national) name for the Ultimate Great Mysterious Force. For the Hopi, it is Taiowa; it is Sakoiatisan for the Iroquois (who may prefer to be called the Haudenosaunee). For the Oglala Lakota, it is Wakan Tanka (Great Spirit). Wakan Tanka is holy, sacred, powerful, omnipresent, omniscient, all-seeing—above everything, and governing it all. Wakan Tanka's wishes are made known through a *shaman* or through visions; his favor can be gained through ceremonies. Actually, says one Minnesotan, "We Oglala Lakota call God by various names. Among our ancestors, God was called Tunka'sila, which means *Grandfather*." He favors this name because it calls to mind God as Loving Creator. One Ojibway woman agrees: "Our relationship to Creator is that of a grandparent's love for a grandchild—that caring, that nurturing. We are of Creator and we are of that Spirit."

Among Native Americans, there may be a sense that this great force inhabits each aspect of creation, or that it presides over a complex spiritual world. The Keetoowah (Cherokee) believe in a Supreme Being, but think that the universe was established by a community of eternal heavenly beings who remain present to the created order and regulate it from the seven-tiered heaven (which begins at the tree-tops). The Diné (Navajo) speak of the Holy People, who assisted the Creator with the process of creation and remain available to assist human beings with their needs. One Oglala Lakota says that for his people, God's Spirit could be in anything—an eagle, a deer: "We cannot measure what is sacred."

In the Algonquian language of the Anishinabe,[7] God may be called Gi'-tchi Man-i-to' (Great Spirit, Life-Giver), but one healthcare worker prefers Gzhemnido (Creator). "Gzhemnido contains all life," she explains; "the physical world, the sun, the moon, and everything. The Creator is huge all right. The Creator that we feel is so powerful. It's not a female; it's not a male." One Anishinabe woman says that when she left the reservation to live and work in a major midwestern city, her family complained, "You're not going to see Creator in the city. Creator is not there because there are too many lights, and you can't see the stars!" But, she says, "I know that Creator is everywhere. Creator is here, and the spirits. When we really become in tune, we see the spirits all the time."

### *Shinto*

In Shinto, the word for Divine Being or deity is *kami*—a term which can be either singular or collective. "The origin of the word itself is unclear," notes the Rev. Koichi Barrish, the *kannushi* (priest) of the Tsubaki Grand Shrine of America. "Some say it is derived from the first and last syllables of *kashikomi*, which means 'that which inspires awe and reverence.' It is also the first and last syllables of *kagami* (the sacred Shinto mirror) which functions as a representation of *kami*." Shinto-followers are followers of *kami-no-michi*—the way of the gods (800 million myriads of them); "the way of the gods" is the literal meaning of the word Shinto as well.

Shinto teaches that *kami* are everywhere. They may be spirits of natural phenomena (heavens, earth, mountains, rivers, seas, islands, forests), or of ancestors or great leaders. Because they are believed to be personal and approachable, *kami* are given names. "When you worship *kami*," one Shinto-follower explains, "you are acknowledging the greatness of nature; you're also acknowledging that certain deities are involved in your life." Reverence is demonstrated by worshiping at shrines, by showing respect for nature (thus deep ecological concern—especially for water), through architecture using materials in their natural state, through the tea ceremony, through arts such as rock-gardening and flower arranging, and more.

From a Shinto cosmological perspective, Ame-no-Minkannushi-no-Okami is the deity of the Origin of the Universe. Four more *kami* were deities of the earliest moment of the birth of the universe. The solar system is said to have been created by "fifteen *kami* in seven generations later." An ancient Japanese creation narrative speaks of the cosmic parents Izanagi-no-mikoto (the male who invites) and Izanami-no-mimoto (the female who invites). Its meaning is that all the solar system is their offspring. Earth is a realm which humans and divine spirits share. The human task is to live up to the heaven-like world into which one has been born.

For Shinto-followers, Amaterasu-omikami (the Sun Goddess) is the supreme deity. "All human beings receive life from her," the Rev. Koichi Barrish explains. "As the apex of all deities, the sun gives life to everything on earth." Sarutahiko-no-o-kami (Earth God—God of the Crossroads, the Surmounter of Obstacles) is the vassal of Amaterasu-omikami, and, Barrish continues, "he is responsible for absolutely everything inside the atmosphere, the leader of all earthly deities." Sarutahiko-no-o-kami is, therefore, the deity of positiveness who guides and corrects human beings. He is also the guardian of *Aikido* (the Japanese program of martial arts, meditation, and development of personal and interpersonal awareness). His wife is Ame-no-Uzume-no-Mikoto, and she is the *kami* of arts and entertainment, harmony, meditation, and joy. Sarutahiko-no-o-kami and Ame-no-Uzume-no-Mikoto are the principal deities of the Tsubaki Grand Shrine of America, which Rev. Barrish serves, but like every Shinto shrine, it houses myriad heavenly and earthly *kami* as well. All receive their due, but it is with Amaterasu, Sarutahiko, and Ame-no-Uzume-no-Mikoto that Rev. Barrish has the most profound connection.

### *Traditional Chinese Religion*

Traditional Chinese religion interweaves aspects of Taoism and Confucianism with Buddhism. We can tease the strands apart to talk about them. Taoism is both a complex system of indigenous Chinese beliefs, rituals, and practices, and a highly influential school of Chinese philosophy. Some people are drawn much more to ritual than philosophy. Others prefer the philosophy and the ancient texts. However, as is often pointed out, apart from clergy, very few people call themselves Taoists. Researchers say that most traditional Chinese people hold some Taoist beliefs and participate in some Taoist practices as part of the basic way of being Chinese—and this is true of many Chinese-Americans. Meanwhile, many non-Chinese Americans, without calling themselves Taoists, have embraced aspects of Taoism like acupuncture, Chinese holistic medicine and herbalism, or the practice of *T'ai-chi ch'üan.*

In Taoism, the Tao is the underlying First Principle of the universe, source and determiner of everything, a force flowing through all life. There is no notion of a personal Ultimate, nor a notion of a sovereign creator of the universe. The Tao is not *worshiped,* but is acknowledged and respected in the effort to become one with it.

In the traditional Chinese worldview, the spiritual dimension and the dimension of immediate experience exist in tandem, and even have similar structure: both realms are bureaucracies with a system of rewards and punishments. Deities (residents of the spiritual realm) may have personalities, and may seem very much like earthly human bureaucrats without much power, ultimately. Reciprocity demands that humans attend to these "gods," and that the gods serve humanity. When a god is perceived no longer to be helpful, it can be dismissed and replaced, just as in human bureaucracies.

T'ien (Heaven), another important notion, refers to the Ultimate Governor of the universe: ever-present, all-seeing, all hearing, who punishes the evil, rewards the good, and empowers the righteous. This notion of Heaven as the timeless, omniscient, omnipresent (if not omnipotent) impersonal governing power of the universe brings us to Confucianism. "Worship" of Heaven is not quite the right concept. Confucianism is about "learning to be human" by cultivating core virtues. The point of the Confucian way of life is to know and to achieve union with Heaven by knowing and fulfilling our obligations to our fellow human beings.

## Non-Theistic Religions

Religion is a constellation of beliefs, rituals, doctrines, institutions, and practices that help us make sense of the world, binds us together with others who see the world in a similar way, and/or binds us back to those who have seen and done it this way in the past. "God" need not be in the equation for religion to accomplish these goals. Jainism and Buddhism are two examples of non-theistic religions.

*Jainism*

"In Jain religion, there is no such thing as 'God' *per se,*" explains a member of Long Island's Jain community. "From the Jain perspective, the universe has been in existence for eternity and it will remain for eternity. Nobody has created it. It is just there. No one person manages it or controls it." His point is that Jains reject any notion of a single, ultimate, omnipotent Creator-of-all to whom human beings are accountable. "*That* Jains don't believe," he says. "Jains believe that *you* are responsible for all your deeds—not some external power."

Jain devotion centers on the notion of the *tirthankara.* The word means "crossing-maker"—someone who can help human beings ford the "ocean" separating *samsara* (the affairs of the physical world; the cycle of life, death, and rebirth) and *moksha* (liberation from that cycle; permanent spiritual enlightenment). *Tirthankaras* are great human teachers who have developed omniscience and then have founded a fourfold order for human society: male and female ascetics, and male and female laypersons. "We have twenty-four *tirthankaras* for the present era," a Long Island pharmacist reminds us. The most recent was Mahavira, a contemporary of the Buddha.

Some Jains are careful to say that "Jains don't worship," while others do use the term. When pressed, it turns out that to them "worshiping" means honoring and seeking guidance from the *tirthankaras.* Jains venerate *tirthankaras* as great role-models. They see in them a reminder of what they hope to become: a human being who has destroyed all of his or her *karmas*—those positive and negative particles clinging to the soul, the results of thoughts and deeds both good and bad—and so has become a *siddha*—a perfected soul who has returned to its original state of perfect knowledge, vision, and bliss.

It also may turn out that when our Jain hosts say, "These are our gods," they are assuming that their non-Jain visitors would not know the term *tirthankara,* and so they substitute a more familiar term. But, says a Jain banker, "We prefer *tirthankara* to 'god.' It is our way of talking. *Tirthankaras* are our teachers, our enlightened souls. We expect them to guide us; they are our guiding force. So sometimes this is how we pay respect to them, by saying god or lord or *bhagwan*—as you would call someone Sir or Reverend."

*Buddhism*

Like Jainism, Buddhism is essentially non-theistic, especially the stream called Theravada (the Way of the Elders), the "original" form, which has come to America primarily from Sri Lanka and Thailand. "We do not *worship,*" explains the Venerable Kurunegoda Piyatissa, renowned abbot of the New York Vihara (monastery). "We do not use that word. We respect the Buddha because he developed high qualities for the long time he existed in *samsara* [the wheel of rebirth], and ten perfections were fulfilled by him." These perfections are generosity, virtuousness, renunciation, development of wisdom, strength, patience, truthfulness, determination, loving kindness, and equanimity. "We are remembering those qualities," the abbot continues. "We respect the Buddha, but we have no such word as worship. Instead, we would say, we *follow.*"

All Buddhists give special regard to the historical figure Siddhartha Gautama (the Buddha), describing him as extraordinary but very definitely a human being. However, Buddhism is a broad tradition with many expressions, virtually all of which have made themselves at home in America. Mahayana Buddhism (the Northern stream) has forms which resemble theism. (Tibetan Buddhism is an example, as are the Pure Land schools of China and Japan.) However, some Mahayana strands are as non-theistic as the Theravada parent tradition. Ninety-year-old Won Buddhism (a Korean form) is one example. The ancient Ch'an (Zen) tradition is another.

"From a Buddhist perspective," explains the Venerable Sevan Ross, a Zen *sensei* (priest) in the Chicago area, "the very act of coming up with the notion of a personal God shows up in the practitioner's ego. It allows the practitioner to be at the center of the universe—which is not where the Buddhist wants to be. Buddhism says that if you're going to reach out for a personal god, you're not going to find a hand reaching back to you. In Buddhism there is the sense that we are not going to be taken care of unless we make a serious effort to understand what this moving moment really is. Once there is some deeper understanding, then eventually, the need for a personal God to rescue the ego will begin to fade to some degree."

From a Zen perspective, does the universe have a "Creator force"? Or, has the universe always been there—with no beginning? "Buddhism does not ask or answer that question," Ross asserts. "Buddhism is really unconcerned with how we got into this train wreck. The point is to get out of it again. The Buddha once said that our situation is like a man who has been shot in the leg with an arrow. Does he examine the arrow and say, 'This arrow is made of ash. Therefore I was shot by someone from such-and-such tribe,' or 'These feathers are the feathers of a hawk. Therefore the arrow was made up in the mountains at this place or that place'? Such things are not relevant! What is relevant is getting the arrow out of his leg!"

"Once we concern ourselves with 'getting the arrow out,'" Ross continues, "then we begin to move our life along. Then, oddly, the relationship between *self* and *other* becomes clearer. And then, the need for a creation story begins to fade away—not because we are ignoring it, but because we have come to understand that our relationship with the universe is not a relationship of self-and-other. We are not alienated so much. Once we get that, the sense of need for rescue, if you will, begins to fade. We realize we are already at home, and when we do, we're not so concerned with these other things. That is why knowing exactly where the universe came from and the exact moment the universe was created is irrelevant from the point of view of a Buddhist."

"We're not *worshiping*," Ross explains. "We are exploring. In its highest form, Buddhism is empirical. We ask, 'What do I really have in front of me here? What is this really?' When I look deeply enough, I may come to understand it. That is what we are doing. That is what meditation is. That is why we are not *praying*. We are meditating because we really want to know what is the truth of this operation as far as one can understand it."

## Reflections

As we have seen, many of the faiths in the American neighborhood are quite comfortable with the notion of "worshiping God." For most of them, God is transcendent but approachable. Some speak of God's attributes as personalities; some personify God's various functions. If we are theists, then how we think about the nature of God and what we think God expects of human beings will give shape to our rituals of faith. If we are non-theists, then we have some other explanation of how the world works and what humanity's place is in it—and that is the foundation of our devotional habits.

As we have learned, some religions place great emphasis on the essential distinction between God and creation, between God and the human self or soul. Others do not. In any case, this bears on how people understand the goal of their rituals of faith. We have learned that in many worldviews, the spiritual realm is a lively place with lots of inhabitants—as when Shinto-followers speak of *kami,* or followers of Afro-Caribbean religions speak of *orisha* or *lwa.* In some accounts, the divine is very, very near at hand, and the curtain between the physical and spiritual realms can be quite sheer.

This brings us to the notion of *ancestors.* One of the remarks sometimes made (too often in a dismissive or pejorative tone) about people who embrace Afro-Caribbean, Native American, and traditional Chinese religion is that they "engage in ancestor worship." "No, we don't," they are likely to respond—if what is meant by "worship" is to regard them as the Ultimate Concern. Rather, they explain, "We *honor* our ancestors." As we are using the term in this book, religion is that which not only binds us together but also binds us back to those who have gone before us. In these many traditional worldviews, life is a continuum. Mutual respect and reciprocity need not be interrupted by human mortality. Sometimes, we will hear the term "the Living Dead." It can be a synonym for ancestor. It can also mean "deceased relative"—with "ancestor" referring to those who went long before us, but do still exert influence. And some communities distinguish between ancestors and the Living Dead, but reverse these definitions. The only thing to do if they come up in a conversation is to ask, "How are you using that term?" And when we hear some of our neighbors speak of "venerating" or "honoring" or "reflecting upon," we are made aware that, in some religions—at times, if not always—"worship" is not quite the right concept.

Now that we have a sense of toward whom or what our neighbors' worship, veneration, or reflection is directed, we can ask: *How* do you go about these things? *How* do you worship, venerate, or reflect? It is to daily rituals of faith we now turn.

CHAPTER TWO

# Daily Devotions

"WHAT I WANT," says a Hindu mother of two, "is for my children to know that every day of their lives is sacred." "What I want for my son," says a young Muslim mother, "is for him to realize that the way I dress, what I eat, and the choices I make about how I spend my time—all of this is part of my daily dialogue with God." The daily dialogue with the extraordinary takes place in the myriad ways people give meaning to the ordinary passage of time. All religions do this. In the Christian tradition, we have the ancient heritage of the "monastic hours" which still may provide a daily framework of formal morning and evening prayer. Christians of every denomination maintain less formal patterns of waking and bedtime prayers, and prayers before meals.

As we inquire about other people's rituals of faith, we need to keep in mind some vocabulary issues. Christians often use the word "prayer" to name a range of things: calling upon God extemporaneously, making up the words as they go along; reciting a set text such as the Lord's Prayer or an Anglican collect; saying a meditative litany, such as the Rosary or the Prayers of the People; engaging in "centering" activity. They might believe that unless God is addressed, it isn't *praying.* On the other hand, some of our non-Christian neighbors carefully distinguish between prayer and *supplication,* or prayer and *meditation,* or between *worship* and *practice.* Some groups do this to emphasize that they are non-theistic; others, because the terms are not interchangeable in their religion's home language.

Whatever they call it, all of the religions we are investigating here have daily things which are expected of (or at least encouraged in) the faithful. The very devout or very observant will take care to maintain this daily rhythm; the professionals have made promises to do so. In this chapter, we will look at daily rituals of faith, most of which resemble what Christians mean when they speak of "praying." As we do, we will hold on to a caveat from an Orthodox Jew. She speaks for adherents of many of America's religions when she reminds us: "My daily ritual life is going to be bigger than my daily prayer life." And, while our common life in our shared neighborhood demands that we all agree on what day it is, religions may have their own ways of defining, dividing, and naming a day. So that is where we must begin.

## What a Difference a "Day" Makes

"Our ancient astrologers were precise," notes a specialist in Indian classical dance. Traditionally, a Hindu day would be divided into eight parts of three hours each. Each hour is fifteen degrees of the rotation. "As a traditional Hindu," a hospital chaplain explains, "I begin every morning's devotions by announcing what day and month and year it is, and by affirming that it is auspicious. I declare my name, my address, my ancestry." The priests are very careful about their rituals, she says. "They have to start some minutes after the sunrise, and all. They are very careful, and they are carefully trained. They try to stay very close to the right time. Then at the end, they make a disclaimer: 'Just in case we did make some mistakes, don't mind those things.'"

"It was interesting to hear my Hindu neighbor talking about how the Hindu priests were so careful about time," says a young rabbi. "That's true in Judaism, too. If you're an observant Jew, you're always looking at the clock! Everything is so time-oriented. Technically, you take all the daylight time and divide by twelve. So, the 'hour' shrinks and grows according to the season. There is a certain time which is the beginning of when you can say the morning prayers. There is a certain time after which you can't say the morning prayers. So time is very important for when you can say what."

"Take the *Sh'ma*," a New Jersey accountant suggests. "It is the recitation of Deuteronomy 6:4 as sort of a creed. To fulfill the biblical requirement, the *Sh'ma* needs to be said within the first quarter of the day—up to three hours after sunrise. But as the solar year proceeds, the time to do things shifts. We need to know: When *is* sunrise? When is three hours later? Praying the *Sh'ma* one minute is a *mitzvah;* one minute later, it's not. We need to know when *is* fifteen minutes past sunset on Saturday, so we can turn on the news. Life has to have boundaries," he says; "like in baseball: the ball is fair—or it's not!"

There is a range in Jewish attention to such clock-detail, just as there is a range of attention to all matters of ritual, observance, and devotional habit. Conservative Jewish practice sometimes resembles Orthodox, but may reinterpret it. At other times, it modifies traditional practice—but not to the extent one would find among Reform Jews.

Where the secular calendar measures a "day" from midnight to midnight, for Jews, Muslims, and Bahá'ís, the day begins at sunset. Keeping track of Jewish time in a detailed way is a challenge, but, "today's technology is a big help," says an observant Conservative professional woman, whipping out her pocket-sized PDA. Hers is loaded with special Jewish clock-and-calendar software. "I can look up exactly when each and every Shabbat starts. It tells me when I have to light candles and when to extinguish them—and, according to which rabbi! There are two different methods for calculating."

For Muslims, the Arabic word *yaum* (day) indicates a twenty-four-hour period. (There is a different word for "daylight hours"; *yaum* is also used to mean "occasion," as in the Day of Judgment.) The names of the first five days of the week are numbered. Friday is called *Yaumu'l-Jum'ah* (Day of Gathering), and Saturday is *Yaumu's-Sabt* (Sabbath Day). A day is punctuated by five prayer-times which shift with the shortening and lengthening solar day, and like Jews, Muslims can get electronic software to help them keep on schedule.

Instead of numbering the days, Bahá'ís name them after God's attributes—so that the very names of the days can be vehicles for theological reflection. The names for Saturday and Sunday—*Jalál* (Glory) and *Jamál* (Beauty)—are also used as month-names.

In the Jain worldview, however, the new day begins at sunrise. Each twenty-four-hour day is divided into sixteen *chaughadiyas* (segments) of about ninety minutes each—eight for daytime, eight for night. Some *chaughadiyas* are auspicious, some are inauspicious, and some are "in-between." Each day has its own pattern of the three kinds, and sometimes there may be two good segments or two bad segments back-to-back. (Sunday morning begins with a bad *chaughadiya,* Monday begins with a good one, and Friday begins with a medium one.) It is always preferable to start something during a good *chaughadiya!* One more thing: for fasting purposes (and devout Jains fast more frequently and more rigorously than just about anyone) a Jain day is thirty-six hours long: a fasting-day begins at sunset, and concludes two sunrises later. For example, fasting on Monday begins at sunset of Sunday, and ends after sunrise on Tuesday.

A Zoroastrian day is called a *roz* (or *rúz*), and each day of the month takes the name of an Amesha Spenta or a *Yazata* (the spiritual entities we discussed earlier)—except for four days a month which honor Ahura Mazda (God) specifically. Every twenty-four-hour period is divided into five parts, called *gehs* (watches), each with its own name. Like Jains, Zoroastrians believe the day begins at sunrise. This makes a difference to a devout Zoroastrian, because there are ceremonies to be done on the anniversary of a birth or a death. A birth which occurs, say, at three A.M. on October 20 belongs properly to the *roz* which began on October 19. "This is what happened with my daughter," says one mother. "It is a little confusing, but we celebrate her birthday according to our religion on the nineteenth, and have her 'American-style' birthday party on the twentieth every year."

## Punctuating the Day

Some religions in the neighborhood have a daily regimen of obligatory ritual prayer—patterns of praise, thanksgiving, remembrance, supplication and such—with specific things to do and say. They are to be done at very specific intervals during the day, and sometimes require the donning of specific articles of clothing or ritual objects. We'll begin with our Jewish neighbors.

### *Judaism: Blessing God*

Ancient Judaism revolved around the performance of ritual sacrifices at the temple in Jerusalem. When the temple was destroyed by the Romans in 70 C.E., the Rabbis (the scholars who collated the scriptures, and who compiled and edited the Talmud) declared that henceforth Judaism would be a religion of prayer and study. Thus the requirement to pray three times a day.

The "bookends" are morning prayer and evening prayer. Their liturgies are similar, calling for recitation of the *Sh'ma* plus the *Amidah* (the Standing Prayer—a long series of blessings, thanksgivings, and petitions) and the *Aleinu* (the prayer which concludes all Jewish prayer services). Psalms, scripture readings, and meditations are traditionally included, and all of this is spelled out in a *siddur* (prayer book). Formal morning and evening prayer can be performed at home alone, and home is where many observant Jews fulfill this obligation. However, some prefer to join a morning or evening *minyan* (quorum) at a synagogue.

Congregational prayer requires the presence of ten Jewish adults. (For Orthodox Jews and some in the Conservative movement, this means men only.) "If you go our evening *minyan,*" says a member of a Conservative synagogue in Michigan, "you will see a few people there who just like to make it part of their day—but most people are there because they're saying *Kaddish* for somebody. (That's the prayer you say in memory of someone who has died.) It's been part of my routine at various points in my life. It's a great way to start the day, a great way to end the day—a great way to frame your workday."

For morning prayer, Orthodox men ought to don a *tallit* (ritual prayer shawl with knotted fringes at each corner) and *tefillin* (also called *phylacteries*—leather boxes containing a portion of the *Sh'ma* on kosher parchment, which one fastens to one's forehead and left arm with leather straps). Men in other denominations sometimes do this also, and *some* Jewish women have decided to use these prayer articles as well. One Modern Orthodox scholar does this, and has grounded her decision on careful study of the large body of Jewish legal literature on the issue of the permissibility of women's wearing of the *tallit* and *tefillin.* But certainly, her practice is not the norm among Orthodox women.

"Even among girls who celebrate becoming *Bat Mitzvah,* it is not typical to wear a *tallit,*" says a Conservative rabbi, "and even less typical to wear *tefillin.* When I became *Bat Mitzvah,* I wanted a *tallit,* but I couldn't have told you why. To wear one is a conscious choice. For a woman to put on a *tallit* feels natural, because it feels and looks like a shawl, and we have other experiences of putting on a shawl. But a *tefilla* is a black box. There's no way it feels 'feminine.' It feels weird, and it looks odd! After I became *Bat Mitzvah,* I went to Jewish summer camp. My best friend at camp put on *tefillin* every morning before services. I watched her do it. So, when I got home, I put on my brother's. It felt strange, but somehow spiritual, and definitely like something I was not ready for. Now, as a rabbi, it feels right and comfortable. The day somehow feels different if I haven't done it."

The language of the mandatory prayers has been a topic of intra-Jewish discussion for decades. "I do pray, absolutely, using the traditional prayers," says one Orthodox woman. "Since Hebrew is a gendered language, God is masculinized in the prayers. I'm not comfortable switching the liturgy, so I don't." The traditional series of morning blessings ("Blessed be God…" for a long list of things) includes three "status-related blessings" by which one thanks God that one was not made a Gentile, a slave, or a woman. "The Reform and Conservative movements have tampered with the texts of the prayers," says one young Modern Orthodox professor, "but I prefer to deal with them as we received them, and to live in that tension." Reform and Conservative Jews do not look at their liturgical changes as *tampering.* Orthodox attitudes are mixed.

"My position on this has moved from where it was ten years ago," says an Orthodox mother of two. "Then, I too would have said that the text is problematic, but we're stuck with it. Now, I have come to believe that we can absolutely drop it. I think, theologically and sort of in a Jewish legal sense, it's much easier to drop things than to adapt and change them. I would get rid of all three. I would prefer that my sons not say them. As a woman, I obviously don't say the third, but I try to delete the first two. That means I must be careful not to say the prayers by rote. I try to remember to eliminate those lines, but most mornings I catch myself thinking, 'Oh God, I said that already!' They just kind of fall out of my mouth."

*Minchah* (afternoon prayer) is a ten- to fifteen-minute ritual: recitation of Psalm 145, the *Amidah,* a prayer of repentance, and the *Aleinu.* It can create an oasis of peace during the busiest period of the day, but it is fair to say that, of those Jews who maintain the discipline of daily ritual prayer, fewer pray the evening service than perform the morning prayer ritual—and still fewer make time for the *Minchah.*

Jewish daily devotional life includes specific *berakhot* (blessings) to be recited before, during, and after meals. Many Jews believe this is mandatory. "In the Mishnah—their first legal compendium—the Rabbis give several reasons for saying a blessing before a meal," explains Melinda Zalma, a recently ordained Conservative rabbi. "One is that all the world is God's, and by not saying a blessing, it is as if you're taking without asking." The after-meal blessing is longer. "The mandate for it is based on a biblical verse that says, 'You will eat, you will be satisfied, and you will bless God.'" There are many blessing-formulas, and the decision of which to use at a particular meal is determined by what is on the menu, and to some extent by which ethnic liturgical tradition you come from. "You'd have to be intentional to pick up on all these prayers," Rabbi Zalma agrees. "You'd have to look them up." But when these many blessings are invoked, the meal is transformed.

*Islam: Engagement with God*

"*Salat* is the foundation of life!" says a Muslim peace activist. She is speaking of the formal prayer-ritual so characteristic of Islam. "At least it's the foundation of conscious life for practicing Muslims. There is the greatest joy in having a regular recourse to the divine presence. Making *salat* doesn't necessarily have anything to do with having a big spiritual experience each time. That's not the point. The point is that *salat* is always there. That door opens regularly, five times a day. The Qur'an says, 'God is closer to you than your jugular vein.' We might not sense it, but God is present and God promises us that if we come into *salat,* that there is an engagement with God in the act of *salat.* You can say to yourself, 'I may not feel it, but it's real and here I am.' What a gift that is!"

If non-Muslim Americans know one thing about Muslim practice, they know that observant Muslims pray five times a day, facing Mecca. The mandate to pray daily comes from the Qur'an. The details come from the *Hadith* (the authoritative record of what Muhammad said and did). *Salat* consists of a series of nearly identical units. The five prayers differ according to how many units are to be performed, and whether they are to be done aloud or silently. The call to prayer is called the *adhan* (pronounced "athaan," with "th" as in "the," but sometimes as "azaan"). It will be repeated as part of the prayer script itself.[8] After the last unit of prayer comes a call for blessings on the Prophet, and the invocation "Peace be upon you."

In between comes *al-Fatihah* (The Opener)—the first chapter of the Qur'an: "In the name of God, the Compassionate, the Merciful: Praise be to God, Lord of the Universe; the Compassionate, the Merciful, Sovereign of the Day of Judgment. You alone do we worship, and to You alone do we turn for help. Guide us on the straight path—the path of those whom You have favored, not of those who have brought on themselves Your wrath, nor of those who have gone astray." This core text of *salat* is recited silently or aloud several times. When you add up the number of times it is said in the required prayers, then add the other occasions one might also say it, it is estimated that a devout Muslim ends up praying the *Fatihah* at least forty times a day.

Just as there is a script of things to say in *salat,* there is also a script of required and recommended motions and postures. At points in the ritual, additional portions of the Qur'an may be recited, and the brief 112th chapter (an affirmation of God's oneness) is always a popular choice. Opportunities for free supplication, either extemporaneously or using set texts, are built into the routine. There are also optional things to say with each posture of the prayer-rite. For example, with each prostration (when you—physically—are at your lowest) you might say *Subhana Rabbî al-'ala* (Glory to the Lord Most High) three times.

At the completion of *salat,* one may perform additional units, or simply make supplication (the posture for which is hands in front of one's chest, palms upraised). Some people like to repeat the phrase *Astaghfiru'llah* (I seek forgiveness from God). And of course, one may return to the words that opened the prayer-time in the first place: *Allahu akbar.*

The prayer-times for each day vary with the seasons. When the days are long, the morning prayer is quite early; in the winter, it will be significantly later. From the perspective of some Muslims, each posted prayer-time opens a window that closes when you come near to the next prayer-time; it is more efficacious to pray at the beginning of the period, and as you get later it is less efficacious, but it still counts. Others insist that you must be rather precise about the timing. Shi'ah Muslims believe it is quite acceptable to combine the midday and afternoon prayers, routinely performing them as a single elongated session.

"We take *salat* very seriously," says a member of a Sufi Order in upstate New York. "It's the foundation of practice. We believe that if you can't do *salat,* how do you expect to do anything else? If God says, 'Let me meet you at the corner of 73rd Street and Third Avenue at three o'clock,' and you say, 'I'm sorry, I'm too busy. I can't make it,' where's your claim to loving Allah? On the other hand, there are sometimes people who just feel themselves unable to make their prayers. That's an interior spiritual struggle. That can happen in an individual. But it's not a Sufi teaching."

The president of the Muslim Student Association of a large urban university says he is careful about the five-times-a-day prayer routine, which he has maintained since he was seven years old. "My family prayed together," he explains. "My parents followed the Muslim practice of not compelling *salat.* They taught my brothers and me by example. Later as we got older, they explained *why* we were praying. When you become responsible, in adolescence, you start praying on your own. You consider it your responsibility. We have a 'reflection room' in the University Student Center now," he continues. "Anyone can use it to pray or meditate, but it's primarily used by Muslims. It works out well."

In order to perform *salat* properly, one must "make *wudu*'"—which means washing one's face, nose, mouth, arms, and feet. Mosques provide special washrooms. At home it is no problem. How do the students at a large, urban commuter university handle *wudu'?* "I find that to be one of the comical scenarios on campus," one student says. "If you walk into the restroom when it's time for *salat,* you'll see a lot of people washing themselves. We try to be as neat as possible, so that we're not a hindrance to other people who are using the place. We do get a lot of questions from non-Muslims who walk in while we're making *wudu'.* We try to explain as much as possible so that when people see someone performing ablutions, they can automatically understand: 'Oh, I get it. He's just getting ready for prayer.'"

An Egyptian-American office manager in her fifties smiles at this eager concern for details. "You know," she says, "Islamic law has always provided for contingencies. If we cannot do prostrations, we are allowed to make *salat* sitting. If we cannot wash with water, we can use clean sand. And if we cannot do that, we can just touch a clean surface and say, 'I intend this to be my *wudu.*' That's what I do at work. I pray every day, even at work. Usually, I go sit in my car and make my *salat* in private."

A young lawyer keeps a prayer rug in her office. When it's time to make *salat,* she just turns off her phone and locks her door for a few minutes. A specialist in a large school district says she is one of two Muslims who work in her wing of the building. They've turned a closet into a prayer space. A young professor reflects upon her own student days: "When I was in high school, I decided that praying wasn't going to be a big deal. My dad had gone in and made sure that the administration provided me and my sisters a place to pray, but we never took advantage of it. We'd wait until we got home. Now, I am less self-conscious, more assertive, but also more integrated—heart, dress, and practice."

*Bahá'í Faith: Obligation and Choice*

Like Muslims, Bahá'ís have a daily prayer obligation—which, says one member, "is about as close as we ever get to ritual." Bahá'u'lláh gave them three obligatory prayers for daily use: the short, the medium, and the long. "We can recite them in our own language," one school teacher explains, "and we can choose any of them on a given day."

Each obligatory prayer comes with its own instructions for timing and performance. The short obligatory prayer may be offered only between noon and sunset. After washing your face and hands, you orient yourself toward the Point of Adoration—the place in Israel where Bahá'u'lláh's remains are entombed. Saying this prayer takes less than a minute, and does not require any special postures or motions: "I bear witness, O my God, that Thou hast created me to know Thee and to worship Thee. I testify, at this moment, to my powerlessness and to Thy might, to my poverty and to Thy wealth. There is none other God but Thee, the Help in Peril, the Self-Subsisting."

If you choose the medium obligatory prayer, then you are obliged to pray it three times that day: sometime before noon, anytime between noon and sunset, and anytime after sunset. As with the short prayer, ablutions are expected; but now there is a specific supplication to be made while washing your hands, and another to say while washing your face. The medium prayer's four short passages combine testimony and supplication, and each has its own posture: standing, bending, standing with palms upward, then sitting.

If you choose the long obligatory prayer, you may say it any time in a twenty-four-hour period. It takes about ten minutes.

There are fifteen passages to be said—again, each in a specific posture, and sometimes with accompanying motions. It is concluded by sitting and saying: "I testify, O my God, to that whereunto thy chosen Ones have testified, and acknowledge that which the inmates of the all-highest Paradise and those who have circled round Thy mighty Throne have acknowledged. The kingdoms of earth and heaven are Thine, O Lord of the worlds!"

So, if you choose to do the short prayer, that's all you must do that day? Yes, says a classroom assistant, although many Bahá'ís set aside time for ninety-five repetitions of the phrase *Allahu Abha* (God is All-Glorious). But whichever obligatory prayer you do, she stresses, it is to be recited in privacy. "That's very important. The only prayer that is to be recited in unison, in public, is the prayer for the dead. There are certain verses we can recite altogether." This is not to say that Bahá'ís never pray congregationally; they do, and they like to select the texts from collections of revealed prayers. Such prayers are provided for every occasion and concern. The difference is that making these prayers is entirely optional, and they come with no special performance instructions.

"I prefer the long prayer," one mother says, "because I can say that at any time. On the days I am busy, I opt for the short prayer. But the long one is my preference. I feel a little more centered, calmer when I do the long one. The short one goes by too fast. I feel like I didn't even get a chance to focus."

"Considering my schedule," explains a Michigan high school teacher, "I usually end up with the short prayer, simply because of what else I have to do in a day. But on days when I am not so busy, if I really want to be centered, then I will take on the medium or long. I think Bahá'u'lláh in his wisdom prescribed the three different prayers just for that reason, so that one could pray, no matter what. The Bahá'í Faith gives us a method of making contact with God every single day, irrespective of the demands of the secular world."

### *Zoroastrianism: In the Presence of Fire*

According to ancient tradition, Zoroastrians (women as well as men) are to pray five times daily (sunrise, noon, sunset, midnight, dawn—once during each *geh*), standing, and in the presence of "clean" fire (the symbol of righteousness). Ablutions are to be performed in preparation for prayer. The prayers themselves use texts from the Zoroastrian scriptures in Avestan and Pahlavi—two ancient languages of Persia (now Iran). While praying, one unties and ties one's *kushti*—the sacred knotted cord that ought to be worn as a belt over a sacred shirt *(sudreh)* at all times by initiated Zoroastrians. There is symbolism attached to the number of threads in the cord, and the number of knots. Minor differences have developed over the centuries between the Iranian and Parsi customs for performing the rite, which includes many supplications and concludes with the *Fravarane:* the Declaration of Faith.

In actuality, though, says a retired chemist, "Most of us don't follow the five-times-a-day routine. One of the most important aspects of Zoroastrianism is the freedom of choice. As a result, individuals say their devotions based on what satisfies their personal spirituality. People can pray once in the morning and once in the evening, or whatever they choose."

However often a person does them, says one community leader, because Zoroastrian prayers are in an ancient language, saying them often has the quality of fulfilling a duty or maintaining a tradition. "We have a general understanding of what the prayer is about: this one is an affirmation of faith; this one is about righteousness; and so on. But I don't think most of us really literally translate the prayers line-for-line. We don't pretend to memorize the translation. Yes, you can get a prayer book with the English translation, and you can read that if you have an interest, but I think most people just have a cursory knowledge that this is a prayer for asking forgiveness, and this is a prayer for affirming your faith. I think the majority leave it at that."

"But there is another thing about our prayers," a priest suggests. "There is supposed to be a vibrational quality to the actual prayer itself. This is what we've been told. You've heard of AUM—the sound which resonated in the universe at the time of creation. Our Zoroastrian prayers are like that. They have certain vibrational qualities which tend to soothe us."

*Hinduism: Putting on the Tilak-Chandlo*

It has long been a Hindu custom to mark the forehead with colored paste to indicate one's devotional path: three horizontal bars for a Shaivite (devotee of Shiva); the u-shaped "Vishnu's footprint" for a Vaishnavite. The members of one Vaishnavite reform movement, Bochasanwasi Shri Akshar Purushottam Swaminarayan Sanstha (BAPS), worship Swaminarayan (their founding teacher) as an *avatar* of Vishnu, thus God himself. All members of the BAPS movement are expected to maintain daily rituals of prayer, scripture reading, and community service, and this includes putting on a *tilak-chandlo* every morning. "In the morning," explains one electrical engineer, "when we sit down to pray, we open our prayer books. We put our pictures of God in front of us, and for fifteen to twenty minutes, we pray to God. But the first thing we do is to put on the red *chandlo*—a round dot of saffron or kum-kum powder in middle of forehead. It symbolizes Lakshmi (Goddess of Prosperity) living in the heart of Lord Swaminarayan. Then we put on the *tilak*—a yellow U. We use sandalwood paste to make this U. At that point we are telling ourselves that *tilak* is God; *chandlo* is the devotee. I, the devotee, am bringing God into my body. So every morning I pray, 'Please God: Come into my body; come live in my heart; live in my *atman*.' Our spiritual guru is the perfect devotee. We want to be like him. So we do *tilak-chandlo* every morning, and tell ourselves to conduct ourselves with morality."

*Sikhism: The Daily Routine*

Sikhs speak of *nitnem*—literally, the daily routine. *Nitnem* includes daily reading or recitation of prayers revealed by the Gurus (the inspired leaders during the early centuries of the religion). As part of their religious observance, *amritdhari* (initiated) Sikhs are required to read this collection of texts every day; other Sikhs may. "I have an hour train ride home every evening," says a college professor. "I just settle into my seat, close my eyes, and do my sunset prayers on the train." One of the morning texts, *Jaap Sahib*, is 199 verses long. Part of it speaks of the nature of God: "Immortal, Omnipotent, Beyond time and space, Invisible, Beyond name, caste, or creed, Beyond form or figure, The ruthless destroyer of all pride and evil, The Salvation of all beings...The Eternal Light, The Sweetest Breeze, The Wondrous Figure, The Most Splendid."[9]

Many families have their own copy of the *Guru Granth Sahib*—the Sikh holy book. It is written in a special script called *Gurmukhi* (word of the Guru), and it contains hymns in several languages. Since it is regarded as a living teacher, having one in the home means providing a proper place for it, and bringing it out reverently for reading. Some Sikhs set aside a daily time for this. Meditation is encouraged as well. Wearing the five symbols of faith—unshorn hair (covered with a turban); a comb; a bracelet; an undergarment; and a *kirpan* (sword)—is a devotional act. But at its most basic level, Sikh daily devotion involves remembering God at all times as "the only Doer and Giver," working hard to earn an honest living, and sharing with those in need.

Most American converts to Sikhism entered the religion through the Sikh Dharma movement founded by Yogi Bhajan (Harbhajan Singh, 1929–2004). Many of them have settled in Española, New Mexico, where living in community makes it possible to support each other in daily discipline. "We are about three hundred families," says a longtime resident. "At four o'clock in the morning, everyone (well, not everyone, but many of us) comes together to practice our morning *sangat.* We recite *Japji,* which is the first song of the Sikhs. And then we do about forty-five minutes to an hour of *kundalini yoga,* and then we do an hour of chanting. After that, we have a little thirty-minute worship service." Altogether, this morning routine takes between two and two-and-a-half hours. So, by six or 6:30 A.M., everyone is ready to head off to their jobs—which is also a daily devotional habit. "Most of us are on the Path of the Householder," a community administrator explains. "You work righteously. You earn by the sweat of your brow, in a loving way. So people go to work." By about six o'clock P.M., at least some of the community will gather to do their evening prayers together. Others will do them at home.

Most of what the Sikh Dharma community does daily is typical of any Sikh family. It is the prominence of *kundalini yoga* in their practice distinguishes this movement from mainstream of Punjabi-American Sikhs (and indeed, most other Sikhs worldwide). "The majority of Sikhs consider the practice of *kundalini yoga* antithetical to Sikh doctrine, in fact rejected by Guru Nanak unequivocally." The mainstream position is that any of the "physical exercise yogas" are acceptable as just that—physical exercise—but not as a spiritual exercise in the effort to reach God.

When a Sikh community (or family) gathers for worship, they do so in a *gurdwara*—a place where the holy book, the *Guru Granth Sahib,* is installed. During the liturgy, one member of the community has responsibility for serving as *granthi*—attendant of the holy book. The *granthi* sits before the *Guru Granth Sahib,* facing the congregation, and fans the book with a whisk, much as a servant would attend a king in ancient times. Sikh liturgy itself involves coming together for *kirtan* (singing) and to take a *hukam* (order) from the *Guru* (the holy book). Someone opens the *Guru Granth Sahib* at random, picks a passage, and reads it aloud—and that becomes the gathering's order for the day.

## Devotional Imagery

Sikhism, which avoids all representations of God, arose in a Hindu context in which imagery for the divine is plentiful, colorful, diverse, and much loved. The better umbrella term for this realm is *Sanatana Dharma* (Eternal Law), because it includes groups like the Hare Krishnas who may not want to be called "Hindu." In the realm of *Sanatana Dharma* there are groups and individuals who do not use statues, portraits, and other such depictions of the divine in their rituals of faith. But many do. So do most Jains and Buddhists, and practitioners of Chinese traditional and Afro-Caribbean religions. As we move from "formless worship" (as Sikhs refer to their approach) to "worship using forms," we do well to think for a moment about how these various groups think of the images they use.

Hindus, Jains, and some Buddhists may use two Sanskrit words as technical terms for these images: *murti* (form or embodiment) and *pratima* (reflected image). Either term is vastly preferable to "idol" in conversation about their devotional practices—although they themselves may say "idol," either because they think that their non-Hindu conversation partner will not understand *murti* or *pratima,* or because they do not realize that "idol" is often used pejoratively. "Our statues help us visualize abstract concepts," says one Buddhist. Symbolism is necessary, she says. The world needs it. A Pure Land nun concurs: "It is unkind to call veneration of these images 'idol-worship.'" American Hindus, Jains, and others may point to the statues in their shrines and say, "These are our gods." Again, sometimes they do that because they think their guest will not know a term like *deva* or *tirthankara* or *bodhisattva,* or because "god" for them means "a representation of divine being."

Theravada Buddhism makes use of statues of the Buddha (usually of the historic Siddhartha Gautama) standing, sitting, or reclining—sometimes of imposing size. The statues are not worshiped, but they are honored and respected. They also teach. There are lessons on self-control to be learned from the calm visage, the downcast eyes, the solidness of the material from which the statue is made.

As Mahayana Buddhism spread north and east through Asia, its catalogue of images expanded. America's Chinese Pure Land temples are full of colorful and complex statuary. What would we see if we dropped in for a visit? We might be greeted by the Guardians of the Four Directions (usually quite large, and made of wood) or Wei-to (the Protector—dressed in armor and holding a gnarled staff or a mace), or a guardian Bodhisattva (a being who has earned the right to enter Nirvana, but instead remains in the cycle of life, death, and rebirth in order to bring all other beings to enlightenment).

On the side walls of the meditation hall there may be small statues of the eighteen *lo-hans* (or, *arahants*)—perfected beings who have listened to and practiced the Buddha's teachings. Typically, each *lo-han* carving has a distinctive, amazingly expressive face, and whatever supernatural power he is said to possess is symbolized by the object he holds or by a wild animal posing with him.

We might see the round-tummied Ho-tei (also called Mi-Lo-Fwo). He is the Happy Buddha—happy that all of his disciples will be happy in the land of no suffering. Ho-tei is one way of depicting Maitreya—"the Friendly and Benevolent One" or "One Who Possesses Loving-kindness." He is a ninth-stage Bodhisattva, one step away from being a fully enlightened Buddha.

In some temples, Maitreya will stand near the entrance; in others, the greeter is Avalokitesvara. "Ah-wah-loh-kee-TESS-wah-rah," says the diminutive Burmese nun patiently, three times—until the visitor to her modest New York storefront temple is able to say the name easily. As the embodiment of boundless compassion, Avalokitesvara may be portrayed with many arms (the better to reach out to all beings), or with a crown of many heads (representing every state of the human condition). Its feminine form, Kuan-Yin, is often portrayed holding a vase from which she pours compassion on the world.

There will be one or more images of Shakyamuni (the Buddha as Teacher), usually flanked with Bodhisattvas or with Amitabha (the Buddha of Boundless Light). There may be a display of dozens of tiny Buddhas or Bodhisattvas, each of which can be illuminated by a devotee—much in the way a votive candle may be lit in a church as an act of devotion.

The nuns who run one small but busy temple stress the usefulness of Buddhist imagery in one's devotional life. They encourage it. "We have a 'lending library' of Buddha- and Bodhisattva-statues," one of them explains, pointing to a bookcase near the door, its shelves full of Shakyamunis, Kuan-Yins, and Ho-teis of many sizes, colors, and styles. "If you need one, you can take one—for free!"

It is commonplace to practice Chinese Buddhism in harmony with Taoism and Confucianism. In a traditional Chinese-American home, one might find statuary of Lao-tse and K'ung Fu-tse together with the Buddha, or classical drawings showing the three of them in conversation. To daily rituals of faith, Taoism contributes practices such as *Ch'i-kung* (breathing exercises) or *T'ai-chi ch'üan* (development of mental and physical discipline through slow, graceful movements). Taoism also contributes statuary of deities such as the Jade Emperor (Yuhuang), ruler of all heavens, highest among all spiritual entities, ruler of earth and humanity, *yin* and *yang*, indeed all of creation; Shang-ti (Lord-Above), ruler of the universe, but not the Ultimate Creator; T'u-ti Kung (Earth God), a local caretaker, responsible for neighborhoods, farms, mountainsides; Ch'eng Huang (God of the City Wall and Moat), a celestial "district magistrate"; and Tsao Chün (Lord of the Stove—the Kitchen God), who observes family members and reports on their behavior to the Jade Emperor. "My mother takes the traditional Chinese gods very seriously," reports one accountant—a second-generation Chinese-American, "but she also goes to the Buddhist temple several times a month."

To all of this Confucianism contributes an emphasis on the veneration of ancestors. So, a home shrine might include framed photos of deceased family members (particularly the paternal grandparents) alongside statues of the Buddha and the Household God. "If you go into my mother's house," the accountant continues, "you will see the Kitchen God and the Property God (the god for your house). The Property God must be set on the floor. The Kitchen God does not have to be on the floor. It can be on a shelf. However, we are not supposed to put the household gods in the kitchen, because it is said that they will be bothering the Kitchen God. So the Property God is usually in the living room, sitting on the floor, and always looking toward the main entry door."

It isn't Tsao Chün (the Kitchen God) that some families place in the kitchen, says a member of a weekly Chinese Pure Land Buddhist study circle. In her community, people think of the kitchen-guardian as a *lo-han*. "A *lo-han* is a disciple in the Buddha's time, but below the Bodhisattva level. Just like human beings have various interests and commit themselves to different things, each *lo-han* has something he is interested in, and committed to. There is one whose commitment is to anything that is being cooked in the kitchen. He makes sure it won't be poison, and that it will be delicious!"

In the New York Buddhist Church (a Japanese Pure Land temple) the centerpiece of the shrine is a statue of Amitabha—

the Amida Buddha. *Amida* means Immeasurable Light or Immeasurable Life, says the priest. The statue reflects these two themes. The right arm is bent upward at the elbow, denoting wisdom and light. The fingers of the right hand point upward, except for the index finger, which makes a circle with the thumb, depicting harmony. The left hand is outstretched—fingers straight, palm up in a gesture of compassion and life. Wisdom and compassion are represented as well by the candles and flowers adorning the shrine. Above it hang pictograms for *Ken* (meaning "to see") and *Shin* (meaning "the truth"). "*Ken Shin* (the one who sees the truth) is also an honorific for Shinran Shonin, the founder of Jodoshinshu, which is the school of Buddhism we follow," one member explains.

The notion of seeing truth and reality as they really are returns us to the conversation with our Hindu neighbors. "I think of *murtis* as providing tangible representation of the intangible," says one Hindu engineer. "They provide this only if you believe they do. If you don't believe, the image is just a piece of rock or clay. One doesn't have to stop with the image, because the mind and intellect are complex. At an initial stage, you can't form an idea of something unless you can make sense out of it. We can't see mind and intellect in a physical sense. God is ultimate consciousness. God is much beyond what we can see, hear, and touch."

"Each image has so much symbolism," says one educator. "If you really want to understand, you need to study each one in depth." From a Hindu point of view, no image can be a vehicle of worship until it is ritually empowered to be. Statues or paintings of deities are pointers toward the divine—and temporary ones at that. Some images are temporary in that they are ceremonially discarded and replaced once a year; all are temporary in that, eventually, the mature soul will no longer need such a window.

From a Jain point of view, the statues or portraits are visual reminders of lessons on how to conduct oneself now. Jain use of *tirthankara*-images is an ancient practice. Jainism has two branches: Digambara and Swetambara. "*Digambar* means, literally, the one whose clothes are the sky," a businessman explains—which means that their monks wear no robes at all.

(They don't think of this as "going naked," however.) "And *swet* means white, so Swetambara monks wear white robes," he continues. That given, it is not surprising that Dibambara statuary is always simple, whereas Swetambara statues are more elaborate, and may be decorated with jewels or with gold or silver foil. In the United States, most Jain temples include *murtis* in both styles.

Swetambara Jainism produced a reform movement, the Sthanakvasi. One aspect of their reform was to get rid of temples and the ritual use of images altogether. They may make use of a *sthanak* (meditation hall), but from their point of view, all you really need is a peaceful space. Wherever you find one, you can position yourself there and seek guidance and knowledge from the *tirthankaras,* since they are omnipresent. "Perhaps in ancient times," says one Sthanakvasi Long Islander, "we Jains looked at our Hindu neighbors and thought, 'Everybody has temples. We have to have one. We will put our *tirthankaras* there. We will get inspiration there.' Perhaps that is one explanation for why some Jains use images now."

## Homage

Once the *murti* has been installed ritually, it is "alive" to the individual devotee or the community of faith in some sense, and must be given daily care—just as one would give an honored guest in one's home. This is called *puja*—the ritual paying of respect or homage. Hindus, Jains, and some Buddhists use this term, although how they perform *puja* and what it means is somewhat different in each religion.

### *Hinduism*

"*Puja* is something many of us try to do daily," says Rathi Raja, a Long Island Hindu educator. "My daily *puja* is very, very simple. The underlying concept is giving back what is already there. You could have the simplest of *puja* which the poorest of persons could perform. You could have the elaborate *puja* of someone who is very well off. The only difference is in the substances you use and the money you spend. The wealthy person might use thousands of dollars of roses or carnations, and the poor person might use one small flower she picked from her backyard."

"There is temple *puja* and there is home *puja*," she continues. "But *puja* is an endless ocean. If you were to start cataloguing the different ways temples do it, you would have a very long list. Our temple follows South Indian traditions. The offering is a big part of *puja* for us. The Hindu Center near us has a strong North Indian flavor, although South Indians go there too. Their *pujari* [ritual expert] conducts a very simple *puja* that emphasizes recitation. The offering part is small. In a temple, there are certain minimum requirements. People go to a place that does what they want to see."

"Now a home *puja* is a smaller version of a temple *puja*," she explains. "The five elements of *puja* represent the five elements of the universe: sky, air, fire, water, and earth are represented in the form of flowers, incense stick, the light. Water is represented in the fruit or food—which is all tradition-based. Then of course, sandalwood, which represents earth, and has a sweet smell. There may be many Hindus who do not know what represents what, but they know that *puja* has these five elements. They bring them all together, and recite some prayers, and offer them. For me, during my festival, I will sit down with my family and do *puja*. And if I want some elaborate—we do a *homa* once a year, and we call a priest in. These are rituals which have to be done in a particular way. You find a priest who suits you."

As a Madhva Brahmin,[10] Deepak Sarma's day is oriented around doing *puja* in the morning, at noon, and at dusk. "The *Brahmin* sense of time is oriented around doing at least the first *puja* in the morning—at least in theory," he explains, pointing out that *Brahmin* means he is a member of "the priestly class," but he is not actually "a priest"; most *Brahmins* are not. "I am not sure how many people in America are able do *puja* daily. Certainly in India, many people do the morning ritual. *Puja* involves sitting down and saying the Gayatri Mantra,[11] then saying a series of mantras to different deities. In my case, since I'm Vaishnava, they revolve around Krishna. Depending on how detailed you want to get with your *puja,* you can do it up to two hours. Some of my relatives in India do it for two hours every morning. Here in Cleveland, mine is only about fifteen minutes. In my tradition, the combination of mantras and thought patterns help you to locate yourself in a monotheistic hierarchy. You are in relationship to Vishnu. There would be mantras, sounds, and hand gestures—sacred movements that help to create sacredness."

"I should point out that my day is completely governed by this," Sarma says. "I can't *eat* until I do the *puja.* The day begins with doing the *puja* in the morning. And I have to take a shower. If I don't shower, then I can't do the *puja,* and if I don't do the *puja,* I can't eat. I work out in the morning. So I might get up at 5:30 in the morning, and I'm hungry, but I can't actually eat anything until I work out and take a shower, and come home, and do *puja.* People will say to me, Why don't you have something to eat at the gym? But I can't do that, because I can't really do *puja* at the gym. I could shower in the gym, but it wouldn't work to do *puja* there. So it completely governs my day. In theory, this obligation governs every male *Brahmin*'s day. And if we push it further, we'd be doing it three times a day. Yesterday, I did it twice. I did it at noon; I happened to be home. I'd worked out at 11 o'clock. I came home, took a shower, did a *puja.* So that's how I think of my Hindu day."

In theory, then, Sarma would be taking a shower three times a day. However, he explains, "people have different theories about how much of a shower is necessary. Some people do symbolic things. You're supposed to bathe, to cleanse yourself. Temples in India have tanks and water faucets nearby, so you can somehow cleanse yourself—at least your hands and your arms—before you enter. Very few American Hindus do that these days."

Hindu *puja* can include waking the image; bathing it; dressing it; offering it flowers, water, various other liquids; providing it with fruit, light, and air (by fanning); and "putting it to bed" at night. As one devotee puts it, "the statues are basically statues. But we treat them like God is here. We have to think and behave as if God is here. So maybe that will bring more godliness in us. When we do things for these *murtis,* we become humble. Greed, lust, jealousy—all these things we get rid of from our life so we can become more pure."

"The Christian onlooker might have a hard time with the notion of bathing a deity and putting it 'to bed,'" says one midwesterner. "When people use images in worship, there is interplay between 'This is God' and 'This is not God.' Think of the Eucharist. Is the bread just a 'symbol' in the sense that it points to a 'meaning'? Or is it an embodied presence that acts on us in some way? My sense of Hindu worship is that the deity acts and interacts in a very concrete way *as* (rather than *in*) images."

*Puja* can also include actions like chanting names of a deity. The number of repetitions varies. Sometimes it might be a chant of 108 names; sometimes, many more. "We also have one chant," one devotee explains, "which speaks of the light of the stars, the sun, the moon, everything. This chant is part of all the ceremonies, to describe God who loves in such a way that there's no need for sun, for stars. He is the light behind the light that makes our eyes see. It's a beautiful chant. We not only have a third eye but a third ear, too. In a sense, God is behind the ears you use to hear."

In Hindu practice, *puja* is linked to the notion of *darshan*—the efficacy of seeing and being seen by an image of the divine. It may include an offering of food, which is linked to the notion of *prashad*—the blessing of distributing and consuming the food the deity has "consumed." It may also include *abhishekam*—the holy bath ritual, which involves pouring liquid on a deity while praising it. For a simple home ceremony, pouring water is the norm.

An elaborate temple *abhishekam* would involve the pouring many different substances, and takes about an hour. "We use water, milk, yogurt, honey, sandalwood paste—all expensive things," a temple administrator explains. "We pour each thing over the image. People say to us, 'Why are you wasting these expensive things?' But it isn't like that," he says, pointing to the *murti* of the goddess Lakshmi, which is being bathed in milk as he speaks. "She gave these things to us in the first place!" When the bathing is completed, the *pujaris* close the curtains while they dry and dress the image. "That is for modesty," a devotee explains. "After you take a bath, don't you get dressed in private?" Then the curtains are thrown open once again, and all who are present receive *darshan* (auspicious sight)—the blessing of seeing and being seen by the divine. "Our temple does one every day—for a different deity," says one administrator. "We follow a schedule—a calendar—but if a devotee wants to sponsor one, the temple staff will accommodate that."

*Jainism*

Jains who make use of *murtis* in their devotional practice, whether Digambara or Swetambara, also believe that someone must assume responsibility for performing daily *puja* and the evening lamp-ritual *(arti)* in the presence of the *tirthankara*-images. Lay people can do this—just as they may at home—but often Jain temples in America have a *pujari* (trained *puja*-performer) on staff. Jains, like Hindus, say that they perform *puja* for *darshan.* However, the Jain notion of *darshan* differs from the Hindu idea, in that Jains think of this auspicious sight as one-directional only. Jains feel it is important to see the *tirthankara*-image, but expect nothing in return. At most, a banker explains, "We just say, 'Give us the guidance, and we will strive ourselves. We will look out ourselves. And with our actions, with our potential, we are going to work on the challenges in our life. But keep on guiding, keep on showing us the right path.'"

When Jains perform *puja,* they first walk around the *tirthankara*-image (or images—most temples have at least three, and so do many home shrines). Next they bathe the image with a series of liquids (usually milk, water, and sandalwood paste). Then they arrange grains of rice on the temple floor in a *swastika*—which, for Jains, is a diagram of the four spheres into which a soul can be reborn. Three dots of rice are placed above this diagram, to represent the Three Jewels of Jainism: Right Faith, Right Knowledge, and Right Conduct. Finally, a crescent with a dot resting within it is placed above the three dots, to represent the principle of *ahimsa* (non-harming) and the goal of *moksha* (liberation from the cycle of rebirth).

Sometimes non-Jain visitors to Jain temples and homes are surprised to see how prominent the *swastika* is in Jain symbology. "I had been in this country only a short time," says a Jain pharmacist. "I had a *swastika* decal on my car windshield. You know, I did not know at that time that this is a problem. I parked my car in the company parking lot, but my director called me into his office. He said, 'Take off that sign. Otherwise, somebody would think that you are Nazi!' That day, I started thinking that we should at least publicize more about Jain religion. I wish people would come to know that this sign is as important to us as a cross is to Christians! It is like a cross to us, or like a Star of David is to Jewish people."

In America, much Jain practice is home-based, partly out of necessity. There are very few temples. A nurse explains, "In the morning, when we get up, just as we take a shower before we start our day, so we do *puja* and then we start our day. We raised the children to do that also. Doing our daily *puja* at home is not difficult. But as far as going to the nearest temple, that is difficult. Back home in India, the temples were always within walking distance. Now, going to temple requires a different level of commitment. So, here we have our own little shrine in our home, or we get together at someone's home for instruction or a ritual."

*Buddhism*

When we enter the shrine room of the New York Buddhist Vihara, we notice flowers in front of the Buddha statue. Is that *puja?* "Yes," says the abbot, Kurunegoda Piyatissa. "That is also a *puja*—an offering. When you offer flowers, it is to venerate, and to meditate. When you offer flowers, in your inner mind you think, 'These flowers are now very good. Tomorrow they will be withered; and later, they will be putrid. And then, they will be decomposed and afterwards, they will disappear. In the same way, one day my life will also be faded away, and forgotten, and my body will decompose.' In this way, *puja* helps us understand the impermanence of life. The flower becomes a lesson of the teacher."

What about water? Do you ever set water in front of the statue? Yes, the Venerable Piyatissa replies, "We do that every day. That is also a *puja*—an offering." "Water is used to wash the Buddha statue," a Mahayana graduate student explains. "Or, you can use it in a bowl as a blessing. In Buddhist texts water comes up a lot. Water is seen as being strong but fluid—opposites being together. There is this metaphor: a leader should be like a river—strong yet flexible, to allow for change. There are many stories or teaching tools in the texts that deal with water."

What about candles? Sometimes we see candles at the foot of a Buddha statue. For Theravada Buddhists, says one *bhikkhu* (monk), candles are simply to make light. However, he continues, the candles give light to dark places, and "as a result of that offering of light, you can see the world. In the same way, it is a certain mark of wisdom. By lighting and by offering light to the Buddha, you may be able to gain wisdom on Buddhist teaching. That is how Mahayana Buddhists believe." Yes, a Mahayana practitioner agrees, "and a candle can also be an aid when learning to meditate. I did this back in college. It is a useful tool because you can sit and stare at the little flame. That will help you focus. Eventually, you don't need the help anymore, but it is a wonderful tool in the initial stages."

Like other devout Tibetan Buddhists, one urban executive maintains a shrine in the corner of one room of his home. Typically, it will have a Buddha statue, representations of certain Bodhisattvas, and the family's *guru* or *lama* (if they have one). "We offer seven bowls with water every morning," he explains. "Then we also light butter-lamps and incense, and arrange fresh flowers. Every morning, I get up, say my daily prayers, do my prostrations before the altar, and begin my day." His prayers and prostrations remind him to take refuge in the Triple Jewel—the Buddha, the *Dharma* (the Buddha's teaching), and the *Sangha* (the Buddhist community). What about the Four Noble Truths and the Noble Eightfold Path? Do lay Buddhists think about these things? "I don't," he says. Studying them is time-consuming, and setting aside time for this is difficult. However, he explains, the Four Noble Truths are contained within the prayers that he recites every morning for about fifteen minutes. "I try to correct my motivation right in the morning: not to harm other people, not to harm all sentient beings. If I can, I will help; if I can't help, at least I will try not to harm. That is our practice."

## Meditation

Talk of practice brings us to consideration of meditation. Ask one prominent Theravada leader if meditation is "praying," and he will insist firmly that it is not. What word would he prefer instead? "Say that we *follow* Buddhism, that we *follow* the Buddha's path that he taught us to take. We *practice.*"

Like many Buddhists, some Sikhs and many Hindus and Jains practice meditation daily. It is common to hear Hindus and Sikhs speak of the goal of the practice as "God-realization." Techniques and terms vary. *Hatha yoga* and *raja yoga* are but two methods brought to America by Hindus. The first emphasizes exercises involving postures and rhythmic breathing. The second involved a system of eight steps of abstinence and observance aimed at control of thought, emotions, and sensations. As we have seen, members of the Sikh Dharma movement incorporate *kundalini yoga* into their daily practice. Some Jains practice *kayotsarga*—the renunciation of physical comfort and bodily motion. You are to stand (or you choose some other posture). Then you try to remain absolutely still, meditating on the soul's true nature as being separate from the body. The goal of this form of meditation is gradually to gain control over all human activities—mental and physical.

Jains may also practice *bhavana*—reflection or contemplation that helps the devotee avoid building up bad *karma.* Laypersons engage in four *bhavanas:* reflection on friendship; on admiration (as an antidote to jealousy); on compassion; and on maintaining neutrality or noninvolvement.

"There is this idea in Buddhism called *mindfulness,*" one graduate student explains. "What I like about it is that it is about the finding of the extraordinary in the ordinary. So basically, you can be walking on the street or cleaning your house or sitting and relaxing—but being mindful of what you're doing.

It is a kind of meditation where you are in the moment, and you're fully aware of what's going on around you. So, as a Buddhist, I think one of the biggest things I do on a daily basis is, whenever I am walking anywhere, I try to be mindful of myself in the situation and those around me as much as possible. It is amazing what you see when you are mindful."

The *bhikkhus* (monks) in America's Theravada *viharas* (monasteries) have a built-in community for daily practice of *vipasanna*—insight meditation. "*Vi* means 'particularly,' and *passathi* means 'to see,'" the Venerable Piyatissa explains. "*Vipasanna* is to see, to understand, to realize, that things are impermanent, that they are subject to suffering. That is because of delusion."

For example, the abbot says, eating a meal is a good time to practice controlling your mind. "When you digest, you may feel hungry, but you have to realize this hunger is not permanent. When you eat, the hunger will disappear; but it will come again. That is the nature of changing. Insight meditation helps us realize the nature of every changing thing in the *samsara.* Now we see how much we have been changed. When we entered this room we didn't have such knowledge of the *dhamma,* but now we have enriched our knowledge. Not only that, we are older, stepping forward to death, because we have reduced our lifetime. When we came to the room it was nearly 3:30 and now it is nearly 4:30. This is the way: not only time is changing; everything is changing." Meditation purifies the mind of greed, hatred, and delusion, the monk explains. "When you can slow down your active mind," he says, "then you can understand better. For that purpose we meditate, because through meditation we can gain insight. There is no other way."

Theravada Buddhism has its American converts, and there are American Buddhist movements which are based on insight meditation, but have not adopted the other aspects of Theravada as a whole. Americans have been aware of and participating in Zen Buddhism far longer. The primary practice of Zen is *zazen* (sitting meditation). This can be done alone, says a Long Islander who embraced Zen a couple of decades ago. "Of course I practice at home—most of us practice at home. Every day I sit for an hour. I like to do this in the morning, but if I have a busy day, I'll do thirty minutes in the morning and thirty minutes in the evening."

A Chicago-based Zen priest offers training in sitting meditation, and recommends it as an early morning practice, "before the mind is horribly active and has had time to put the ego together." People come to his *zendo* (meditation hall) on a daily basis to join him in *zazen* (sitting). Followers can do this at home, of course, and many do; but some people like the daily support of a group.

"Meditation is the main part of our practice—sitting meditation," says the head minister of a major Won Buddhist temple. She *does* speak of prayer and praying—silently and aloud. To whom are Won Buddhists praying? "You are praying to your Buddha nature inside you," she explains, "praying that everyone named in your prayer might be transformed, might be transported."

"Water is the symbol of purification. Each day, when we see a new day, we begin by offering water to Buddha before we meditate. In the morning, it is meditation-in-silence. During the day we practice meditation-in-action, in an effort to build a stronger community and a better society. It is a way to keep the meditative state of your mind throughout the day. We describe it as having about thirty percent of your awareness being awareness of your breathing and your inner center. You are aware of your inner world: your feelings, your behavior. Your focus is on *you.* With your other seventy percent, you are engaging the outer world. You are meditating as you fulfill your duties."

## Day-long Prayer and Purification

This notion of meditating while fulfilling other duties relates directly to the notion of prayer as inseparable from daily activities. We are turning once again to theistic religions.

*Native American Religions*
"Every single day, every single thing we do, it's all with the Creator in mind. That's how things are done in Native ways," says a Nashotah Cree mother. "Whatever we are doing, we are praying. When we are praying, we are praying for every single person on this earth, every single being on this earth. When that prayer goes up to the Creator, it encompasses every single thing that is of the Creator." A Keetoowah writer says she was taught to think that every step she takes is a prayer of thanks to the Creator. Therefore, she says, "Walk lightly on Grandmother Earth, give thanks, and respect others."

"Native peoples don't need an intermediary when praying to God," says an Ojibway healthcare worker. "We don't go to medicine people to talk to the Creator." "Our daily prayer comes from the heart," says an Oglala Lakota community worker. "You don't need a prayer book. If a person wants to do it right, it's a discipline. You would get up before sunrise—like three o'clock in the morning. First you pray in the Four Directions, and then you remember the Morning Star. Then you pray up to Heaven, and then down to Mother Earth. You would have a pitcher or cup of water handy, and after the prayer, you take a drink and give thanks for the water of life." There are, of course, mealtime blessings to be said. Then, at the end of the day, the routine is similar. "Again, you pray to the Four Directions, and then you would have a short prayer or prayer-song, giving thanks to the Creator, to all of creation, to all of the cosmos, and to the human beings—the four-legged and the two-legged."

The Anishinabe (Ojibway) People make *smudging* part of their daily routine. It is also a good way to open a meeting, says a health center administrator. "We pray all the time around here," she explains. "We smudge the medicines we dispense, to bless them. We also do it to open our staff meetings. It helps us focus. Today we are using sage for our smudge, but we could use tobacco or sweetgrass or cedar."

Her co-worker has lit some kindling in a large seashell, and is wafting the embers with a feather, carrying the shell clockwise around the perimeter of the room, finally placing it in the center of the conversation-circle. "The sage is at the center of creation, which is what the smudge-pot represents. When we use our smudge, it is for the intention of blessing our space—in front of us, behind us, to the right and to the left, above us and below us. We petition Creator—however you want to refer to the Great One. We ask Creator to come to our space, to take good care of us, and to bring the spirits around us from the Kingdom, to help us in this way."

*Shinto*

Many Shinto-followers keep a *kamidana* (deity-residence) in their home. "The Shinto day begins and ends with gratitude," explains the Rev. Koichi Barrish, priest of the Tsubaki Grand Shrine of America. Outwardly, Shinto rituals have remained unchanged for millennia. "Every morning," says a dental hygienist, "my father stands in front of the *kamidana* and claps twice. Then he bows, says a brief prayer, claps twice again, and turns away." Why the clapping? "We send and receive vibration to and from the *kami,* and we offer respect," the Rev. Barrish explains. Beyond this ritual, daily acts of purification are the very essence of Shinto. "Physical cleaning—house-cleaning—is pivotally important," the priest continues. "*Kami* won't come to a dirty place. *Kami* are deities of higher vibration; they won't come to a place with low vibration."

The priest's daily routine involves *gishiki* (Shinto ceremony). "*Gishiki,*" the Rev. Barrish explains, "is direct communion with the fountainhead of cosmic life." The effect, he says, is that "intuitive knowledge is brought to the surface of the modern mind, and the natural result of that is deep humility and gratitude for the gifts of life." *Chohai* (daily ritual) begins early in the morning with self-purification, then ritual purification of the shrine grounds and building, and the food offerings for the *kami.* He invites the *kami*'s cleansing action. He waves the *haraigushi* (wand) in order to sweep away stagnation. Everyone present recites the *O-harai-no-kotoba* (the Great Words of Purification).

Later, on a typical day at the shrine, worshipers will come for special prayer ceremonies. After each such ceremony, they can enjoy a sip of purified *sake,* which they are—in effect—sharing with the *kami.* They and the priest will also be able to enjoy the food dedicated to the *kami* in the morning ritual. Because this food is now imbued with "clear energy," it is believed, it gives special strength to all who partake. The priest's daily duties include performing *gishiki* requested by individuals and families. Such ceremonies are a means by which the priest helps people deal with whatever is happening in their lives.

The Rev. Koichi Barrish's own daily practice includes the performance of *misogi* (purification with water). He has been performing *misogi* for over twenty-eight years, and every morning for more than thirteen. *Misogi* is purification in moving water—a waterfall, a river, or the ocean. Recently, he has been using the river near the shrine. "*Misogi* is unmitigated experience of nature," he says. "If you've ever been camping in the summer, and you've gone into a really pristine mountain river, you'll remember how incredibly alive you felt when you came out. *Misogi* is like that. It is a wonderful way to enhance your connection to Great Nature. You can do it once, and have a life-changing experience. For me, it is best to do it every day."

## Mantras

Literally, a mantra is "an instrument of thought." A mantra can be a single syllable or a verse which is believed to be of divine or cosmic origin. Chanting a mantra is a way to focus one's concentration, a way to change what is possible in the world. So, repetition is important. That is why, in Tibetan tradition, one may write out the mantra (sometimes dozens or even hundreds of times) and place it in a prayer wheel. With each turn of the wheel (or cylinder), the prayer is repeated exponentially. Similarly, the mantra can be written on a prayer flag. Each fluttering in the wind is a repetition of the prayer.

*Hinduism*

"Every day," one woman explains, "I go into my prayer room. I utter God's mantras, and I utter God's name. Since Hinduism allows different paths for worshiping God, I choose the path that is most comfortable for me. I believe that doing mantra and doing God's name is as powerful as doing meditation yoga. Some people want to reach God that way, but for me as a common person, I go to God, I pray to God, and I utter his name three times, I utter a couple of mantras three times, and that satisfies my need to offer devotion. I pray a Krishna mantra. I do it three times. I would do Gayatri Mantra three times. Then I utter Lord Shiva's mantra, which gives you strength in calamities. So uttering those mantras and thinking about God three times a day gives me the satisfaction of reaching God. I don't do meditation. That's not me. Some people believe in ritual. They follow ritual, doing *puja.* Me, no. I just believe in mantras. That's how I try to reach God."

Many Hindus make chanting the Gayatri Mantra part of their daily devotions: "O Absolute, Ultimate Source of the Three Dimensions [earth, atmosphere, heaven]: we contemplate your light—the universal source of wisdom; may Divine Grace illuminate our intellect." Its Sanskrit text comes from the *Rig Veda.* In fact, this mantra is sometimes called the Mother of the Vedas, because (in a sense) it summarizes the teachings of this form of Indian sacred literature. "Twice-born" Hindus (that is, members of the upper three castes) are taught this mantra as part of the rite of passage into the Student Stage. Thereafter, they are to recite it every morning and evening—preferably sixteen times.

However, the simplest and most profound mantra is "AUM." For Hindus, AUM (also, "OM") is the Primal Sound from which the universe evolved, carrying the meaning of infinite completeness and eternal wholeness. A midwesterner explains it this way: "We say *'AUM, Shanti, Shanti, Shanti.' Shanti* means 'peace and quiet.' The sound AUM is a very spiritual way of cleansing your body. Every morning, we do AUM. The deeper you take the sounds, the more you cleanse your body."

Some Hindus use a *mala* (a string of prayer beads) to keep track of their mantra-repetitions. "We do five *malas* every morning," explains a member of the BAPS movement (devotees of Sri Swaminarayan). His *mala* is a string of 108 beads, with a 109th larger bead which acts as the counter. "A *mala* is holy," he says. "You must wash your hands before you touch these things." He keeps his in a protective bag, even when he is using it. He whispers "Swaminarayan" as he touches each bead, going around the string until he reaches the starter-bead, then doubling back. "Sometimes we do it five times sitting down, one time while standing on the left foot (with the right foot up), and one time while walking around the deities."

Private spiritual practice for committed members of the Krishna Consciousness movement involves chanting the *Maha Mantra* up to two hours per day. It is a simple pattern using only the words *Hare, Krishna,* and *Rama.* Essentially, it means, "O energy of the Lord—known to us as Krishna and Rama"; and implies a request to be engaged in God's service. "We believe that chanting changes things," says a West Virginia monk who came to New York City and chanted in Union Square for four days soon after the September 11, 2001 attacks. "Chanting expands what it is possible for God to accomplish in that space."

### *Jainism*

AUM is important to Jain practice, and, like Hindus, Jains think of it as primal, eternal sound. However, Jains add another layer of interpretation. By thinking of it as AAAUM, it is also the seat of the five benedictions of the *Navkar Maha Mantra* (the Great Salutation Formula). Whether a renunciate or a layperson, whether or not one uses *murtis* (images), the *Navkar Maha Mantra* is the most important, most basic Jain formula, and can be recited at any time of day. "This mantra is what most people I know recite on a daily basis," says a bank officer. "It is pretty short, and it comes in very handy."

Because devotees actually bow as they chant, this formula is sometimes called the *Namaskar Mantra.* It is also known as the *Pancha Namaskara* (the Fivefold Salutation) because it pays homage to the five categories of spiritual beings: the *arahants* (enlightened souls), the *siddhas* (liberated souls), living spiritual leaders, teachers of the scriptures, and *sadhus* (ascetics). Its text praises the virtues of all categories of supremely spiritual people without mentioning any particular person by name, honoring them equally.

Regardless of the name by which it is known, it summarizes the essence of Jainism: liberation requires that we renounce worldly life. To do this, we must work our way up the chain of spiritual discipline, progressing from layperson, to monk or nun, to inspired teacher, and ultimately attaining the omniscience of *arahant* status—which leads directly to liberation, and the becoming of a *siddha*—one who has attained perfection, and so is now formless, and out of our reach.

*Buddhism*

"The evening is very interesting for us," says a Won Buddhist minister, "because that is when we chant to return to our inner center. During the day, we have been very much engaged with the outer world, so our mind is so busy, so noisy, that it is hard to meditate. So we begin with chanting meditation. The words are *Namu Amitabu.* Pure Land Buddhists use this chant, but it has a different meaning for us than for Pure Land Buddhists." Won Buddhists interpret it as 'I yield to' or 'I am returning to' the Amida Buddha—the Buddha of Compassionate Light and Life that is within me." From a Won perspective, she says, "There is a compassionate Buddha within, an internal light and internal life within ourselves. This is a different way of speaking of your 'Buddha-nature.' So we are coming back to that source within ourselves. By chanting *Namu Amitabu,* we are coming back to the center of our being. That helps us to center and balance ourselves."

While a mantra may be an aid to meditation, some also function somewhat like a creed—a very brief affirmation of a core belief. Tibetan Buddhists prefer the mantra of Avalokitesvara (the Bodhisattva of Compassion): *Om mani padme hum* (I am aware of the jewel in the lotus of the heart).[12] For Pure Land Buddhists the mantra is *Namu-amida-butsu* (also *Namo o-mi-to fwo* or *Namo Amitabha Buddha*). It means, I rely on the Buddha of Boundless Light.

This practice is called *nien-fwo* (prayer recitation) in Chinese. In Japanese, it is called *nembutsu.* It has a proper method, beginning with the three aspects of the proper frame of mind: sincerity, faith, and aspiration to be reborn in the Pure Land. You adopt an appropriate sitting posture and, if possible, have an image of the Buddha on which to fix your eyes. As you give voice to the six syllables of the mantra, your ears help your mind to stay fixed on the goal of passage into the Pure Land. The Pure Land is not the same as Nirvana. It is one of the many heavenly realms of Buddhist cosmology—a heavenly state in which beings will be free from temptation, and blessed with the best conditions to practice *dharma* and achieve Nirvana. The majority of Chinese Pure Land Buddhists are devotees of the Avalokitesvara, the Bodhisattva of Boundless Compassion—often portrayed as Kuan-Yin (a female figure). Kuan-Yin devotees have their own preferred mantras.

The Nichiren Order teaches that the Lotus Sutra is the most genuine embodiment of the Buddha's teachings. Their core practice, therefore, is affirmation of this by chanting the *Odaimoku* (Sacred Title): *Namu Myoho Renge Kyo* (I take refuge in the sublime Lotus Sutra). The Lotus Sutra itself teaches the merits of embracing, reading, reciting, teaching, and copying out the Lotus Sutra. The Buddha is said to have taught that anyone who venerates it or who reads, recites, teaches, or copies out even a single one of its verses—or simply dedicates oneself to chanting the *Odaimoku*—performs a compassionate act on behalf of all living beings. Nichiren Buddhists chant *Namu myoho rengekyo* as they perform their cross-country walking meditation. As they walk and chant, they bow to the Buddha-nature of everyone they pass. In this way, they hope to increase peace in the world.

### *Islam*

Muslim mystics (some—but not all—of whom call themselves Sufis) engage in a daily practice not unlike mantra-chanting. It is called *dhikr* (with the *dh* pronounced like the "th" in "this"; sometimes pronounced "zikr"). *Dhikr* means recollection or remembrance. "Remembering what? Remembering the continual presence of God—that Allah is nowhere else, is not another place," explains a translator of early Islamic literature, herself a member of a Sufi Order. "God's right here. Everything in the universe may distract us. If we get lucky, everything in the universe may also remind us of this. The Sufi effort, in a sense, is to move from allowing the universe to distract us to allowing the universe to remind us."

*Dhikr* involves repetition, and beads can be helpful in keeping count. "They're very convenient," the scholar agrees. "I call them *tasbih* because my Sufi Order comes from the Turkish tradition. The Arabs call them *subha. Tasbih* and *subha* are two forms of the same root-word. Anyhow, the beads have been around in Muslim tradition for centuries and centuries. They come from India originally, and the Catholic rosary comes from the same source." A graduate student says that, in his Order, the practice is to begin by reciting *La ilaha illa'Llah* (There is no god but God) 165 times. "We have ninety-nine beads, and they are marked off in sets of thirty-three; so that is one-and-two-thirds times around the *tasbih.* In the science of numbers, there is a reason for that; other Sufi Orders might do something else. Next you do 165 of *Ya Allah.* After that, we say the 112th chapter of the Qur'an thirty-three times (it's very short). And finally, thirty-three *salawats* (requests for God's blessing on the Prophet). I do this every day."

## Supplication

The gates of prayer are always open, says Jewish tradition, and one can enter those gates with extemporaneous protest, rage, and complaint as well as gratitude and joy. Spontaneous requests are always appropriate. Jews are encouraged to maintain a running conversation with God—and so are the followers of many other religious paths. The making of supplication has been called a basic human activity, but in some religions we find a well-developed library of supplication literature, and the engaging in non-obligatory supplication is a cherished daily ritual for some. We will look at three examples: Judaism, Islam, and Zoroastrianism.

*Judaism*

In the Jewish repertory of supplication texts, one prayer, the *Tefillat ha-Derekh* (Prayer for Traveling) is to be recited before embarking on any journey. "Its origin is in the Talmud," a young scholar explains. "Basically, any journey out of your village was perilous. So it made sense that whenever you left your home to go somewhere else, you'd say a prayer to God to protect you, and to grant you peace. It's the kind of prayer you can use at different times. A lot of people use it when they are going on long journeys—definitely when going on a plane. Some people carry it around on their key chains and use it every time they drive their car."

Then there is the *Shehecheyanu:* "Blessed are You, O Lord, Creator of time and space, for you have given us life, saved us, and brought us to this time."[13] Technically, says one rabbi, "the *Shehecheyanu* is mostly about arriving at a new point. It can mark newness, and it can mark a significant event. It's said on all the holidays. It's said when someone does something for the first time—like the first time someone is called to the Torah. It is also said when you wear new clothes. Some people think you should stick to these defined times when using it. Other people have expanded upon this, and use it to mark all different sorts of passages of life." Still others say it in order to transform whatever they are doing (studying, shopping, hiking, gardening—whatever) into a sacred moment.

"I am quite fascinated by *techinas* (*techinot,* if we want to use the proper plural)," says an Orthodox professor. "*Techinas* are Jewish women's supplications—although some were written by men—and they are in Yiddish." This literature dates from the seventeenth century. They provide a way to talk to God "Jewishly" about women's concerns: infertility, pregnancy, childbirth, post-partum depression, hysterectomy, menopause, divorce, and more. The old *techinas* are being translated, and new ones are emerging as well, as the genre is being claimed anew in some circles as an authentic vehicle for today's Jewish women to call upon God, to bind themselves back to the spirituality of Jewish women of past centuries, and to strengthen their own present sisterhood.

*Islam*

For some Muslims, *du'a'* and *dhikr*—supplication and remembrance—are dimensions of the five-times-daily *salat.* For others, they are vehicles of beyond-the-mandatory devotion in their own right. *Du'a'* literature is associated with Sufism, but not all Muslims who make a special place for supplication in their daily routine would call themselves Sufis. "For me," says an Alabama graduate student, "*du'a'* and *dhikr* are about being aware of God's actions and attributes—his Beautiful Names. When I perform *du'a'* or *dhikr,* I am calling on God in a certain case. For example, when I am writing a paper, I would ask God the Most Knowledgeable, the Most Articulate, to help me be articulate and accurate."

Many Islamic supplications are taken directly from the Qur'an. An example is the Throne Verse (2:255), which begins, "God: there is no god but He, the Ever Living the Ever Watchful. Neither slumber nor sleep overtakes Him."[14] One New York social worker learned it as a child in Pakistan. Now she wears it as a gold medallion on a chain around her neck. "I pray it every time I set off on a journey—even the shortest errand in the car. I never start my car without praying it first."

Other supplications come from the *Hadith*—the authoritative record of the Prophet Muhammad's own practice. Many are very short, but one notable exception is a litany traced back to the Prophet through his son-in-law Ali.[15] This is the *Jawshan al-Kabir* (The Great Armor),[16] a one-hundred-stanza meditation on God's "Beautiful Names." It takes one hour to recite in its entirety, but many who pray the *Jawshan* read just ten stanzas per day, working their way through the whole every ten days. Like many Turkish-American Muslims, one graduate student says the *Jawshan* is very meaningful for him. He keeps a copy of it on his dashboard. "Whenever I get in the car," he says, "I read a few stanzas. It calms me, and centers me. It helps me be a better a driver." He recites it in Arabic (as is customary), but he likes to study its meaning in Turkish and English translations.

In third category of *du'a'* are the supplications composed or collected by Islam's great spiritual masters. A great-grandson of the Prophet Muhammad known by the honorific Zayn al-'Abidin (Jewel of the Worshipers) left a legacy of supplications sometimes called "The Psalms of Islam."[17] The collection is especially revered by Shi'ah Muslims, for whom Zayn al-'Abidin is their Fourth Imam (fourth authoritative leader of the community after the Prophet's death). A Shi'ah graduate student says she reads from this collection every day. However, many Sunnis love it as well, attests a Syrian-American family in Maryland.

*Zoroastrianism*

For Zoroastrians, the *Gathas* are the words of the Prophet Zarathustra. They are the record of his teachings and of his relationship with God, thus an example for a Zoroastrian's own practice. One devout member of the Washington community observes how Zarathustra's relationship with God was intensely open and personal. No topic was off-limits, it seems. In the *Gathas,* we hear Zarathustra asking God questions like, Who fixed the course of the sun and of the stars, and the waxing and waning of the moon? He brings God his concerns for his personal safety, and his anxiety about his ability to fulfill his calling. He asks for guidance, but always retains his ability to think for himself. For members of the Zoroastrian reform movement especially, Zarathustra's example offers encouragement to engage God directly, and to be certain that supplication made lovingly and with good intentions will receive some sort of an answer.

## Reflections

In this chapter we have learned of many ways in which devout people maintain a daily dialogue with the divine—or if not with the divine, then with themselves. Some have called it "praying"; others call it "meditating." For still others, neither of those terms is quite right, and they have introduced us to their own vocabulary of worship or veneration. We have seen the same elements and objects in use in one religion and another—beads, water, statues, flame—but with different intent. These daily rituals of faith are ways in which our neighbors create some sacred time and sacred space each day—or affirm that every day is holy. Now that we know something about the daily devotions of our neighbors, let us turn to weekly and monthly practices, and the phenomenon of congregationalizing.

CHAPTER THREE

# Coming Together

AS WE LEARN ABOUT how members of America's many religion-communities pray or venerate or practice or observe, we are keenly aware of the much greater variety of storefront and free-standing sacred spaces dotting the landscape than was the case a quarter-century ago. We wonder what goes on inside. In some religions, it is obligatory (or at least highly desirable) to meet as a community regularly. In others, in their original context their ritual spaces would be open all the time; people would come and go as they felt the need. Only on holidays would there be anything like a "group activity." In the American context, adherents of all of these religions do meet regularly—weekly or monthly, bi-monthly or occasionally—and not just on major holidays.

In this chapter, we will learn about mandated regular communal practices, and consider other ways religion-communities come together regularly for worship and practice.

## Obligatory Weekly Observances

*Judaism*

It has been said that the Jews get the credit for inventing the weekend, and Judaism does seem to be the first religion to have established a weekly day of rest. Called Shabbat (Sabbath), it begins eighteen minutes before sunset on Friday, and ends about an hour after sunset on Saturday. There is a tremendous range of Jewish commitment to Shabbat observance, with liturgies for home and synagogue. Some people "do it all." Others maintain some or all of the home traditions and rarely go to synagogue. For still others, synagogue attendance trumps home-based rituals. Some attend synagogue just on Friday evening, some just on Saturday, and others try to get there both days.

"Shabbat is definitely where my Jewish calendar conflicts with the secular calendar," says one young professional woman. "Every week it begins and ends at different times. So, in the summer, that makes it hard to go out on a Saturday night, because sunset is so late in the evening. And in the winter, it is hard to get home from work and begin the Sabbath on time, because Friday sunset is so early. Sometimes Shabbat starts at four o'clock."

"I look forward to the Sabbath as the one day in which I will, for the most part, refrain from my normal activities," says a political scientist who calls himself "a Post-Modern Jew." "Shabbat is on my mind by Wednesday, because I have to make sure that I have done all of my marketing in advance. If I am inviting people to join me, I will have done a lot of the preparation by Thursday night, so that by Friday, I will be able to have everything in order by sunset. It is the one day of the week that one can count on dessert at my house—in fact, a good dessert!

And it is the one meal where I'll generally see friends. Interestingly, being mindful of Jewish time on Friday night means, paradoxically, that it is the one night when I'm *less* mindful of time. A Friday night meal will just go on and on."

"The real mark that the Sabbath is about to begin," he continues, "is that I am making a hurried stop at the corner grocer to pick up the quart of milk I might have forgotten (and won't be able to get for the next twenty-four hours), but more importantly, a bouquet of flowers. I *always* bring home flowers to begin Shabbat. I really don't notice who is carrying their flowers on other days of the week, but I often think, as I see people carrying their flowers on Friday afternoons, 'Aha! That person must be going off to celebrate Shabbat—even if they don't know it!' You see, there is this notion of *Hiddur Mitzvah* (which means, 'beautification of the *mitzvah*' or 'beautification of the commandment'). It means that one doesn't engage in a commandment as an onerous act of obligation that one is seeking to get out of the way; one wants to beautify it, and make it one's own. So, to personalize Shabbat, and to beautify it, I bring home flowers."

The traditional Friday evening dinner is a liturgical event, and while the essentials can be found in one's *siddur* (prayer book), there are Shabbat how-to books available as well. It begins by gathering the family and lighting two candles, which should be able to burn slowly enough to last for at least an hour, and will be allowed to burn themselves out. "I light the candles," one mother explains. "We circle our hands around the flames three times, then bring our hands up to cover our faces, then we say the Shabbat blessing." The dining table is to be covered with a white tablecloth. A platter bearing two loaves of *challah* (special bread) covered with a cloth are placed in the center, along with special goblet called a *kiddush* cup (sanctification cup) which will be filled with kosher grape wine. The meal begins (at least in homes of Ashkenazy heritage) by singing the Shabbat hymn *Shalom Aleikhem* (Peace be unto you)—a song welcoming the Shabbat angels into one's home.

Next comes recitation of special blessings for one's spouse and for one's children, followed by recitation of the *Kiddush*—a prayer which, in recounting the story of Creation and the

Exodus out of slavery, celebrates God as the source of life and justice. For this prayer, the *kiddush* cup is filled to the rim with wine. (In many families, it is the custom to stand for this.) The prayer is said while holding the cup in the palm of one's hand, symbolizing that all good things come from God. It concludes with the formula "Blessed are you O Lord, Who sanctifies Shabbat"—to which everyone responds, Amen! Everyone now takes a sip of the wine, and there is to be no conversation until the goblet has made its way around the table.

Everyone now engages in a ceremonial hand-washing using water poured from a pitcher into a bowl at the table, or into a nearby sink, while reciting the thanksgiving for bread, and thus for the entire meal. This recalls how the priests in the Jerusalem temple would have purified themselves in order to perform sacrifices—the Shabbat table replacing the temple altar in our time. The *challah* is passed so that everyone may take and eat a piece dipped in salt (as temple sacrifices would have been). The ritual part of the meal is over until the blessings after the meal; the rest of it focuses on food and fellowship.

While the home is the center of Shabbat observance, attendance at synagogue services—albeit optional—can be very satisfying. Some attend every week; others, less frequently. The services for Friday evening and Saturday morning are quite different from each other. Orthodox services are the longest. A Conservative Friday night service is about an hour or hour-and-a-half. Reform services are significantly shorter, and often at a fixed time.

The first part of the Friday evening service is called *Kabballat Shabbat*—Sabbath-Welcoming. The tradition was begun by Jewish mystics during the Middle Ages, a rabbi explains. "It incorporates beautiful imagery of rebirth and renewal and peace. There are a lot of psalms, and lots of ritual. For example, at one point everyone turns and faces east in silence to watch Shabbat come in, as it were." Then comes the usual daily evening service, which includes the *Sh'ma* and the *Amidah*, and beautiful melodies to sing during this part as well.

In Orthodox and Conservative synagogues, the Saturday morning service can last for several hours, and has many more parts to it. There is something of a warm-up service of psalms.

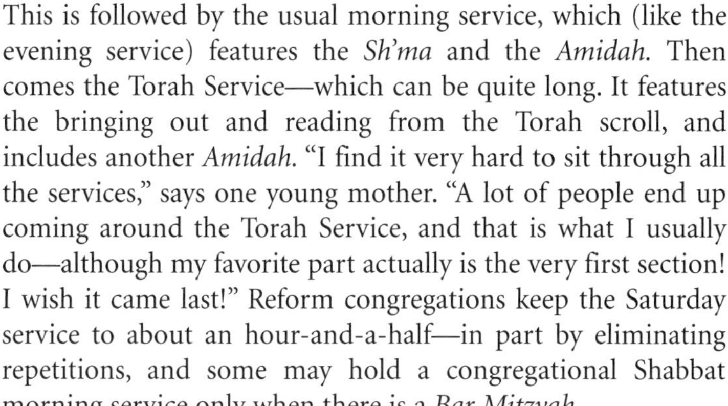

This is followed by the usual morning service, which (like the evening service) features the *Sh'ma* and the *Amidah.* Then comes the Torah Service—which can be quite long. It features the bringing out and reading from the Torah scroll, and includes another *Amidah.* "I find it very hard to sit through all the services," says one young mother. "A lot of people end up coming around the Torah Service, and that is what I usually do—although my favorite part actually is the very first section! I wish it came last!" Reform congregations keep the Saturday service to about an hour-and-a-half—in part by eliminating repetitions, and some may hold a congregational Shabbat morning service only when there is a *Bar Mitzvah.*

"Saturday night, if we're home," says a young educator, "we do *Havdalah,* the ceremony which marks the departure of Shabbat. You light a special braided candle with two wicks, you inhale the aroma of spices which are kept in a little box, and you share a goblet of wine over which the end-of-Shabbat blessing is said."

To observe Shabbat fully, however, there is more to consider than candle-lighting rituals, Friday night dinner, and synagogue attendance. This is a twenty-five-hour interval during which life is to be lived quite differently from the rest of the week. There are many things a Jew is supposed to do to make Shabbat special, and there are also many things one is not to do—for the same reason. On Shabbat, Jews are not to take part in creative activities, and the Mishnah lists thirty-nine to be avoided—things like writing, gardening, cooking, sewing, building, cutting, and carrying things from public to private space (and vice versa)—from beginning a new task or completing a task already in progress. Interpretations vary on all of this, but it is common to consider that observing Shabbat includes taking a twenty-five-hour break from talking on the phone, spending money, and driving the car. "I don't shop on the Sabbath," says one grandmother. "I don't handle money." Her neighbor says, "I like to go to Saturday morning services, but the synagogue is five miles from where I live. My compromise is that I take the bus there, and walk home."

While refraining from certain kinds of activities plays an important part in giving Shabbat its character, so does participation in “activities of rest”—which include leisurely walks, napping, playing non-competitive games, reading a good book, or having a lively discussion with friends. How stringently one observes Shabbat is a matter of denominational allegiance, individual sensibilities, family background, and more. “The concept of *mitzvah* has a different quality in Reform Judaism than in Orthodoxy,” says a Reform rabbi. “In Orthodoxy, it’s a belief that God actually commanded you to do something. God will punish you if you don’t, and will reward you if you do. In the Reform context, you do it because it’s a way of personal, spiritual growth. The reward is in feeling nearer to God.”

*Islam*

Like Jews, Muslims have a mandated weekly day of observance, but it is *Yaumu’l-Jum‘ah*—the Day of Gathering—rather than a day of rest. It coincides with the Western calendar’s Friday. Observant Muslim men take seriously the obligation to gather at the nearest *masjid* (mosque) for the Friday midday prayer, which usually begins around 12:30 or one o’clock. (Women are not required to attend, but many do.) *Salat* is performed as always, but time is provided as well for a *khutbah* (sermon)—which is often given by the imam, but could be given by someone else. Usually, this is a two-part discourse. The first part is usually an explanation of a Qur’an passage chosen by the speaker, while the second part addresses a topic made relevant by current events.

Congregational *salat* is performed in rows, shoulder to shoulder, with everyone facing toward the Ka‘aba in Mecca. Traditionally, Muslim women pray behind men (although there are a few mosques in the United States where the women have always prayed on one side of the hall, and the men on the other). This men-in-front, women-in-back arrangement is sometimes as simple as that. But in some mosques, the women are expected to go behind a fixed partition or a curtain, or they pray in a balcony. Where mosques are in found space (a townhouse, for example), the men may be on the ground floor, and the women on the second floor, with the imam’s voice piped over a speaker; or, it may be the other way around. Occasionally, mosques have separate entrances for women and men. In some countries, Muslim women rarely go to mosques, and so the notion that women *shouldn't* be in the mosque has been imported into some American communities. Sometimes they are turned away with the excuse that "there isn't enough room." Sound Vision, a major American Islamic educational foundation, has published articles from time to time reminding American Muslim men that such behavior is not Islamic.

Traditionally, only a man can lead *salat* if both women and men are present, although a woman has always been able to lead prayers for a congregation of women only. Recently, a small but vocal movement has emerged which insists that women's leadership of community prayers is authentically Islamic under all circumstances, and that women should never be denied access to the main door and main floor of the mosque. American Muslim women are far from being of one mind about whether women's leadership of mixed-gender prayers is worth the struggle, or even whether it is truly desirable.

"The issue arises in the American context," a Muslim hospital chaplain explains, "because there has developed an expectation that the imam of a mosque is supposed to be a kind of clergyperson—a leader who represents a congregation to the larger society." Most of the discussion misses the real point, she says. "The real issue is, 'Can women be the leader (that is, president of the board) of a congregation? Can the women who lead Islamic organizations—be they for women only, or mixed—sit on the Imams Council in their city?' These things happen already. The term 'imam' could indeed be readjusted to include mosque presidents and heads of associations, and that would make perfect sense in the American context—and Islam, historically, has always adapted to the universe it's entered."

### *Bahá'í Faith*

Like Judaism, the Bahá'í Faith has a day of rest, but it is supposed to be on Fridays, and most American Bahá'ís find this very difficult to observe. However, there is another regular mandated observance which contributes much more to the Bahá'í Faith's unique character. The Bahá'í calendar—different from all others—divides the year into nineteen months of nineteen days. Each new month is to be welcomed with a Nineteen

Day Feast—which does not necessarily require food! "It is a spiritual feast," says an elementary school teacher, "but we have snacks as well." The Nineteen Day Feast's purpose is largely administrative: the local community comes takes this opportunity to worship together and to take care of any necessary decision-making, she explains, "And then we have the fellowship, sharing food with each other."

## Full-Moon Gatherings

In some religions, the mandate is not to gather weekly, but to heed the phases of the moon. Full-moon days are very important for Hindus, Buddhists, Taoists, Shinto-followers, and others. For some, the new moon calls for special observances. There are rites to be performed, and in the American context, this provides a good reason for the community to assemble at the temple or shrine. Hindus who set their festivals according to a lunar calendar divide each twenty-nine- or thirty-day month into two two-week periods. "I tend to look at the month's schedule in terms of *ekadashi* (fasting)," explains an Ohio resident. "In a lunar month there occur two days when you fast. Twice a month—once each fortnight, you fast."

For Shinto-followers, a special ceremony marks the beginning of a new lunar month. As with Shinto, Chinese traditional religion places much emphasis on the lunar cycle. "I don't follow the rules too strictly," says an accountant, the daughter of a very traditional Chinese-American, "but on the first and fifteenth days of the lunar month, we are not supposed to eat meat—only vegetables. My mother is very strict about this, but she does not force it on the rest of us. On the first and the fifteenth, there is always a gathering at the Buddhist temple, and my mother always goes. There is a free vegetable meal for everyone, but my mother always gives a donation." In fact, the nuns at New York's Chinese Pure Land Temple of Wonderful Enlightenment report that they draw about four hundred worshipers for full- and new-moon observances. (Two hundred is a large gathering for other regularly scheduled events.)

"On the first and fifteenth days is also when we should change the fruit," the accountant continues. "We put fruit in front of the statues of the gods—the Kitchen God and the Property God. There should be an odd number—like three oranges. And if you burn incense, you should burn three sticks. Everything is in three. So, we put out three fresh oranges on the first, and again on the fifteenth. Also, on the first and the fifteenth we are not supposed to wash our hair. Before I got married, my mother was very strict. I did not wash my hair on those days! Now that I am married, I am not so particular about this, but she is *very* particular about it!"

The rough equivalent of full- and new-moon observances for Tibetan Buddhists is the practice of offering special prayers on the tenth and twenty-fifth of every Tibetan calendar month. A prominent leader in America's Tibetan Buddhist community says that while it is less important for Tibetan Buddhists to have a temple to attend here in America than it would be for Christians to have a church, a temple is still the best place for these twice-monthly observances. Where there is no temple, getting together with friends will do. "We used to meet in a home," he explains. "We were about six or seven families, and we always had prayer together. Unfortunately, sometimes it would become more social than prayerful. Only some of us 'practiced.' But when the month's prayer would be held at our home, the family members of all of my friends who did practice would come. Then we *would* say our prayers *and* have our dinner together."

## Congregationalizing

Members of certain religions are required to gather regularly for group rituals of faith, no matter what. For others, coming together as a congregation has become part of their normal routine because the American context makes spontaneous visits to the temple difficult. Sometimes, when traditional observances fall midweek, some communities translate them to the weekend so that more members of the community will be able to participate. For these reasons and more, voluntary congregational gathering has become a hallmark of being religious in America; and Saturdays and Sundays have become the *de facto* days for this. Also, because numbers and resources make it necessary in America, people, rituals, sacred texts, and objects of veneration are brought together in a way they are not "back home." In this section, we will look at some of the many forms of congregational worship and practice.

*Devotional Gatherings*

Typical elements of devotional gatherings include singing, reciting set texts, hearing scripture lessons, and fellowship (often with simple refreshments or a meal). Members of the Bahá'í Faith call this a "Devotional." We have borrowed their term for the section heading, and will start out by looking at what they do.

While the mandate is for Bahá'ís to meet every nineteen days (for their Nineteen Day Feast), most of them meet weekly in addition. "The Bahá'í Faith has an international administrative body called the Universal House of Justice (located in Haifa)," a graduate student explains, "and it has advised us that in this current Five Year Plan, we should engage ourselves in three core activities: study circles, children's classes, and devotional gatherings. All of these activities help each of us get involved in our community, according to our own needs and strengths. So, in our city, we hold 'Devotionals' called Sunday-at-Eleven. Different ethnic groups are taking responsibility for planning. One Sunday a month, we have a Spanish Devotional. The last weekend of the month is an African-American Devotional. I've even been to a Hip-Hop Devotional."

"At the university," a medical student reports, "we have Devotionals every other Thursday. On the Thursdays in between, we have a discussion based on the theme of the Devotional of the previous week. The style varies. When you go to a really well planned out, creatively energized Devotional, it is an amazing experience. I have been to some Devotionals where students have acted out scenes from the history of the Bahá'í Faith, and these were done so reverently, with talented performers. That's a spiritual experience in itself."

One characteristic of the Hindu BAPS movement is that members are expected to meet weekly at the *mandir* (temple) for *sabha*—a spiritual discourse and congregational prayer and song. It is their custom for women and men to sit apart, to show respect for each other. In some temples, women sit to the rear of the hall, behind the men. In others, the men's and women's sections are side by side. "Spiritually, women and men are equal," one member explains, "but they pray separately." Similarly, Hare Krishna communities (who, like BAPS members, are Vaishnavites) like to meet at their temple once or twice each week. This is a chance for the lay devotees to worship together and to share in fellowship. "Here in New York," a monk explains, "on the Lower East Side, we meet on Tuesday and Friday evenings; the Brooklyn temple meets Wednesdays and Sundays." There is chanting, a discourse by one of the monks, prayers, and a vegetarian meal.

A significant part of the evening is spent chanting the *Maha Mantra* which so characterizes the movement: *Hare Krishna Hare Krishna; Krishna Krishna Hare Hare; Hare Rama Hare Rama; Rama Rama Hare Hare.* Everyone does this at home during daily personal devotions, but when they are in the temple as a group, they can do it as call-and-response. "Group chanting is called *kirtan*," a devotee explains. "It is usually done standing. Individual chanting is called *japa*." Devotees use a *mala* (string of prayer beads) which they keep in a drawstring carrying bag, even when counting the beads as they chant. "*Bhajan* is worship in the form of singing," a monk explains. "This is usually done seated. All of these activities are elements of *bhakti yoga*—the path to God through devotion. So is *puja*. *Bhakti* is the most popular Hindu path. *Bhakti* is what we do exclusively for the Lord. It is free, non-reactive activity. It purifies, frees us from entanglements."

"Keep in mind," says one Hindu educator, "that for every *mandir* you see in America, there are hundreds of homes where Hindus are doing their own thing. There are so many people who have devotional sessions in their own home on a regular basis. *Satsang* is an overall concept. There is a North Indian community in my neighborhood that holds *satsang* on Sunday mornings. Someone will read out something their guru has had to say, and people will share their thoughts. At the end, they do *arti* [the lamp ceremony] and they distribute *prashad* [blessed food]. This happens every Sunday morning. This type of Sunday *satsang* is all over the place. You will find a lot of Hindus who don't go to temple very often. Also, a lot of Hindu traditions are done in the home, or organized by a family in a space to which the priest is asked to come. It may not be a temple. If you go to a temple, you will see rites of worship; some things are done in the public forum. But a lot of Hindu traditions are not done there. These things are not so visible. But if you get acquainted with the Hindu community, you'll see them."

"I will share one more thought with you," says a Hindu attorney. "The home should be a temple. If my home is not a temple, the outside temple where I go has no meaning to me. Most of our time we spend at home. So, my relationship to my wife, to my kids, to my neighbors—that is the essence of the temple. Serenity, purity, high-quality relationship, peace, prosperity, harmony should be in the home. If I am able to develop that in my home, then my home is temple for me. So I should not do at home what I don't do in the temple. I don't drink in the temple, so I don't drink at home. Nobody cheats in the temple, so I should not cheat in the house. If my home is not temple, my mind is restless. But if my home is temple, then my mind is at peace."

In the Punjab, the *gurdwara* (Sikh house of worship) would be open every day, and many people would make it their routine to visit it daily. In America, it is more likely that the *sangat* (community) has an established pattern for meeting weekly. In the main gathering room, the *Guru Granth Sahib* (the Sikh holy book) will have been brought processionally to its throne, where its attendant fans it continuously, as one would a king. As devotees arrive, each one reverences the holy book by kneeling before it, touching one's forehead to the carpet, and placing an offering nearby. Everyone sits on the floor, men on one side and women on the other. Devotional singing is an important element of worship. The service begins with hymns taken from the holy book, which are sung to traditional melodies and accompanied by harmoniums and tabors. There will be a reading from the *Guru Granth Sahib* (chosen at random), and a discourse explaining it or some particular tenet of the faith.

Toward the end of the service, *karah prashad* will be distributed. This is a lump of pudding, meant as a symbol of acceptance of the teaching read from the *Guru Granth Sahib.* Literally, *prashad* means kindness, graciousness, favor, aid; so one youth leader also thinks of receiving *karah prashad* as a symbol of the blessing of coming together. "Remember the last words of the *Mool Mantra,*" says one teacher: "*Gur Prashad,* 'realized only by His grace.' We should always remember that when we take the *prashad.*"

Anyone, regardless of gender or age, can play a leading role—tending the holy book, leading the singing, playing an instrument, distributing the *prashad.* The service closes with the *Ardas,* said standing. This is Sikhism's congregational prayer. Afterward, all are expected at *langar,* a simple vegetarian meal. When it is served in traditional fashion, everyone sits in rows on the floor, so that everyone is of equal status. And, although vegetarianism is not a religious requirement for Sikhs, the *langar* is vegetarian so that people of all religions may partake.

The realities of life in America have necessitated some adaptation of Zoroastrians' preferred way of worshiping. Zoroastrians would like to be able to drop by a fire temple at any time. However, the enthronement of a consecrated, continuously-burning fire is a complex undertaking, and most see a North American fire temple as a distant hope at best. So, in the American context, for most Zoroastrian communities, a *Darbe-Mehr* (prayer hall) will do. The community might meet there weekly or monthly for informal prayer, fellowship, a potluck meal, and sometimes, a *Jashan* (formal prayer rite with fire) officiated by a *mobed* (a person who is authorized to perform ceremonies). "*Jashan* is a very general term," one *mobed* explains. "It comes from the Avestan word for 'worship.'" A *Jashan* can be performed for a festival or memorial occasion."

During the *Jashan,* the priest chants continuously while he adds sandalwood kindling and incense to an urn in which a fire has been lit. "All Zoroastrian ceremonies are done in the presence of fire," explains a leader in the New Jersey community, "because fire symbolizes Ahura Mazda and his spirit of righteousness." The flames rise and ebb as the priest chants, fans, and adds more fuel. The prayer texts vary, depending on the occasion, and the ritual can take an hour. All of the elements of creation are represented on the platform where the priest, dressed in white and wearing a mask so as not to pollute the fire, sits to perform his task. Fire is present, obviously. But also, the priest explains, "from the plant kingdom, we have fruits and flowers. We have a glass of milk to represent the animal kingdom. We have metal (in the form of utensils), which represents the earth. The priest represents humanity. But the entire sacredness of creation is deployed in the performance of the *Jashan.* So water is there. Milk and water. Water, next to fire, is one of the most important symbols of divine creation. Along with fire, it is the most powerful cleansing agent. Cleanliness and purity are at the basis of our religious concept."

The American context has provided challenges for Zoroastrian ritual leadership. Traditionally, the Zoroastrian priesthood is an hereditary office. A boy born in the priestly class who decides to become a *mobed* is sent to India for about three weeks of training, followed by ordination in a fire temple. Like *mobed,* the terms *ervad* (or *herbad*) and *dastoor (dastur)* also mean "priest," and the three terms do get used interchangeably. However, *ervad* may denote a student of theology, and *dastoor* often designates an especially learned priest. Very recently, some communities have trained and authorized men not of the priestly class to perform certain duties and ceremonies. They are called *mobedyar.*

Some of the ceremonies of America's First Nations have survived the period beginning in the early 1800s, during which it was illegal for them to practice their religion in the open. The passage of the Indian Reorganization Act of 1934 granted them a certain level of home rule. The passage of the American Indian Religious Freedom Act of 1978 took this recognition an important step further, making it "the policy of the United

States to protect and preserve for American Indians their inherent right of freedom to believe, express, and exercise the traditional religions of the American Indian, Eskimo, Aleut, and Native Hawaiians, including but not limited to access to sites, use and possession of sacred objects, and the freedom to worship through ceremonials and traditional rites." Now it is possible for Native Peoples to get together regularly and openly, and some do.

As a consequence of governmental repression and Christian missionary activity, Native American practice now falls into four categories. Some members of America's First Nations are devout Christians, but maintain their Native practices in tandem with that. Others embrace their tribal religion exclusively. Still others belong to new religious movements which blend aspects of Native and Christian religions together to create a distinctive new religious movement. The Native American Church is one example.

Finally, many embrace what is sometimes called "pan-Indian" or "trans-tribal" spirituality. "Some tribes and family systems are in transit," explains a Lakota leader. "They lack their traditional rituals. There is a need for them to adapt and apply—to integrate aspects of the faiths of various Nations." Native American practice and theology is not generic, though, he emphasizes. He considers himself fortunate to have grown up in a community which was able to maintain the integrity of its Oglala Lakota heritage. So, for example, the ritual use of peyote—a fixture of the Native American Church—is something he has seen, but does not do. "Even as a child," he explains, "I knew that peyote originated in the Southwest. It wasn't our way; it wasn't Lakota."

While some of America's Native Peoples may gather weekly or monthly, it is more typical to assemble (even pulling people together from several states) for larger ceremonies that are held as needed by the community. To take the Keetoowah (Cherokee) as an example, in winter, ceremonies are held inside. In summer, rituals may be held outdoors, in a forest where a Stomp Grounds—a Sacred Circle—is established. Traditional dances such as the Eagle Dance and the Green Corn Dance are always done in circular fashion.

To nurture her devotional life, the Keetoowah administrator of a New York healthcare facility belongs to an Intertribal Women's Prayer Circle which meets about once a month. "We are from many different religions," she explains, "just about every nation you can think of: Navajo, Apache, Shinacock, Cherokee, Blackfeet, Ojibway, Mohawk. Typically, there are ten of us. Sometimes the kids come, too. And sometimes, we have men come. We choose to do things in a traditional way, but we are really being pragmatic with what we do." Sometimes they choose one Nation's way of prayer or ceremony; other times, they combine elements from several. "Our tradition is not frozen in time," she explains. "It is living. It is organic."

Use of the tobacco pipe may be an element of Native communal ceremonies. "Everything on this earth is given us for medicine," says an Ojibway teacher in Michigan. "Tobacco is for prayer. I am against the abuse of tobacco. I teach that tobacco is medicine, and we should not abuse medicine. I grow my own out back in the garden. It's natural—no chemical additives; not a brown tobacco."

"The pipe is from the past," says an Oglala Lakota man. "It was brought to us by the Spirit with instructions. The Pipe-Keeper keeps the original pipe. The pipe can be used in a special ceremony, or any gathering, but not by yourself," he explains. "Passing the pipe is like the Holy Eucharist in church. Smoking the pipe is communion with God. That's the way it is interpreted."

### *Group Meditation*

The line between these devotional gatherings and group meditation sessions is a fine one. In this section, we will look at some forms of regular gathering where meditation is the core activity, although there may also be chanting, instruction, and a meal.

The New York Buddhist Vihara is typical of America's Theravada monasteries, in that it provides several opportunities each week for laypersons to practice *vipasanna* (insight meditation) with the *bhikkhus* (monks). At least one of these will be held in Sinhalese, but since these centers are attracting an increasing number of people who are not Sri Lankan, most sessions are held in English. One soft-spoken woman says she meditates at home every day, but she prefers to come to *vihara* as often as she can. "When you are in a spiritual place like this," she explains, "it is easier to focus."

Most Zen practitioners also like the support of a group—at least occasionally, if not once a week. At the moment, a businessman we'll call John Smith belongs to a small *sangha* (practice-community) that comes together weekly. "Our routine is to do that on Sunday mornings," he explains. The session runs 8:30 to 10:30 A.M.—which includes an hour to an hour and a half of sitting. "At the end of the sitting, we usually have a *dharma* talk: a teacher gives a talk about Zen's teachings, and how they function in our lives. Or, we do catching up. We ask each other how practice is going, and what we've learned in the last week since we met."

Some Zen communities maintain the tradition of employing a monitor to keep an eye on everyone as they sit, and to tap them on the shoulder with a "swatter" as necessary to bring them back to consciousness, to get them back into focus. "You can do this for yourself, though," Smith says. "You can use a *mudra* (hand position) where one hand sits inside the other, with thumbs touching. Then if your thumbs start coming apart, you know that you are falling asleep; you are losing focus. You can correct yourself, if you notice it." His teacher does not like to employ a monitor. "After all, you are practicing for your own enlightenment."

Once every two months, Smith continues, his *sangha* has a *zazenkai* (all-day sitting) which lasts from 8:30 in the morning until four o'clock in the afternoon. "Now we don't sit the whole time. We'll alternate forms of meditation. We sit for twenty-five minutes; we do walking meditation for five or ten minutes; we sit for another twenty-five minutes; and so on. We have a break for lunch, and we have a *dharma* talk. Then we have what for us is a very important part: a face-to-face session with the teacher. You talk about your practice, and he or she questions you about your practice, to find out how you are really doing. He will ask you insightful things. Face-to-face teaching is a very important thing. It can be very powerful—almost threatening sometimes. There is a lot of pressure on you, because you go in and the teacher says, 'No, that's not it. Go back and go deeper!' Sometimes, though, they will say, 'Try this,' or 'Try that.' They are looking for that one thing that will get you to the point where they want you to be."

This practice-group follows a Soto Zen teacher. "In Soto Zen," Smith explains, "you have a breakthrough all at once. It is based in just sitting. In one famous Zen story, someone asks a monk, 'What are you thinking about when you are sitting and not thinking?' And the monk answers, 'Non-thinking!' Non-thinking is about releasing all thoughts as they come up. You are just breathing and releasing all thoughts."

Zen practice can also involve liturgies, says the administrator of a small-town *zendo* (meditation center). "Sitting is not the only thing we do together. We have a whole book of liturgical practices—like chanting, bowing, and prostrations. We do prostrations once a month or so, but Korean Zen Buddhists make 108 prostrations each day. (That is an interesting practice. It does keep you in good physical shape, for one thing!) The first time I encountered Zen full-prostration bowing, it was a little off-putting! But you know what? I came to understand that I'm doing this because I bowing to the Buddha—who is really 'me'! I am bowing to the Buddha in myself, because we are all Buddhas. That is what we believe. We all have the Buddha-nature. It is about realizing that, and experiencing that, and accepting that."

Another form that Zen community practice takes is called *oriyoki.* Literally, it means "taking just enough," and it might be described as "eating-meditation." It replicates the Zen monastic practice of eating in a mindful way from a bowl. "We do this at our *zendo* occasionally," says one Long Islander. "You are served, and you eat mindfully—without watching television, without reading the paper, without having a conversation with someone, but just experiencing the food. As you do, you are also being mindful of the fact that, when you take something, it is important that you have respect for whatever you have taken, and that you eat everything that you take. No leftovers, no scraping stuff into the garbage. After the meal, you take water, and you put it in the bowl, and you scrub the bowl, and you drink it! Then you've eaten everything. It is powerful!"

*Oriyoki* as eating-meditation brings us naturally enough to *chado*. "As an inveterate tea-drinker," says one New Yorker, "I was thrilled when I finally got to experience a tea ceremony. How surprised I was to realize that *chado* in essence is a method of meditation." One Shinto priest has been performing the traditional Japanese tea ceremony in his urban American home for several years. Many people associate *chado* (The Way of Tea) with Zen, but he argues that it is a Shinto practice. Like *misogi*, a tea ceremony is a means of purification. "*Misogi* purifies you outside; the tea ceremony purifies you inside," he explains. "Also, it is about having a pure heart and pure mind. Before offering the tea, we always purify. We purify the tea-powder, and the tea-bowl, and the people before we offer tea. We purify each offering."

It is impressive how deliberately everything is done by the tea ceremony host. It is a study in care, in being fully present in each tiny detail, each step. Nothing is casual. Everything is elegant in its simplicity. "Each tea ceremony performer uses a special cloth, and recognizes that the cloth has power. The color is very important," we're told. Today our host is a woman, and she is using cloth of deep orange color. Men use a purple cloth, she explains. "In Japan, people recognize that purple is a sacred color. Also, the kind of cloth is very important. This is silk." The priest interjects, "The tea ceremony performer never washes the tea ceremony cloth. If we were to wash it, its sacred power would be passed into the water. Also, we never wash the altar. However, every half-year, we change the *haraigushi* [the fan-like ceremonial wand made of white paper streamers], because it becomes dusty. We also dust the shrine."

Jain meditation, as we have seen, takes several forms. All may be practiced alone, but some Jains prefer to practice with others. "At our temple," says a banker, "a small group of people gathers every Friday for meditation—*samayik* we call it." *Samayik* is the practice of "staying in equanimity" for a forty-eight-minute interval. Being in *samayik* means giving up attention to all worldly affairs, from attachment and aversion, thus letting go of passions and desires. To perform *samayik* an devotee dons simple, white clothing and settles in a quiet spot where he or she can recite the *Navkar Maha Mantra,* read from scriptures, or meditate. This practice provides the layperson a glimpse of what being a *sadhu* (renunciate) is like, since *sadhus* live in this state constantly.

*Chanting*

While it might seem to an outsider that spending two hours chanting is a form of meditation, the head nun at one of New York's many Chinese Pure Land temples does not concur. For her, the term "meditation" could only mean the kind of silent sitting associated with Zen (Ch'an in Chinese). It is another method. Chant is chant! Group practice for Pure Land Buddhists (Chinese and Japanese alike) includes the chanting of *sutras*—collections of the Buddha's teachings. The congregations of New York City's many Chinese Pure Land temples typically meet on Friday evenings and Sunday afternoons. On Sundays, many temple communities gather for about two hours of hymn-singing and chanting. If there are memorials or other ceremonies to be performed, these take place after lunch.

Just before breaking for lunch, the community chants the "Lunch Offering." While saluting each of the Ten Directions (north, south, east, west, northeast, northwest, southeast, southwest, up, and down), gratitude is given to the Buddhas of the past, present, and future. Thanks must be given at four levels, one woman explains. "We give the Buddha all respect because he has attained Enlightenment. So we give him all thanks, and ask him to lead us on the right path. We thank our parents, who gave us life and education; and our teachers, who are there to help us on the way. We thank all sentient beings. (Even though I am going to the grocery store and paying for my rice, if there is no farmer, I won't have any rice.) And also, we thank our country, for without a system, who knows what we would be living in?"

In some temples, a narrow table runs the length of the meditation hall, from entrance to altar, with everyone facing the center; in others, tables are placed in rows facing the Buddha statues up front. At some temples, seating is on traditional cushions, but American-style chairs have become the norm at many. On the table are *sutra* books—one for each person. Traditional chant-books are put together accordion-fashion.

You turn the pages from right to left as you work your way down columns of Chinese characters; and when you get to the bottom of the last page, you just turn the back cover over and keep right on going. A monk or nun sets the pace by tapping a temple-block, and the chanting begins. Often the pace is intense. Even with a transliterated text, it is hard for a novice to keep up with the syllables.

"We don't chant the same thing each time we gather," says one regular participant at a one of Brooklyn's many Chinese Buddhist temples. "And we don't use the same chant-books each time. We also have a book with our hymns in it. Today we sang the *Grand Offering Before Buddhas.* It begins 'Blessed be ever-dwelling Buddhas in all places.' We praise the healing Buddha, the incoming Buddha, and Amitabha (the Buddha of Boundless Light), in addition to Shakyamuni Buddha—the historical Siddhartha Gautama. What we chant depends on the time of year and the needs of the congregation. We have a schedule. On the first Sunday of the month, we chant a *sutra* about the Bodhisattva of Compassion. That is for repenting of our sins. On the second and fourth Sundays, we chant the name of the Holy Buddha, and do some sitting meditation. Today is the third Sunday, so we did the Diamond Sutra."

Why the chanting? Pure Land Buddhists believe that the Buddha has prepared a "Pure Land" for them—a "last step before Nirvana" to which they will be transported when they die, if they but call with sincerity upon the name of the Buddha of Boundless Compassion. So, says our guide, "We chant because it insures that at the end of our life, we will be greeted by the Buddha. We chant in order to repent of our sins and to become like the Buddha."

Some devotees make three prostrations before they begin chanting. This is called refuge-taking. They are making the classic Buddhist testimony: I take refuge in the Buddha; I take refuge in the *Dharma* (the Buddha's teaching); I take refuge in the *Sangha* (which, for Mahayana Buddhists, means the entire Buddhist community—not just monks and nuns). When the chanting has finished, they will do this again in thanksgiving.

New York's Japanese Pure Land Buddhists meet at their temple on Sundays for meditation, chanting, and a sermon by the resident priest or one of the laypersons. Once the congregation has gathered, there is silent meditation. "We place incense in an incense bowl," the priest explains. "Incense is used for calming down your mind. Smells can make a difference." The priest strikes the gong twice, to signal that silent meditation has commenced. Later on, a thin, gentle-sounding bell is struck and the *sutra*-chanting begins. "I lead," says the priest, "and all the other members of the *sangha* (congregation) chant together." Traditional Japanese Pure Land chanting is done on a very low pitch—a somewhat sustained monotone, but occasionally shifting to a higher level, then returning. The chanting remains steady, but is accompanied by tapping of hollow wooden sticks—slowly and rhythmically, then accelerating. The gong and various bells also punctuate the chanting. All of these percussion sounds serve a practical purpose, indicating where they are in the *sutra*. Group chanting typically involves repeating the single line *Namu amida butsu* (I take refuge in the Buddha of Boundless Compassion). This generates a tangible feeling of oneness, of being united with others in chanting.

"Mostly, we use a monotone chant," explains a lay teacher who, like many members of this congregation, is not himself ethnically Japanese. "We also have in some cases special chants that have a melodic line, and that's indicated in special Japanese notation. We chant the Triple Jewel in Pali, in Japanese, and in English. To do that symbolizes that the teaching of Buddha started in India, then went to Japan, then came to the United States. There's a big discussion about what's translatable and what's not. The chanting is in Japanese, but we try to keep everything else in English."

When Muslims recite the Qur'an formally, it is intoned. This is indeed a form of chanting. But, as we learned in chapter two, the Islamic devotional life includes *dhikr* (recollection or remembrance). *Dhikr* can take the form of repetition of a word or phrase—a practice associated with Islamic mysticism. Some Muslim mystics are happy to be called Sufis, and while definitions and descriptions of Sufism vary quite a bit, many will agree that Sufi practice entails initiation into an "order" and meeting regularly as a "circle" under the guidance of a *shaykh* (elder, teacher). "Our Sufi circle meets every Thursday evening," a graduate student explains. "We start with the early evening *salat.* Then we'll do a litany composed by our founding master. We'll have some tea, and maybe some nuts and dried fruit. Our *shaykh* will give a talk and then open it up for discussion. By 8:30 or nine o'clock, we'll do *dhikr.*"

This circle's congregational *dhikr* follows a predictable routine. "The chanting begins with us seated in a circle like servants and making small movements of the head from the right to the left. During certain recitations there are different positions," the student continues. "After a while, we'll do the standing *dhikr,* which involves a lot of movement. The entire circle rotates. The standing *dhikr* is the longest part. There are different movements to be done and different Names of God and phrases to recite. It's very intense. When the *shaykh* indicates that we've finished, we sit quietly for a little while and then close with the night *salat.*"

### *Temple Puja*

In many cities of the United States, Hindus have gone to great lengths to construct *mandirs* (temples), or to establish them in found space—in what was once a grocery store, or a church, or a warehouse—in which the traditional *murtis* (images) can be installed. In a given temple, which images to install (and even what color they will be) may depend greatly on what region of India was home to the founders. It can also depend on how much money can be raised. A temple will have a principal deity, but usually many others as well.

Temples in Nashville and Flushing are dedicated to Ganesha, the Remover of Obstacles, a deity embraced by virtually all Hindus. One temple near Detroit is dedicated to the Eternal Mother because of the founder's particular devotion to her. The main shrine of the temple in Memphis features Sri Venkateshwara (the Operator—a form of Vishnu).[18] In addition, it is home to eight other deities which the worshiping community selected by ballot. One temple in upstate New York has installed shrines in both North Indian and South Indian styles, so that everyone's sensibilities could be accommodated.

In traditional Hindu temples you will see clusters of *murtis,* often arranged in alcoves. If Shiva is there, then look for Nandi (the bull), his vehicle. In Hindu iconography, deities are often portrayed with their means of transportation, which are also related to their attributes. Ganesha's vehicle is the rat—useful to the remover of obstacles, because a rat can gnaw through anything. Look for the rat crouched facing Ganesha, meeting his gaze. Saraswati, the goddess of wisdom, knowledge, science, and the arts, is often depicted with a swan—the symbol of discernment. There may be a tableau featuring Rama, Sita (his consort), Hanuman (the monkey-king), and Lakshmana (Rama's half-brother) standing together just so. This is not a random grouping, one devotee explains. It depicts a moment in the Hinduism's great *Ramayana* epic, which means the grouping is in itself an icon: "They have won the war against the forces of evil; Rama has come back from Lanka, and has established the Righteous Kingdom at Ayodhya, and now he is there in glory, as the one who rules the perfect *dharma*." For Hindus, she explains, the images—their poses and the way they are grouped, evoke some aspect of the Hindu narrative, much in the same way as does a church's stained-glass window of a man holding two tablets overhead, or of a man and a woman leaning admiringly over an infant. "There is a kind of narrative connected with the image. You see it, and instantly, you recall the whole of the story."

In chapter two, we learned a bit about *puja*—worship by means of acts of hospitality. Jain and Hindu temples provide the place and the resources to do *puja* on a scale that cannot be managed at home. One Jain temple in Michigan holds five or six big *pujas* a year. Hindu temples may keep a calendar of deity observances, and announce when *abhishekam* (holy bathing) will be performed for Lakshmi or Lord Shiva or whomever. In addition, they may also post the requirements for special occasion *pujas* if a member of the community would like to sponsor one.

"Keep in mind that there are some *Brahmins* who are very, very well trained, so they could do almost anything you could do at temple at home," says Professor Deepak Sarma. "What's unique about a temple is that it might actually have spaces that are better designed to do a big *yajna*—a big fire-sacrifice. You need a good ventilation system, so temples will do that." Some people do *yajna* (which they may call *homa*) seasonally; others do it monthly. Still others do it when something new has happened in their family.

American temples usually have someone on staff (a *pujari*) whose job is to do all the necessary rituals every day. While there may be lay people dropping in each day, Saturday and Sunday can be very busy. “Let’s say there is a particular deity you want to see—a *murti* of a particular deity,” Professor Sarma suggests. “You go to the temple to see that particular deity. At home you can have pictures of that deity, but you lack the scale. There is something quite overwhelming about being in the midst of all the rich imagery in a temple—and the smells and the sounds, to watch the reverence of the people as they come through.” *Puja* always increases *punya,* good karma, no matter where it is performed. In fact, he says, depending on the attitude of the person doing it, “a *puja* done at home can result in as much *punya* as an expensive *puja* done in a temple—if not more! On the other hand, just going to a temple is a *punya* in and of itself.”

It can also be fun. For America’s Hindus, going to the *mandir* is often a social as well as a spiritual experience. “You get a religious experience that is socialized in a way you don’t have at home,” Professor Sarma points out. “And one of the problems is, in America, sometimes the social experience of the temple takes precedence over the reverence aspects.”

### *Arti*

As we have seen, a simple Jain *puja* can be done at home; and so, for that matter, can *arti,* the evening ceremony of light, which has short, medium, and long forms. However, most Jains prefer to do *arti* at the temple. When they can, they make it their practice to come regularly and join in the ritual with the staff member who makes sure all the daily temple rites are performed. Sometimes, coming for *arti* can be combined with an opportunity to participate in other Jain group practices. For example, as we saw in chapter two, *bhavana* is a characteristic Jain form of contemplation that helps the devotee avoid building up bad karma. It can be done at home at any time, but some

Jains prefer to practice it together. The Jain Society of Greater Detroit holds *bhavana* at the temple at least once a month.

"One of the main reasons behind *arti*," says a Long Island pharmacist, "is when you pay reverence to somebody, you praise his virtues, and you get inspiration to be like him. And, to pay maximum respect to the *tirthankaras* fully, wholeheartedly, we do *arti*. It's not done to gain you a reward. It is not like a reward in the sense of material concern. Rather, you do *arti* to show respect for the *tirthankara,* and to think about his efforts—how he became pure soul. And I want to be like that. That's the basic principle. The basic principle of Jainism is this: each soul has the potential to be that pure. *Arti* is for maximum inspiration."

"Light symbolizes spiritual enlightenment," says a Hindu classical dancer. "And in the morning—when we light the first lamp—light is like a goddess, like Durga. In the evening also, when we light the lamp, we have a special prayer—*arthi*—where we wave an oil lamp." A Hindu in rural New York says, "I try to remember to light an oil lamp once a day. Lately I have been doing it in the morning. I put on the water for my tea, and then I go in the dining room and do my prayers with the oil lamp. I just light the lamp. And I touch the flame and then touch my forehead. And I just ask that there be peace and love between our family, between our children and us, between husband and wife, between relatives and friends, and the whole world. That I say, and that's it. And by the time I am finished, my tea water is boiling."

In a Hindu temple, lamps come in all different shapes and sizes. "One temple in India has such a big lamp, they have to have ladders to climb up and fill it," the dancer explains. "Once they light it, it will continue for a three-month period. Fire is one of the five basic elements. Fire and the lamp are witnesses for all our rituals." *Arti* is a remnant of ritual practice described in the Vedas, the most ancient Hindu scriptures, Professor Sarma stresses. "You are honoring the deity with fire. It is the idea that this is how people communicated with the deities. The nice thing about fire is that it creates smoke, and the nice thing about smoke is that smoke rises. That is the way you communicate with God. We can talk to God without actually having to talk, as it were."

*Sweating*

Let us turn to America's First Nations for our last example. For Oglala Lakota as for Diné (Navajo), Potawatomi, Keetoowah, and others, community rituals of faith include use of a sweat lodge. Is sweating a form of prayer? Of meditation? Of chanting? Yes! All three.

The Oglala Lakota prefer to speak of a "purification lodge" and a "purification ceremony" rather than of "sweat lodges" and "sweating," says a former resident of the Pine Ridge Reservation. "Basically, purification is a ceremony that is used prior to anything else. It is the first thing you do before you do anything else—like, you would do it before you got married. It's a time of prayer and song. It is communication with Great Spirit, but sometimes there are no words. It is a time for petition and intercession, but also a time of individual and corporate focus on humility."

Purification practices vary. Some people do them weekly. Others do them monthly or occasionally. Depending on the community and the leader, one *could* have a co-ed purification ceremony, but some Natives say that is a distortion of the practice. "Many teachings only let men 'sweat' men, and women 'sweat' women," one man explains. "Others let families go together." Every leader has his or her own style, so the "liturgy" varies considerably, too. Some say the purification lodge symbolizes Mother Earth's womb; others say it represents the center of the universe. Many say the darkness is a reminder of Creator's presence. The shape and size of the purification lodge varies also. Invariably, it has a small opening in the frame (probably closed by a blanket or tarp). Always the door faces the west. Once inside, you turn in a clockwise manner.

"Our sweat lodge is a small tent-like thing with a pit in the middle," explains a Detroit member of a pan-tribal community. "It looks a little bit like an igloo. We heat rocks to a bright red. We bring them into the center of the lodge. When people pour water on them, steam is created and it gets hot, kind of like a really hot sauna. The purpose for that, in the physical aspect, is you are sweating out the toxins. Spiritually, it's going through a little uncomfortableness to ask God for that help, that purification. Going in the sweathouse is like you are crawling back into the womb. You come out born again, cleansed, purified. It's a beautiful ceremony. The helpers—spirits, angels, whatever you want to call them—manifest themselves while we are in the lodge. You'll see them in various ways."

"Originally," explains one Minnesotan, "the purification lodge came from my people, the Oceti Sakowin Oyate [the Seven Campfires Nation, which includes speakers of the Lakota dialect]. It is one of our oldest ceremonies. Through the transition of intertribal contact, other people have adapted it. They create their own protocol. They have their own jargon. But the original meaning of the purification lodge is *ini kagapi*—which means 'to give life or give breath, or rejuvenate the spirit of life.' Entering the lodge through a low door teaches humility—similar to Western theology's teaching about the humility of Jesus Christ," he continues. "You are going in wearing little or no clothing, which means you are leaving all marks of status and ego outside. You would perceive yourself as becoming one of the four-legged ones."

Another man puts it this way: "There's a saying, 'When you come to our ceremonies, you either come in humble, or you're going to be humbled in that ceremony'—not because the wrath of God taps us, but because you're going to feel like a dummy if you come in full of ego. I have these grandmas going to these lodges with a lot of hot rocks. It gets really warm in there, but grandma's sitting there, not sweating a bead. But then there's this big guy, this huge warrior, laying on the floor gasping for air. That's why the elders are so respected. They've learned that you're not dealing with things of the flesh. You're dealing with things of the spirit. Once you get that, you'll see Creation for what it is. You'll see people for who they really are. And you'll know who to stay away from."

The Diné (Navajo) make offerings to Earth, Wind, and Water, then invite the "Holy Ones" to join them in the sweathouse. According to their tradition, the Holy Ones are residents of the world which preceded this one. They symbolize the very beginnings of thought and language, and it is said that they sang the earth into being. They sang all creatures and the rivers into existence. Their singing organized the seasons. So, to perform the sweathouse ritual is to rehearse the very act of creation itself. There are songs to be sung, including songs for prosperity and beauty.

For the Oceti Sakowin Oyate (Seven Campfires Nation), participating in a purification lodge is one of the ancient Seven Rites. "It is the first and oldest one," says a community worker. "It is a purification ritual to keep your body and spirit in balance. Similar to Christianity, it is an opportunity to confess, to ask for forgiveness and mercy, to be granted mercy, and to be purified." The Vision Quest is another. "You have to be at least twelve years old to do the Vision Quest," explains one Lakota leader. "Both boys and girls do this. It is very individual. You go through your own protocol. You consult with the *shaman* or medicine man, and he will instruct you on what to do." Other nations do this, too. An Ojibway healthcare worker explains, "A basic principle of our teachings is that we are spirits having a human experience—not the other way around. That's why we have a connection with the spirit world, with the Creator, with the angels—a connection to the ancestors, to the helpers. It's all the same to us. There's a very thin veil between the spirit world and our world. That's why visions and dreams come to Native people. That's why we go on our fasts. The Creator will tell you something in whatever way you can understand it."

Others of the Seven Rites are Spirit-Keeping (veneration of ancestors), Making Relatives (the ceremony by which an outsider could be made an official citizen of the Nation, or a member of one's family or clan), Making Woman (puberty ceremony), and Throwing the Ball (a community unity ceremony). It is often said that the Throwing the Ball ceremony is lost, but, says an Oglala Lakota activist in California, "a few individuals are trying to bring it back into use." The seventh of the Seven Rites is the Sun Dance, and we will consider it in our next chapter.

## Reflections

We now have some idea of our many neighbors' routines of devotion—daily, weekly, monthly. We have only scratched the surface, though. There are many details we have omitted, and much more left to be explained about the meaning of these rites and observances. Suffice it to say that for people who go to great lengths to be sure that the neighborhood has a temple and a professional ritual-performer, and who weave these practices into their busy American lives, none of these rituals are meaningless or "empty" acts of devotion!

In this brief discussion we have not included everything, of course. We have not mentioned Taoist community ceremonies yet, because in America, they are most likely to be occasional (a funeral, a healing, a thanksgiving ceremony) rather than regularly scheduled. A Taoist priest is contracted to perform a ritual; and a single Taoist ritual can last more than one day—sometimes even more than a month—even though they have been simplified for the American context. For example, a three-day ceremony might have thirty parts, including such elements as lamp-lighting, publishing the announcement, invocation of the spirits, purification acts, chanting, making offerings, and drawing a *fulu* (talisman)—that is, ritual creation of a power-filled line-drawing.

We have not mentioned the Afro-Caribbean religions in this chapter because, as one priest puts it, "It's not every Saturday or Sunday that we say, 'Hey, we're doing something.' Mostly, our ceremonies are agrarian-based, and seasonal." We now turn to questions of how our neighbors mark the passage of the year, and consider their annual cycles of holidays.

CHAPTER FOUR

# Holidays

OUR NON-CHRISTIAN neighbors sometimes refer to the first of January as the "Christian New Year"—which, of course, it isn't, exactly. It is a hold-over from Julius Caesar's revision of the ancient Roman calendar in 46 B.C.E. Where the ancient Roman calendar set the start of the year as the first of March, the solar-based Julian calendar made the first day of January New Year's Day throughout the Roman Empire. However, the Council of Tours (567 C.E.) abolished the use of the first of January as the start of the year for Western Christians. For the next thousand-plus years in the West, a new year was said to begin on Easter, or on Christmas, or on the Feast of the Annunciation (March 25). In some times and places, there was even a return to the very old Roman notion of the first of March. Medieval and Renaissance Christian New Year carols reflect this when they extol signs of spring as they "wish you a Happy New Year." In 1582, the calendar reform under Pope Gregory brought the beginning of the year back to the first of January. Since non-Catholics took their time agreeing to this, it was 1752 before England and its colonies wished anyone Happy New Year on the first of January!

Even as our non-Christian neighbors speak of the Western secular calendar as "the Christian calendar," many of them are well aware that it does not really represent the fullness of the Christian year. Virtually every religion in the neighborhood has its own extraordinary method of making the world meaningful by marking the ordinary passage of time. In this chapter, we will learn about the annual rhythm of some of America's many religions.

## New Year Celebrations

We'll begin with New Year observances, not because they are the most significant, but because virtually every religion has them. Almost every religion has some way of acknowledging that the annual cycle of celebrations and commemorations is beginning once more. Certainly, Christians do. However, liturgically, Eastern Orthodox Christians consider the first of September as the beginning of the year, while for Roman Catholics, Anglicans, and some Protestants, the liturgical year begins a new cycle with the first Sunday of Advent. But there are also groups of Christians who regard Easter, or the beginning of the academic year, or the occasion of their own congregation's "homecoming festival" as the start of a new church year. So, even if we have only Christians in the neighborhood, there are a dizzying number of annual cycles at play. It should then come as no surprise that when it comes to some of our neighbors' religions, the answer to the question "When should we wish you 'Happy New Year'?" is not a simple one. However, in almost any season, we have the opportunity to say "Happy New Year" to *someone!*

*Winter*
*Oshogatsu*—Japanese New Year—is observed on the first of January, and that has implications for America's Japanese Buddhists and Shinto-followers. For Japanese Pure Land

Buddhists, says a member of the Manhattan congregation, the emphasis is on New Year's Eve. "Our New Year service is very big. Our priest turns down the lights, and he alone chants an ancient melody for maybe half an hour. We are supposed to reflect on the year gone by, and how we can improve ourselves in the year ahead. It's my favorite event of the year!"

For Shinto-followers, delightful New Year customs are many, and the Tsubaki Grand Shrine of America (near Seattle) takes responsibility for maintaining them as authentically as possible. The festival begins, in a sense, in December, with rituals for winding up the old year. "Year End parties give people an occasion for a symbolic washing away of the old year's irritations, frustrations, and misfortunes with *sake* (rice wine)," a devotee explains. "Some days or weeks later, they will exchange cards and visits among friends and relatives, and they will toast the new year, expressing their hopes and expectations, wishing each other well, and anticipating the good things to be." In between, there are rituals to attend to, and decorations to hang. New Year preparations include a ceremonial housecleaning followed by the preparation of traditional cold dishes, so that no one has to bother with cooking tasks for the first three days of the New Year. "Actually," says a Japanese-American dental assistant, "females are not supposed to be in the kitchen for those three days, so we prepare all the food in advance. Also, for those three days, each item of food for every meal means something—each food is symbolic of long life, or good luck—something like that." The closing act of the old year is eating the year's final plate of Japanese noodles.

Late on New Year's Eve, some people will head to their local shrine in order to visit it just after midnight, while others wait until daytime—right after they go outside to watch the first sunrise of the year, or simply as soon as they can. "*Oshogatsu* is an amazing time to be a Shinto priest—an amazing time to be around the shrine," says the Rev. Koichi Barrish of the Tsubaki Grand Shrine of America. "Thousands of people visit our shrine to receive *fuku* (blessings)." Since most American Shinto-followers live at some distance from a shrine, they can also welcome the New Year in front of their miniature home-shrine. The second of January is the day to begin new things. "We would always write our resolution in calligraphy and hang it on the wall," says one New Yorker wistfully. "For my brother in Hawai'i, it is pretty easy to do all these things. It is harder for me here. I am not really connected to the Japanese community. But Shinto is the way I think."

Followers of Chinese traditional religion also mark the beginning of a new year in winter. The Chinese twelve-month lunar calendar begins with the second new moon after the winter solstice, which can be as early as January 21 or as late as February 19. While the Chinese have various ways of calculating the *number* of a given year, and some will tell you that 2005 C.E. is equivalent to Chinese year 4702, it is more common to determine what year it is according to a rotation of twelve animal names: rat, ox, tiger, rabbit, dragon, snake, horse, sheep, monkey, rooster, dog, and boar. According to this system, 2005 is the Year of the Rooster. Why these names? A much-loved story tells of twelve animals who came to bid farewell to the Buddha as he lay dying, and the traditional order is the order in which they arrived. In Taoist understanding, each animal represents a unique *yin-yang* balance of five basic elements: metal, water, wood, fire, and earth.

Preparation for Chinese New Year includes spring cleaning, assembling new clothes, making food for two weeks of merrymaking, and decorating the house (with red predominating). On the twenty-third day of the last month of the year, the family must deal with the Tsao Chün (the Kitchen God). According to Taoist teaching, Heaven has provided every family with a Kitchen God to keep watch over its affairs. In return, an annual report is due to the Jade Emperor, Taoism's highest deity. So, on the eve of this report, each family offers its Kitchen God a traditional sticky candy in the hope that it will prevent him from being able to open his mouth (should he plan on giving a bad report)!

The Kitchen God aside, the New Year's dinner can be a meal of thanksgiving, for which each item on the menu has rich symbolism. Festivities continue for two weeks, and may include firecrackers (where permitted), visits to friends and family, distribution of money gifts in red envelopes to the children, dragon-and-lion dancing, and finally, the Lantern Festival. "Chinese

New Year is a big event for my mom," says one New Yorker. "Every day has something particular that we are supposed to do. On the twenty-eighth day of the month, we should clean the house to wipe away all of the bad luck. On the twenty-ninth, we have to put the Good Luck sign on our door. This represents the Door God. Then on the thirtieth, the whole family gathers. The first day of the new year is a day for eating only vegetables—no meat; nothing with blood. But we can eat oysters, because oysters are considered as not having blood. On the second day of the new year, if you are married, this is the day you go back home—not on the first day. On the third day, we are not supposed to visit anyone—because that is the day that, if you meet someone, you could have an argument! So, we try to avoid meeting anyone on the third day."

*Spring*

For America's First Nations, the springtime has been regarded as the beginning of a new year. The Keetoowah calendar follows the agricultural year, and includes festivals for both the Spring New Year and Winter New Year. "The Oceti Sakowin Oyate (Seven Campfires Nation) have been hunters, traditionally," an Oglala Lakota leader explains. "For us, the coming of springtime is not associated with planting as much as with the renewed ability to gather medicinal plants." There are special ceremonies to be done by the medicine men. The community celebration includes special songs. As with all Lakota ceremonies, the spring ceremonies begin with prayers to the Four Directions and to heaven and earth.

"The Buddhist year begins from the last day of the Buddha," says a Theravada monk. "It was on the full-moon day known as *Wesak* when he passed away. From that day on, the Buddhist year started." In the early years, he explains, the Buddhist calendar was simply lunar, with twelve months of twenty-eight days; there was no need to adjust it to the solar year. Eventually, when the need did arise, it became customary to insert a "leap month" every four years.

Sometimes called "Buddha Day," *Wesak* is celebrated universally by Buddhists, but *when* it is celebrated in relation to the solar year, and *what* it commemorates, varies from one stream of Buddhism to another. Some Buddhists regard *Wesak* as the celebration of the Buddha's birthday. For others, it commemorates three occasions at once: the Buddha's birth, enlightenment, and passing away—occasions which may be celebrated on three separate calendar days by other Buddhists. Some laypeople try to spend the day observing the Five Precepts—even if they pay little attention to them throughout the rest of the year. That means they are to spend the day refraining from killing living creatures, from taking what is not given, from engaging in wrong sexual conduct, from false speech, and from indulging in intoxicants.

One of the features of Buddhism in America is that all of Buddhism's many streams can be found here (and all of their subdivisions on top of that). In a given American city, many "Buddhisms" will be represented, each with its own customs. In many cities, Buddhists have decided to compromise on a common date and to have what Sevan Ross, a Zen priest, calls an "inter-Buddhist celebration." At the celebrations in his city, "the story of the Buddha's birth is told in some way—sometimes with puppets or other things the kids will like. There is not any darkness to this day. It's a bit like a combination of Christmas and Easter. There are gifts—but not too many. We pour sweet tea on the baby Buddha. There is a light party atmosphere."

Having an inter-Buddhist celebration makes a bigger impact on the neighborhood's consciousness. It also draws the Buddhist community closer together. Celebrating Buddha Day was the main reason for the founding of the Buddhist Network of Greater Baltimore, which has held an event every May since 2000. "We celebrate by offering a service in which the various communities each share some aspect of their traditions. Everyone is always welcome to attend, both Buddhists and non-Buddhists," says network member Jeff Covey, a Zen practitioner.[19] Participants say it is a wonderful occasion for developing friendships and sharing of Buddhist teachings and practices.

All lunar calendars "slip" in relationship to the solar year, so most have a method for keeping holidays in their proper solar seasons. In spite of this, the calendars used by some religion-communities have gotten "out of whack," and reformers have stepped in with solutions which, as is typical of human nature, not everyone accepts. This means that, in America, there may be people who practice the same religion, but with different schedules for New Year's and the other holidays. We know this is true within Christianity. America's Sikhs and Zoroastrians also struggle with these issues.

In 1999, Sikh reformers inaugurated the Nanakshahi Calendar, which took the birth year of Guru Nanak (1469 of the Western calendar) as its point of departure. This new calendar is based on the length of the tropical solar year, with a leap-day every fourth year, and prevents Western-style calendar dates for Sikh observances from fluctuating from year to year. The names of the month are taken from the Sikh scriptures, the first month being *Chet.* Accordingly, Sikh New Year falls on March 14, and 2005 C.E. is the equivalent of Nanakshahi Year 537. Some traditionalists have never been happy with this innovation. Nevertheless, says a member of the Sikh Coalition, the Nanakshahi Calendar has many advantages, and has been accepted by most North American Sikhs. In fact, he says, the custodial body for Sikhism's holy places has now adopted it, which means that it is now acceptable to most Sikhs worldwide.

Zoroastrian New Year is called *Naw-Rúz,*[20] and ought to be associated with the Spring Equinox. However, American Zoroastrians differ on calendar issues, even though they are a very small community. There are three versions of the Zoroastrian calendar in common use, and all of them have found their way here. According to the two traditional calendars, *Naw-Rúz* falls in late summer. Recent reformers prefer the Fasli (seasonal) calendar, which fixes it permanently on March 21 of the Gregorian calendar. However, as one Zoroastrian Sunday school teacher explained to his adult class, tradition dies hard. "Most people—including me—are so used to the old calendars that, in spite of agreeing that the Fasli calendar is more accurate, they are reluctant to change to it." Only about fifteen percent have adopted it, he thinks, and a single American Zoroastrian family may include followers of two or three calendars.

Regardless of these human efforts to measure it, in the Zoroastrian worldview, time moves inexorably forward toward its final goal: the *Frashokereti* (the "Making Wonderful")—

when all of creation will be restored to its original perfection; when the first day of the month will merge with the thirtieth day of Endless Light, the result being one timeless moment and the total annihilation of evil.

The roots of the Bahá'í Faith, like those of Zoroastrianism, are also in Iran. The Bahá'í Faith also uses the ancient Iranian holiday of *Naw-Rúz* as the beginning of its year, which the Bahá'í calendar has always aligned with the Western secular March 21. Unique among the religions, the Bahá'í Faith divides the solar year into nineteen months of nineteen days. The remaining four or five days of the solar year left unnumbered and are called *intercalary days.*[21] Why nineteen? The Farsi word *vahid* means "unity," which is a central teaching of the faith; and in Persian numerology, this word has the numerical value of nineteen. Bahá'ís believe their method of ordering time in units of nineteen was divinely revealed.

"As a teacher who is Bahá'í," says a midwesterner, "I have to pay attention to the academic calendar. What keeps me on track with the Bahá'í year are the feasts—our first-of-the-Bahá'í-month meetings—because I know when the next one is coming up; that, and our holidays." Bahá'ís like to socialize together on *Naw-Rúz,* which falls on a workday evening more often than not. "One nice thing," says one high school teacher, "is that—since Bahá'ís don't consume alcoholic beverages—I can go out for Bahá'í New Year's Eve party on a Wednesday and be pretty well assured that I am going to be in fine physical shape to go to work the next morning!" Technically, Bahá'ís are not supposed to work on their New Year's Day, and some do try to observe it in this way. "I do take our New Year off," this teacher notes. "I have talked to my boss about it, and she's said it is all right to use personal-leave days for that."

Given the Bahá'í year's peculiar rhythms, why such pains to institute a calendar such as this, especially considering that the Bahá'í Faith arose in the nineteenth century, when the Western calendar's worldwide use was nearly established? The Bahá'í sacred texts are ambiguous on this point. However, "calendars are tools we use to organize and regulate our lives, especially our collective lives," Dale Lehman, host of the "Planet Bahá'í" website, reminds us. "The calendar has a fundamental impact on the way we think and the way we interact with each other. Bahá'u'lláh came to 'recreate' the world, to revitalize the spiritual life of humanity and to revolutionize the way we live. This revolution seeks to touch all aspects of our lives, from private acts of devotion to the governance of our communities and the world as a whole." Since the Bahá'í calendar names the days and months for attributes of God, it serves a devotional as well as a time-measuring function. Eventually, Lehman speculates, "it may prove to have a significant effect not only in organizing the affairs of all people, but also in drawing them nearer to the Source of their being."[22]

"For Hindus," a Hindu hospital chaplain explains, "since time is infinite, there is no beginning and no end. It just keeps going around and around. It keeps going, not in the sense of spiraling. It simply exists. But at our more limited level, we need calendars—and we Hindus have many." In spite of modern governmental calendar reforms, some regions of India persist in setting their festivals according to a solar calendar, while others use a lunar calendar for this purpose. These Indian regional differences have been transplanted to America. "In the same family, we may use two or three calendars at the same time. It is entirely possible that each Hindu family you meet will have its own opinion as to when the Hindu year begins," she continues. "Our lunar New Year's Day will be, perhaps, in March or April. But the solar New Year's Day may come two weeks or a month after that. We celebrate both. Any excuse to make feast and eat!"

For some Hindus, the annual cycle is less important than where we are on the timeline of Brahma's life. A single "Brahma day" is equal to so many million solar-lunar years that the numbers boggle the imagination. Time proceeds in *mahayugas* (great ages), each with four stages which are many thousand years long. The fourth stage is called *kaliyuga* (the age of strife), and it is subdivided into sixty-year cycles. To put this in Western calendar terms, we are now in the midst of the *kaliyuga* which started in what we would call 3102 B.C.E.; we are in a cycle which began on March 30, 1987, and will end in April 2047; Brahma is now fifty-one "years" old, and the world has eons to go until he has fulfilled his lifespan.

"One talks about Brahma in mind-boggling numbers," says a Hindu educator, "but the average Hindu does not care about those billions of years because everything is just viewed as a cycle. Everything repeats itself; nothing dies. There is no such thing as an original point. Bhagavan has always been there, and there is no beginning. The concept of beginning is only a concept in time and space—and time and space themselves belong to Bhagavan. This is the way the whole universe is viewed, so this creation as we humans see it is just a manifestation of Bhagavan. There was never a point when it was not there. It is just going through a cycle. You plant a seed, and a tree grows; it dies, and it becomes something else—part of the land of something—and somewhere else a seed grows. Who are we to know the connection?"

The bottom line for Hindus, says another devotee, is this: "If you are interested, you can find out a lot about time; you can also not make a big fuss about it!"

*Fall*

For Jains, the point of departure for numbering the years is Mahavira's attainment of Nirvana. Jains believe this took place on *Diwali* (the traditional Indian Festival of Lights), which means that *Diwali* is New Year's Day for Jains. *Diwali* comes in late October or early November of the Western calendar, so the Jain year 2531 commenced on November 11, 2004. In Jain New Year observance, the emphasis is on bolstering one's spiritual development. According to Jain tradition, eighteen kings were present as Mahavira left his physical body and achieved *moksha* (liberation). "They decided to keep his knowledge alive symbolically by the lighting of lamps," explains the priest of the Jain Center of Northern California. "However, the light of the Lord Mahavira's knowledge cannot be kept alive by just lighting lamps. That is just an external approach. We also need to light up our internal lamps by practicing what he taught, and that requires self-effort." So, on *Diwali,* Jains might fast, or perform mantras with a *mala* (a string of prayer beads), or resolve to increase their practice of good conduct.

It is safe to say that most Americans are aware of the rhythm of the Jewish year to some extent. We are accustomed to hearing about *Rosh ha-Shanah* (New Year), which can arrive as early as September 6 and as late as October 4. Add the fact that Jewish days begin with sundown, and we can say that in 2005, the evening of October 3 and the day of October 4 fell on *Rosh ha-Shanah.* Thus began Jewish year 5766. 5766 years since what? Since "the creation of the world," based on the numbers provided by the genealogy in the book of Genesis. However, says one rabbi, there is no need to get hung up over scientific data suggesting that the earth is far, far older than that. The six days of creation are "days" according to God's time, not ours.

The long, communal *Rosh ha-Shanah* worship services focus on God's sovereignty and the Day of Judgment. "The *shofar* (the ram's horn) gets blown a lot—actually up to one hundred times during the day," a Conservative rabbi explains. "You do it after the Torah service, and after the additional *Amidah* (standing prayer) that comes right after that. It is often said to be a wake-up call. According to one *midrash,* it represents the ram that was sacrificed instead of Isaac, and recalls a deal Abraham struck with God. Abraham says to God that since he (Abraham) had been *willing* to sacrifice his son, then 'in the future, whenever my children down the line blow the ram's horn, you'll remember my willingness, and forgive them.' So in some ways, the *shofar* is a reminder to God, too."

*Rosh ha-Shanah* launches the Days of Awe—a ten-day period of reverence for Jews. So, in addition to exchanging wishes for a "Happy New Year," the customary greeting for the first evening of *Rosh ha-Shanah* is *L'shahah tovah tikatevu*—May you be inscribed [in God's Book] for a good year. "After that," an Orthodox educator explains, "it's *gmar tov* (which means 'a good sealing')—the notion being that the righteous are inscribed for a good year immediately; and so as not to cast aspersions on anyone, we assume that they have already been inscribed as soon as the holiday begins, and we wish them a good final sealing."

"But actually, there are four Jewish New Year's Days," one educator explains. The "first month" is *Nisan,* and Passover begins on the fifteenth of *Nisan.* So Passover is the New Year for the festival cycle. "Then there is *Tu B'Shevat,*" which comes in January and is the New Year for the tree—kind of an arbor day," she continues. "And there is a New Year for livestock on the first day of the month of *Elul* (in August), both of which are related to calculating your annual tithe. So Jews are unique in that we can say Happy New Year to each other four times a year."

*Every Twelve Moons*

"The Islamic calendar kind of sneaks up on you because it is entirely lunar," says a Muslim administrator. "It does make you have a sense of the phases of the moon in a way that would not happen otherwise." Islam marks time according to a lunar calendar exclusively. And, since a lunar year is about 354 days long, Islamic New Year falls about eleven days earlier on the secular calendar than it did the previous year. Islam has no agriculturally based holidays, so there is no need to keep Islamic months, dates, or observances aligned with solar seasons. Furthermore, the Prophet Muhammad himself is on record as having specifically rejected such systems of adjustments. So, for Muslims, a new year begins every twelfth crescent moon—the first day of the Islamic month of *Muharram.*

Years are counted from the first day of *Muharram* for at least two reasons. It is believed to be the anniversary of God's act of creating life and death itself. It is also the anniversary of the *Hijra*—the nascent Muslim community's departure from Mecca for the safety of the northern Arabian city of Yathrib, which they would rename Madinatu'l-Munawwarah (the Radiant City) or Madinatu'n-Nabiy (the City of the Prophet)—Medina, for short. Thus on February 10, 2005, the First of *Muharram* (Islamic New Year) marked the beginning of 1426 A.H. (after the *Hijra*). This is not a festival day, however, and Muslim observance of it is rather low-key. It is thoughtful, however, to offer wishes such as, "May the new year be filled with peace, happiness and joy for you and your family."

## Holy Days

In addition to its New Year observances, each and every religion in the American neighborhood has a wealth of holidays. Some of them involve colorful celebration, while others are more somber; some merit taking the day off from work or school.

*Sikhism*

Sikh holidays center on the religion's founding prophet, Guru Nanak, and his nine successors, with observances on all of their birth and death anniversaries. "Guru Nanak's birthday is a big celebration," an information-technology specialist explains. "We get together at our *gurdwara* [house of worship], we sing religious hymns, and we speak about stories of Guru Nanak." Traditionally, however, Sikhs have celebrated Guru Nanak's birthday in the month of *Katik,* in late November of the secular calendar.

*Holla Mohalla,* an annual celebration inaugurated in 1680 C.E. by the tenth and the last Sikh Prophet, Guru Gobind Singh, is another important holiday. It falls on the first day of the month of *Chet* (mid-March), which has also become the first day of the reformed Sikh calendar. In a world where the underclass had been denied the right to bear arms and ride horses, Guru Gobind Singh made these things a standard part of life for all Sikhs. *Holla Mohalla* commemorates this innovation with such activities as martial-arts demonstrations and competitions, congregational worship, political conferences, recitation of the Sikh scripture, replacing the *Nishan Sahib* (Sikh flag) at the local *gurdwara,* and conducting *Amrit Sanskar* (the Sikh initiation ceremony). In addition to local festivals, a fair continues to be held at Anandpur in the Punjab, the home of the Golden Temple and the very first *Holla Mohalla.*

The biggest holiday, most Sikhs would say, is *Baisakhi* Day. A young technology consultant explains: "This celebrates the momentous day when the first five followers were initiated into the religion. It was a difficult time. The Sikhs were being persecuted. A crowd of some hundreds of thousands had shown up for this traditional Punjabi spring festival, hoping Guru Gobind Singh would give them some comfort. Instead, he asked for someone to give up his life for this religion. I mean, it was a test to see who truly understood the message and was willing to give up everything for this message and for carrying it on."

According to the story, the Guru asked, "Who will give his head for the faith?" When the first man stood up, the Guru took him away into a tent. The crowd heard what sounded like a beheading, and out came the Guru with a bloody sword. This was repeated four more times, and each man who went into the tent had come from a different region and class. Then, to the astonishment of the crowd, Guru Gobind Singh now brought the five men out of the tent garbed in fine clothing. He presented them to the gathering as the Five Beloved, and offered them sweetened water.

Then, the consultant continues, "the Guru himself—and this is another ultimate act of humility—he himself got baptized by those five. He said, 'You baptize me now, because I want to join this faith as an official follower.' So we celebrate that. *Baisakhi* Day reminds us of who we are, why we are the way we are, why we look the way we do. It is time to remember, to try to understand, and to grow spiritually."

"When I tell the story," says a youth leader, "I say that Guruji took the five who were willing to give up their heads into the tent. We don't know what he did in there, but the five came out reborn as *Khalsas* [pure ones]—which is our goal also. We must die, figuratively—our ego must die—so that we can be reborn as one with God. We are striving to become *Khalsa*."

"*Baisakhi* Day is such a huge holiday for Sikhs," says a young professional, "and for school kids in America, it's tough to celebrate that because people don't even know who we are. Now that I am more mature, I'm able to explain why I have a long beard, why I have hair down to my waist, why I tie it up in a turban. Other people are more mature, too. They are more willing to ask me questions and to try to understand my religion. So this year, when *Baisakhi* Day came around, I took the day off from work! I told my boss, 'I am going to go celebrate. It's a very important day for us.' And of course my boss said, 'Go ahead. It's something you need to do. That's great.' So it's easier to do it now."

*Hinduism*

One can't possibly celebrate every Hindu holiday there is, explains a specialist in classical Indian dance. Every Hindu family has its favorites, and their style of celebrating will reflect the part of India in which the family has its roots. For example, a holiday may be celebrated in North India as a quiet family occasion, but as a big community event in the south. Such nuances have made their way to America as well.

"A lot of times, people celebrate the birthday of particular gods," one professor explains. "I happen to care about the birthday of Krishna, because I am a Vaishnava who worships Krishna above all. For me, August 27 is an important day. I am sure I should know Rama's birthday also, but as cool as Rama is, and even though he is an *avatar* of Vishnu, he is not quite as interesting to me as Krishna. And, although Krishna's birthday is very important to me, it has nowhere near the importance for me as a Hindu that Christmas or Easter has in the Christian tradition. The historical narrative in Christianity is so profound, that those days are far more significant than Krishna's birthday. Krishna's birthday really is a celebration, but it seems to me that Easter and Christmas are celebrations of a different kind. They have a very different flavor to them. And, there really isn't any single story that is as pivotal to the entire Hindu narrative as the Easter story is to Christianity."

"My favorite festival is *Navaratri* (Nine Nights)," says a Hindu educator. Also called *Dussehra,* this great Goddess festival comes around in October. It is a time both of fasting and of celebration. Essentially, it commemorates the triumph of the forces of good over the forces of evil, but there are many regional differences in the festival's underlying narrative and the way it is observed. Depending on what part of India one is from, the focus of the entire nine days may be on Durga (consort of

Shiva, also known as Goddess Beyond Reach). In this tradition, the emphasis is on Durga's triumph over the force of evil. For Gujarati Hindus, the Goddess is called Amba or Mata. In the South Indian tradition, the days of celebration may be apportioned among various manifestations of the Goddess: three for Lakshmi (Goddess of Wealth, consort of Vishnu); three for Parvati (Daughter of the Mountains, another name for Durga, consort of Shiva), and three for Saraswati (the Goddess of Learning and the Arts, of Speech, and of the creative process). In this tradition, on the ninth day, one is to abstain from work and perform Saraswati *puja* by offering the instruments of one's profession or trade to God. That is, the scholar offers books, the farmer offers a plow—and, says one research scientist, "I offer my test tubes." He is especially fond of this holiday, but he does not take the day off. Instead, each year, he brings an image of Saraswati into his chemistry lab, and offers his test tubes to her. The first time he did this, his co-workers were quite flabbergasted. Now they look forward to it.

The day after *Navaratri* is called *Vijayadasami* (the victorious tenth day of conquest), and for many is a day of rededication of oneself to one's profession. Some call it *Vidyaramba* (beginning of study), the day on which young children begin to learn the alphabet. "The North Indian tradition is for people to meet each other at a given place to burn the effigy of the evil king Ravana," says the leader of one New York Hindu community. The celebration recalls that in the *Ramayana,* one of India's two greatest epics, there was an evil king Ravana, and a good king Lord Rama—an *avatar* of Vishnu. "There was a fight between these two forces," he continues. "In the end, goodness prevails. Lord Rama kills Ravana. On this particular occasion, like the Fourth of July, there are fireworks, but they are embedded in the effigy. Our community did it one time here. We brought the Ravana effigy from India in parts, and assembled it here. It was about forty feet high, and we put the fireworks within the effigy. Then we lit it. You have to get permission from the town. We had the fire department there. About twenty thousand people came. It was about six years ago. The town objected. The local residents complained about the ashes and the sound, and that the effigy was too high. So now celebrate without the effigy. We've scaled back, in the interest of harmony."

Two major festivals, *Holi* and *Diwali,* are explained differently in the various regions of India, and all of these interpretations have been transplanted to America. Both have roots in marking the change of seasons by an agrarian culture. "The spring comes; the winter is over," one Hindu attorney explains, "and right at the edge of winter going and spring coming—that fine line—is *Holi.*" Some Hindus associate *Holi,* the spring Festival of Colors, with Krishna; but many do not. Regardless, the temple deities may be dressed in especially colorful outfits; and as part of the fun, people throw colored powder on each other. "It is a very nonviolent function," the attorney continues, "but it looks like people are roughing each other up. We do it on Long Island. Also, there are a lot of folksongs associated with this festival."

*Holi* has another special feature, says the attorney. "If I am not on good terms with you, this is the day to offer reconciliation. If I take a box of sweets, or a gift or a flower bouquet, and go to your house personally, and if you accept that, that means that we are friends now—no more enmity. This is the only day socially accepted for diffusing tension and enmity. So each year, you have the opportunity to reconcile on this day. That is why people become very happy. The old misunderstanding is gone. Let us celebrate with colors. This is the social thought behind it, to reconcile the differences."

"My favorite holiday is *Diwali,*" says a Long Island mother. "Everyone loves *Diwali.* Since coming to America, we have modified the way of celebrating it. Back in India, we would wake up very early in the morning, take a bath, and have homemade sweets. My mother would do *arti,* and we would have fireworks. Over here, we don't wake up early in the morning. And we buy sweets. I don't bother to make them at home. I take my easy way out. Mostly I just continue the prayers. We do Lakshmi *puja.* Then we get together with our friends. Sometimes, there are public celebrations and cultural programs. It has been modified over here, but we still have a good time. We adapt."

In explaining *Diwali,* the Festival of Lights, some Hindus emphasize the triumph of good over evil, as told in the epic *Ramayana.* Others associate it with Krishna and reverence for the cow. Still others see it as a time to welcome Lakshmi, the Goddess of Wealth. This five-day festival comes in late October or early November, and is a time for new clothes and jewelry, fireworks, decorating one's house with twinkle-lights and oil lamps, and lots of food. On *Diwali,* says a member of a midwestern Swaminarayan congregation, "we present God with about a thousand freshly cooked items. It is a beautiful occasion. We fill the whole shrine with food. It is all vegetable-food." And of course, it all gets eaten.

The much-loved annual Ganesha festival comes in late August or early September. "It is one of the biggest festivals in the state of Maharastra, where I come from," one woman explains. Traditionally, devotees bring home a new clay image of the elephant-headed deity for the several days of celebration—which includes special *pujas* and processions. The Hindu Temple Society of New York, for which Ganesha is the main deity, is famous for this. "If you go to our temple during this holiday," says one devotee, "you will see that the Ganesha statue is decorated differently each day—one day with green apples, another day with marigolds." Thousands of people join in as the huge Ganesha-*murti* is transported through the streets of Flushing. The idea is that, all the rest of the year, Ganesha's devotees come to receive his blessings in the temple; but on this occasion, Ganesha takes his blessings out into the streets for the benefit of anyone and everyone. At the end of the festival, traditionally, devotees take their temporary clay Ganesha-images to a body of water—the ocean, or a lake, or a stream—and immerse them, figuratively sending Ganesha off to his celestial abode, taking humanity's misfortunes with him. In America, some families have modified this, while trying to maintain the spirit of the festival. "I have a little silver Ganesha statue," a Long Islander explains. "During the festival, I use it in worship every day. I do the *puja, arti, prashad.* I do not do these things the rest of the year, but for five days during the festival, I do."

Finally, some Hindus create their own annual festivals. "One of my Long Island friends has a five-day devotional festival in her basement," one woman explains. "An average of two hundred people come. She has a guru she is devoted to, and she invites him to come and run meditation and spiritual classes, and to do a small *puja.* People come for about two hours each day, and then she offers them food—which is important culturally. She has been doing this every August for years. She'll invite anybody she meets—not just Hindus or close friends. This too is part of Hindu worship."

*Jainism*

Jain holy days follow a lunar calendar adjusted to the solar seasons. Two holy days center on Mahavira—the final *tirthankara* for this eon. Jains commemorate Mahavira's attainment of *moksha* (liberation) on *Diwali* in the late fall, and celebrate his birthday in April. The holiest season for Jains, however, comes in late August or early September. Swetambara Jains call it *Paryushan Parva* (Coming Together Festival), and it lasts for eight days. Digambara Jains call it *Das Lakshan Parva* (Ten Virtues Festival), and for them it is a ten-day observance. In both cases, this is a period of rigorous fasting, special rituals, review of Jain principles, formal forgiveness-asking, spiritual review, and renewal of faith. "The last day of *Paryushan* is the first day of *Das Lakshan,*" explains Smriti Shah, an educator at the Jain Center of Greater Boston. According to Digambara custom, each of the ten days represents a virtue. The first day's virtue is forgiveness, and that is also the focus of the last day of *Paryushan.* So the two traditions of observance overlap, making it a very auspicious day for all Jains. "For both sects, the whole day is about forgiveness," Shah continues. "If there is somebody you have hurt, or someone who has hurt you, the goal is to forgive and let go."

During *Paryushan / Das Lakshan Parva,* the Jain Center of Greater Boston plans a full calendar of activities. "We are one of the few centers to observe both," Shah points out. "We do both because we want to present a united picture of Jainism. Why bring those old separations here to America?" The regular daily and weekly rhythm of faith-rituals such as the singing of religious songs, *arti* (the ritual of light), and *puja* (paying of respect to the *tirthankara*-images) is amplified with special lectures by experts in Jain philosophy or *sadhus* (renunciates whose vows still permit them to travel). The community's children—seventy to ninety of them, ages four-years through high school—take responsibility for performing *puja* (for both Swetambara and Digambara traditions) for one of the auspicious days. The kids are to arrive at the temple freshly showered, wearing clean clothes. "They learn what to do and why they do it. They come with all the *puja* articles—a coin, a flower (which is optional), rice, a fruit—and they make those offerings. We explain to them what the offerings represent. We explain what it means to bathe the *murti* [image] in water or sandalwood paste. That way, if they have a better understanding, they will follow it in the future. Otherwise, when they become teenagers and college kids, they lose interest."

Because one of its goals is the cultivation of the next generation of Jains, the Jain Center of Greater Boston has developed other ways of engaging the children of the community in this important festival. The children learn the basics at their monthly Sunday school class. For the festival period itself, score sheets have been developed for three age-groups, and the children can earn points each day for things like recitation of the *Namokar Mantra* and other Jain prayers, not eating after sunset, visiting the temple, reading Jain stories, visiting the temple and performing *arti,* following Jain dietary customs, and donating food to the needy. Older children also earn points for fasting. But no matter how the points tally up, in the end every child gets a prize.

"In the past, we have given out books appropriate to each age-level, or we have given out puzzles and games related to Jainism," Shah explains. "Now we give out trophies—about seventy to a hundred. The goal is to teach our children the things you can do during *Paryushan*—what people would do in India. We are trying to instill some habits. Even at home, children can pray, they can read, they can control what they are eating and the amount of television they watch, they can avoid violent video games. These are things under their control."

*Shinto*

For Shinto-followers, the annual cycle includes celebrations and commemorations virtually every month. We will learn about a few of them, beginning with *Koshinsatsu Takeagehiki*—which comes right after New Year's. *Koshinsatsu Takeagehiki* is the annual Shinto festival of purification by burning. It is the time for Shinto-followers to remove old ritual objects and charms from their household shrines and exchange them for fresh ones. Devotees can just drop off the old objects at the shrine and purchase new ones, but some people like to attend the bonfire ceremony at which the used items are burned.

In early February comes *Setsubun* (Old Japanese Lunar New Year), which marks the end of winter. On this day, it is customary for people to throw soybeans to shoo away bad fortune and invoke the good. This can be done at home, but the several hundred people who can make their way to the Tsubaki Grand Shrine of America in Washington State each year for *Setsubun* get to share the fun with each other. After a purification rite and the bean-throwing, the High Priest shoots an arrow from a large Japanese bow to break the power of misfortune. In other parts of America, the customs are modified. "In Japanese tradition," one young northeasterner explains, "we have these human-like beings called *Oni.* Some of them have red skin. At home in Japan, people would dress up like *Oni* and go around the neighborhood. We would throw soybeans at them. We don't do that here. We just throw a few beans. Then you are supposed to eat as many soybeans as your age plus one. My grandmother is ninety-two, so she can't keep up! That is too many soybeans to digest at once!"

The Great Spring Festival Ceremony, in early April, is one of Shinto's most formal occasions—one of only two for which the doors of the inner shrine are opened. The faithful make food offerings, and the priest prays for everyone's health, happiness, safety, and mutual prosperity. The central prayer of the Great Spring Festival asks for the true experience of human life in harmony with *Kami* (that is, with Nature), for renewal and revitalization with fresh *ki*—power from Divine Nature.

*Natsu-matsuri* (Summer Festival) lasts for almost the entire month of June—the time when the crops are in the greatest danger of being destroyed by insects, blights, storms, or floods. The festival seeks the blessing of the *kami* during this delicate time.

*Nagoshi-no-Oharai* (June 30) is a day of Great Purification in the yearly cycle. A large sacred ring made of loosely twisted reeds is set up, and during the ceremony people walk through it to be purified of any stagnant *ki* (natural energy) from the first half of the year, and to receive fresh *ki* to carry them through the second half of the year successfully. At the conclusion of the ceremony, the paper effigies which were used in the ceremony are deposited into the river near the shrine. As one adaptation to the American context, everyone brings a dish to share at the potluck meal which follows. Since the turnout for this ceremony is large, this festival also provides an occasion for the shrine-association to meet and conduct any necessary business.

Traditionally, the Autumn Festival takes place from September through November, with some observances celebrating the harvest, and others marking the traditional absence of the *kami* during October. "I love the Moon Festival," says one New Yorker. "It comes with the full moon of September or October. We put two *daikon* (Japanese radishes) on a plate, along with fresh vegetables and other goodies. The radishes are supposed to be the moon's 'chopsticks.'" December brings the end of year and preparation for *Oshogatsu* (New Year festival)—and the cycle begins all over again.

There are many other colorful holidays as well. For people who can make their way to Granite Falls, Washington, all of them can be enjoyed in every detail at a fully functioning Shinto shrine, and its resident priest is also willing to perform all of the Shinto rituals by proxy for people who cannot come in person. Hawai'i has many shrines as well. In other parts of the United States, visiting priests may take care of these needs.

### *Buddhism*

Buddhists in America bring or borrow their holiday celebrations from many different Asian contexts: Sri Lanka, Thailand, China, Korea, Japan, Tibet, Vietnam, Laos, Cambodia, Burma, and more. Distinctly Western Buddhist communities have also been established. As we saw in our discussion of Buddhist New

Year, Buddha Day (*Wesak*) is celebrated by virtually all of America's Buddhist communities—although there is variation as to when it comes and exactly what it commemorates. In addition, each Buddhist community is likely to have its own cycle of other observances. Here we will highlight only a few.

In mid-August Japanese Buddhists to observe *Obon* with drumming, singing, dancing, and the Floating Lantern Ceremony. Its name is derived from a Sanskrit term referring to unbearable suffering. It is linked to the story of one of the Buddha's disciples. The disciple's mother was trapped in the Hungry Ghost Realm. "There are six different realms you can be born in," explains a Pure Land priest. "The Hungry Ghost Realm is one of them. It is a little bit like Hell. You are hungry, and you can't eat. You want something, and you can't get it. Everyone there is trying to get everything for themselves. It is a realm of greed." Guided by the Buddha, the disciple finally succeeds in liberating his mother from the Hungry Ghost Realm once he has offered food to the monks at the end of the summer Rain Retreat. The monks dance for joy, which is why dancing is an important part of *Obon* observance.

"We always celebrated *Obon*," says a teacher who grew up in Hawai'i. "We had paper lanterns at home in front of our Buddhist shrine, and I always danced at the ceremony at my parents' temple. I went back recently, but it wasn't the same. The crowds were smaller, there was no Japanese drumming, and the women were not wearing the full kimonos. It was a bit sad."

While it has joyful aspects, *Obon* is also an occasion for remembering the dead, a time especially for offering respect to ancestors three generations back. Dancing entertains the ancestors, and shows them respect and gratitude. "But you also honor all the dead," one Pure Land priest explains. The traditional way of doing this is with the Floating Lantern Ceremony. Small lanterns are lit and launched in a stream, the ocean, or a lake with prayers that everything in this world and the next may "be happy, good, and peaceful."

The New York Buddhist Temple has been performing the Floating Lantern Ceremony since 2002, but in 2004 it transferred the ceremony from mid-August to September 11. "In Japan, they do it on August 6, to remember the atomic bombing of Hiroshima," says the Rev. T. K. Nakagaki, the temple's priest, "so there is precedent for moving it." Temple members and other volunteers make some one hundred fifty lanterns of paper and Styrofoam; people write messages of peace on them, or the name of someone who has died. "We can't do too many more than that," the Rev. Nakagaki explains, "because we would need more kayaks to pull them out into the river." About a thousand people assemble on Pier 40 at dusk to listen to the chanting (and sometimes, drumming) and to watch members of the New York Kayak Company tow trains of lanterns out into the Hudson River.

Japanese Pure Land Buddhists have a memorial service on January 16 to remember their founder, Shinran Shonin (1173–1262); on May 21, they celebrate his birthday. Unlike Theravada Buddhists, they celebrate the Buddha's birth, enlightenment, and death on separate occasions (April 8, December 8, and February 15, respectively). "Actually," says a member of the congregation, "we observe these occasions on the Sunday before. That's when we have our regular service. We don't hold a separate service for these."

"Here in New York City," the Rev. Nakagaki explains, "we combine remembering the Passing Away of the Buddha with a Pets Memorial. It's not necessarily an innovation. When the Buddha passed away, different animals gathered. Not only humans gathered. We have a scroll of the passing away of the Buddha, with all those different creatures around."

As a reform movement, Won Buddhisn (which originated in early twentieth-century Korea) has several distinguishing holidays. On the first Sunday of June, Won Buddhists celebrate their founder's entry into Nirvana, and celebrate the lives of deceased spiritual and physical ancestors. "Since we believe in rebirth and reincarnation process," the Rev. Chung Ok Lee explains, "this memorial service connects all things in the universe, and stresses the interdependence and interconnectedness of our past, present, and future lives." The annual Won Buddhist thanksgiving celebration occurs on the first Sunday of December. "Gratitude is a very important part of our teaching," one minister explains. "We see the unbroken circle as the symbol of interconnectedness of all existence, so we are part of a whole.

We receive limitless support and love from the universe, our parents, all living beings, and *Dharma.* Won Buddhist Thanksgiving is a distinctive way of celebrating this."

A third holiday focuses on bringing spiritual transformation through deep prayer and meditation. It recalls that, in the early days of this tradition, the first nine Won disciples dedicated their lives to enabling civilization to become more spiritual. "For that reason," she says, "we put nine candles on the altar, symbolizing the first nine disciples." Light is very important in Won holidays and ritual. "Light symbolizes your wisdom," the minister explains. "Wisdom in Won Buddhist tradition is to see things clearly as they are, instead of the way you want to see. So we always put a candle on the altar when we do holiday celebrations."

Many Chinese Buddhists make much of Kuan-Yin festivals. These include her birthday (nineteenth day of the second lunar month), the day she became a nun (the nineteenth day of the sixth lunar month), and the day she attained Enlightenment (the nineteenth day of the ninth lunar month). Observances include temple visits, setting birds and animals free, abstaining from meat-eating, doing charity, taking gifts to orphanages and homes for the elderly, and observing the Five, Eight, or Ten Precepts with extra seriousness. Devotees spend the day in quiet contemplation of the Great Vows of Kuan-Yin to save all sentient beings and to forsake the bliss of Nirvana, and on her virtues of loving-kindness, compassion, and wisdom. They may spend the day making merit by prayer-recitation, *sutra*-reading, and meditation on the happiness of others, and then transfer all that merit to all other sentient beings. (Of course, Kuan-Yin followers try to do things like this every day of the year!)

*Islam*

Fasting is the prelude to one of Islam's two canonical holidays. *Eid al-Fitr* (pronounced "eedul-fitr")—the Festival of Fast-Breaking—marks the end of the month of Ramadan. "I love Ramadan," says one journalist. "It's my favorite thing. My community meets pretty much every night at the mosque, so the month is one enormous festival. We fast all day, we come together, we eat together, and then we pray. So, we see each other every night, but the big blow-out, of course, is at the end." *Eid al-Fitr* occurs on the first day of the Islamic month of *Shawwal.* The joy and thankfulness of fulfilling the month-long obligatory fast is demonstrated through special prayer as a community in the mosque, visits with family and friends, special foods, and gift-giving. A special charitable donation is also made, either a specific amount of food or money in the amount equivalent to the cost of a family meal.

*Eid al-Adha* (pronounced "eedul-ahd-hah")—the Feast of Sacrifice—is the more major of the two Islamic festivals. It begins on the tenth day of the month in which *Hajj* (pilgrimage) is made to Mecca, about two-and-a-half months after *Eid al-Fitr,* and is associated with the *Hajj* ritual, which itself dramatizes some of the events of the Abraham/Ishmael/Hagar story. Since God substituted a ram for Abraham's son, Muslims who have the means are expected to sacrifice rams (or other unblemished male animals—goats, bulls, camels) on *Eid al-Adha* (or to purchase, or contribute toward the purchase of, an animal which is slaughtered professionally). The meat becomes the centerpiece of the holiday meal, which is shared with family and friends but is also distributed to the poor worldwide, making this holiday a huge event of outreach and address of world hunger issues. (Much of the meat is canned and used throughout the year by relief organizations.)

The celebration of *Eid al-Adha* extends over three days. "It is supposed to be a bigger festival than it often turns out to be," one woman comments, "because everyone is involved in the Ramadan fast, but only a few people are involved in the *Hajj.*" Nevertheless, she says, it always means special prayer- and fellowship-time at the mosque. *Eid al-Adha* is a time when Muslims like to gather for community-wide or extended-family meals—which may include special entertainment or educational events. "Also," she continues, "this holiday places more focus on the kids. On *Eid al-Adha,* a lot of people take a vacation, and people buy presents for their children because we remember Abraham's offering of his son and the redemption of that child. *Eid al-Adha* is a celebration of the living child."

Some Muslims observe other occasions as well. *Laylat al-Qadir* (Night of Power) is one of the odd-numbered nights during the last ten days of Ramadan. It commemorates the night on which the Prophet received the first revelation of the Qur'an. It is observed by night-long prayer, Qur'an recitation, and special acts of charity. The Prophet's birthday is a traditional observance in some communities, but without basis in the Qur'an, the Prophet's *Sunnah* (example), or the example of his Companions. On the tenth of *Muharram* (that is, the tenth day of the first month of the Islamic calendar), Shi'ah Muslims commemorate the martyrdom of Imam Husayn (the grandson of the Prophet) and his family at the Battle of Karbala. This is called *Ashura* (tenth), and in fact, many communities have daily observances at their mosque for the nine days leading up to it.

*Judaism*

Jewish holidays often fall on the fifteen day of the lunar month, when the full moon would provide extra natural light for celebrating. Traditionally, the beginning of a new month would have been broadcast by messengers of the high court in Jerusalem, but Jews living outside Israel would not have been able to get the message. So Jews in diaspora traditionally have celebrated holidays for two days instead of one, just in case they miscalculated. Since modern methods of calculation and communication eliminate the ambiguity, America's Reform Jews observe holidays for one day only, Orthodox observe them for two days, and Conservative congregations may opt for either practice.

As we have learned, *Rosh ha-Shanah* (New Year) is followed by a period known as Days of Awe. This leads right to *Yom Kippur* (the Day of Atonement)—a twenty-five-hour period of total abstinence from food and water, the only day of fasting mandated by the Torah. There are special synagogue services on the evening that commences the fast, and the next day until the fast ends at sundown.

"Being a leader rather than being a participant gives *Yom Kippur* different meaning for me now," says a young woman who has been a rabbi for just two years. "Leading services has caused me to think more about what the occasion means, because I have to give sermons. That has really added to my experience—because I have to prepare and think about it.

Traditionally, before the High Holidays, we are supposed to take the month before to reflect upon the themes, to think about our relationship to God and to the people in our lives. I find I don't really do that preparation unless I have to give sermons and think of things to say during the service."

*Yom Kippur's* evening service begins with *Kol Nidre* (All Vows). "One of the things I have really enjoyed now that I am leading services is singing *Kol Nidre,*" says a new cantor. "The tune is beautiful. I find I connect more if I am singing it, because I am concentrating on the words and on the feeling. *Kol Nidre* is such a great mood-setter. It underscores the solemnity of the occasion, and its grandness—that it is something to be taken seriously."

Just five days after *Yom Kippur* comes *Sukkot* (the Feast of Booths, or Tabernacles)—a week-long festival that is sort of a Jewish Thanksgiving Day. Jews build and eat meals in a hut or a lean-to decorated with natural things, commemorating the temporary shelters the Israelites had to use while they spent forty years wandering in the wilderness after their Exodus from Egypt. "So we're supposed to live in booths," explains Rabbi Jack Bemporad. "But why do we do that? Because the booth is a symbol of the body. It's very fragile. It's something that is vanishing. It's passing. Yet we have to make it beautiful. The booth has to have an open roof so we can look at the stars: in spite of the passing, there are eternal things. So that forces us to confront the question of, while we do perish and life is transitory, what values do we embody?"

The week concludes with the holiday of *Simchat Torah* (the Joy of Torah)—a celebration of the completion of the annual Torah lectionary. On this occasion, the Torah reading begins with the end of the book of Deuteronomy, which tells of the death of Moses, and finishes with the opening verses of Genesis, which launches the cycle of lessons once more. "On *Simchat Torah,*" says Rabbi Bemporad, "it's true that you celebrate the Torah: you walk around with it, you carry it. But the real meaning is, 'What is the Torah's teaching, and how do I embody it in my life?'"

Most Americans are well aware of *Chanukah* (dedication), because of its proximity to Christmas. It commemorates an event recorded in the book of Maccabees, when the Jewish community took back the Jerusalem temple, which the Greek occupying force had turned into a shrine for their own purposes. Once the Jews had purified the space and made it ready for use again, they went to re-light the *menorah*—a candelabra of seven lights. Sadly, they discovered, there was only enough oil for one night; but miraculously, the oil lasted for eight. *Chanukah* customs center on the home. Candles placed in a special *menorah* (candle-stand) are lit each of the eight nights (one on the first night, two on the second, and so on), and are allowed to burn all the way down. Gifts are exchanged. Technically, however, *Chanukah* is not nearly so important a holiday as to merit the attention it receives in the American context.

*Purim* comes sometime between late February and early April, and commemorates the heroism of Queen Esther on behalf of the Jewish people. The *Megillah* (Scroll) of Esther is read, and some communities do this at a *Purim* carnival. "I always have mixed feelings about *Purim*," says a young New York professional woman. "You feel like you should be partying and having a lot of fun, and I just never experience it that way. Part of the problem for me is that the days of *Purim* come at a time of year when the weather is always sort of overcast. Even when I think back on services I attended as a child, I remember that they were loud and overcrowded, and I wasn't comfortable. The best *Purim* readings I've been at are where the people take on the different voices of the different characters, and really emphasize the puns in the text. So I have a dream of hosting my own *Purim* party some year with just my friends. We'll do a dramatic *Megillah* reading in Hebrew—maybe with English for some of the major parts. That would make it a fun thing... but I have to learn to read the *Megillah* first!"

*Pesach* (Passover)—the Feast of Unleavened Bread—is an eight-day recollection of escape from slavery into freedom through divine intervention. In traditional homes, cleaning in preparation for *Pesach* includes scavenging for every speck of leaven, and exchanging the dishes, pots, pans, and utensils for ones which leaven has never touched. Because of its importance in Jewish self-understanding, Passover is observed by most

Jews—even if only by means of a *seder* with one's family. The Passover *seder*—the highlight of this season—is a ritual meal during which the story of the Exodus is recounted, using food items as symbols along the way. The script for this is called a *Haggadah,* and can be fine-tuned to suit one's family or community. "I do enjoy *seder* night," says a Michigan poet, "and since I wrote a version of the *Haggadah,* anybody who shows up at our house doesn't have much choice about the way the service is going to be conducted. They do it our way! We sing everything we possibly can."

The story of Passover celebrates coming out of slavery in Egypt. But the Hebrew word translated as "Egypt" can also mean "a narrow place." "Actually," says Rabbi Bemporad, "it's plural; it means 'a double restriction.' Passover is about freedom from a twofold restriction—both physical and spiritual. The whole lesson of Passover is 'How do you get from slavery to freedom?' In the ritual, God becomes a symbol of liberation. So then you have to ask yourself, 'In what way am I a slave right now, and how can I be liberated from it?' For example, if I drink, if I am an addict on some level, then how do I get over that? What does it mean to be free, and what does it mean to be a slave? The whole ceremony, the whole *Haggadah,* is a means of coming to terms with that. It's a ritual, but it has profound moral significance."

There are other annual Jewish observances. There is *Shavuot* (Feast of Weeks; also called Pentecost), which comes in late spring, seven weeks after Passover. It commemorates God's gift of the Torah, and with it the life of *mitzvah* observance. "From a biblical perspective, it is a big occasion," one Orthodox educator points out. "It should be just as important as Passover, but it simply is not given as much attention. It's the most neglected holiday of them all, because it really doesn't have much in the way of rituals and customs attached to it." The Jewish calendar marks days for commemorating the destruction of the temple by the Babylonians in 950 B.C.E., the horrors of the Holocaust, the establishment of the modern state of Israel, the victory of the Six-Day War of 1967; and so on. All will figure in the life of a synagogue.

*Bahá'í Faith*

"Besides our New Year, there are nine annual Bahá'í holy days," explains a schoolteacher who raised two children in the faith. Some holy days center on Bahá'u'lláh's herald, the Báb: his birthday (October 20); his declaration of his mission in 1844, which began the Bahá'í era (May 23); and his martyrdom in 1850 (July 9). Most holidays honor events in the life of Bahá'u'lláh himself. His birthday is remembered on November 12. The Festival of *Ridván* (April 21 to May 2) is a twelve-day period which commemorates his declaration of his mission in 1863. The first, ninth, and twelfth days have particular significance, and the first of *Ridván* is also the day of annual Bahá'í Local and National Spiritual Assembly elections. The Ascension of Bahá'u'lláh (May 29) commemorates Bahá'u'lláh's death.

"On those days, we are supposed to suspend work," the schoolteacher continues. "But if there are individuals whose work situation does not allow them to suspend it, there is flexibility. But children should not attend school." There had to be compromises, however, when her kids were growing up. "If there were certain days when they had a test or exam and just could not miss, then I sent them to school. We didn't substitute another day. One thing was for sure: I always made sure we observed that day in some form, whether it was with prayers, or readings from scriptures, a special dinner—something to make my children know it was a special day."

*Ayyám-i-Há* is a four- or five-day celebratory period of parties, gift-giving, and acts of charity during intercalary days, which are placed just before the last month of the Bahá'í year (which is also the annual Nineteen Day Fast). Bahá'ís are encouraged to invite friends, relatives, neighbors, and coworkers to whatever festivities are planned, and to include them in the gift-giving. *Ayyám-i-Há* means "Days of the letter 'H'"—a letter which stands for the Divine Essence. Thus, while *Ayyám-i-Há* is a lot of fun, it is also a time of preparation for the period of fasting. One businesswoman says she uses the intercalary days to build her list of intercessions for her devotions during the fast itself. "During *Ayyám-i-Há,* normally, if I think about someone, I decide to pray for them during the nineteen days. I keep a list. Then, every morning, after I pray the special prayer for the fast, I remember each of those people in prayer."

*Afro-Caribbean Religions*

Vodou ceremonies are based on a lunar calendar, one priest explains. "Certainly, we'll have ceremonies around the equinoxes, but we also mark the whole planting cycle. In Haiti, for instance, in July, there will have been massive ceremonies for planting. Very little takes place in August, because it's the rainy season. In September, when crops are beginning to emerge and you're getting ready for the harvest, there are many more activities. Then in November, the Haitian equivalent to winter, plants are not growing as much; it's not as prolific a time. So we begin to have ceremonies for the dead, for the ancestors. Things just stay quiet for a while because the harvest has just taken place, and the ground needs to rest. Traditionally, All Souls' Day (November 2) is the last of the ceremonies for November, and there won't be anything throughout December. We have two months without ceremonies, to acknowledge the earth's resting that way. So we have to think of ways to translate these agriculturally connected observances into our northern, urban context."

After this period of quiet comes a big celebration on the first of January. "This is a big day for all of the *lwa* [spiritual entities]," she continues. "All of the spirits are called down on that day, but it is also Haitian Independence Day. We don't segregate Haitian history and politics and revolution from Vodou. It's all one and the same, because it's our religion that helped bring about our independence."

The routine is similar for followers of Lùkùmì (Afro-Cuban religion). Patron Divinity Services occur several times a year, the purpose of which is to establish and understand one's relationship to one's personal *orisha* (spiritual entity), to honor ancestors, and for thanksgiving. Ceremonies include singing, drumming, and dance, all of which facilitates individual and community healing.

Vodou ritual takes place in a *hounfó* (or *hounfor*)—the temple and its grounds. A *hounfó* would have altar rooms, where private things can be done; but it would also have a *péristyle*—

a public interior space that is large enough for a congregation to gather for ceremonial dances. A *péristyle* is distinguished by having a large tree or pole in the middle—the *poto mitan* (centerpost)—that serves as the channel through which the *lwa* enter the ceremony. Ceremonial dances are held in this covered area.

"Vodou is very much about ritual, about performance," one priest asserts. "It's kinesthetic. It's about animating the Divine presence. If you look at the flags I have in my house, it isn't an accident that they are sequined. The sequins shine in the light, and they shift in the light. That's animation!" The symbol of the Vodou priest's power and authority is called an *ason*—a gourd rattle covered with a web of beads, and girded by a small belt. "When I shake my *ason,*" she continues, "there is sound within and without. The bell rings and the glass beads dance on the surface of the *ason.* That's animation, too."

For practitioners of Lùkùmì and Vodou alike, animal sacrifice is a major component of worship. "Our rituals are absolutely misunderstood," says Dowoti Désir, a Vodou priest. "People always ask, 'Do you really kill chickens?' And I always say, 'Yes! And I eat them! And you eat them, too—only somebody else kills them, preserves them, puts them in a plastic container, and puts them in the supermarket for you.' Me, in a ceremony—yes, I'll have a chicken in my hand; and yes, I eventually take away its life. But I also acknowledge the fact that I'm doing it. Essentially, I apologize for taking away its life. I didn't give it; it's not my right to take it away. But at the same time, I know I need it. The ancestors or the spirits have told us this is part of what we must do. Besides, we are all instruments of something else in our lives. In Vodou, we understand that."

"When I need to use a rooster in a ceremony," Désir continues, "I ask its permission. I ask its forgiveness, because I am fully aware that at any point in life, it could be *my* head that is being taken away. I have to acknowledge that. That fowl's head could be *my* head. Having your head taken away probably won't happen in a ceremony like this, but when you don't get the job you need, or something horrible happens to you on your way to work, or your child has a debilitating illness—essentially, it is the same. When such things happen, it is as if your head has been removed. In a Vodou ceremony, when you take the life of that creature, you feel its warmth, you feel its blood, you feel it expiring in your hands. So you know you have power that way. You can misuse that power, but you can also do good with that power. And you can't ever say, 'I don't know what I'm doing!' So there is a critical issue of accountability in our rituals. If I ever even accidentally hurt a human being, or do something inadvertent to end someone's life, I will know what that means, because I know what it means to do the same things with a hen or a rooster within this context of worship and ritual."

In 1993, the United States Supreme Court legitimized Afro-Caribbean religious practice. Among other things, the court indicated that to have ruled otherwise would have called into question kosher and *halal* slaughter of animals, which are ritual practices in their way; and that it hardly made sense that the *slaughter* of animals for human consumption could be legal, but not the *sacrifice* of animals which would then be consumed by humans. Furthermore, as Afro-Caribbean religious leaders themselves stress, every sacrificial animal is put to use afterward. Nothing is wasted—not even the bones, hooves, or feathers; and the meat is consumed by the community. "Not only our *familie*, but *everyone* in the community gets fed," Désir says. "The ironic thing is that sometimes the very people who shun us, who were vilifying us several hours before a ceremony, end up eating our food. For years, we've fed them. They are still part of our family, even though they may not acknowledge it."

### *Native American Religions*

The annual and occasional celebrations of America's First Nations take a number of forms, usually guided by the lunar calendar. As an agricultural people, the Keetoowah (Cherokee) hold an annual Green Corn Festival and Ripe Corn Festival (Thanksgiving). Festivals are held annually for other reasons as well: *Atahuna* is held for reconciliation and forgiveness, and *Busk* for purification. *Uku* is the Priest's Festival. All told, the Keetoowah have seven major annual festivals, and each celebration can last for several days. The festivals provide the community with opportunities to recall its history, reconnect with its ancestors, and educate its children. Participants make the garments they wear for the ceremonies—traditional clothing, moccasins, and shawls. Traditional foods prepared in traditional ways are served.

"When we start our gardens," says a Nashotah Cree resident of Detroit, "there are certain prayers we do, and songs, and actually even dances. There are certain prayers that are offered to the Three Sisters: the corn, the beans, and the squash. There is a corn dance and a squash dance. They are tended by the females. We grow the tobacco we use in our daily ceremonies. Special prayers for the men and boys that work with the tobacco are given. Then, when we pick berries and medicines, there is a different set of prayers."

In the Oglala Lakota tradition, a community leader explains, "each month would have a traditional name, according to the moon. December would be the Moon of the Popping Trees. It is called that because it gets so cold in North Dakota that the wood actually makes popping noises." Wintertime is a time for special prayers to the North Wind and the North Spirits, says his friend. "We ask the North Wind not to harm anybody, because the North Wind is the most treacherous. It can take a life."

"I grew up on the Pine Ridge Reservation," says one Oglala Lakota youth worker. "We'd always go to the Sun Dance when we were kids. It was something we did every summer, around August. It was part of vacation—part of life." The Sun Dance is one of the Seven Rites of the Oceti Sakowin Oyate, of which the Lakota are a part. It is a Northern Plains tradition, but other people often participate. "It's become a pan-Indian thing," the youth-worker continues. "You'll hear of Sun Dances down south—even in Mexico. They go on throughout the whole continent. You know, for me, it's something that you can't take out of context. And by context, I mean more than time and place. I mean knowing how to do it—how to set the tone. I went to one out east, and it just didn't seem right. I just never went back. For me, a Sun Dance isn't a Sun Dance unless it happens in Oceti Sakowin territory. When I was a kid, there were still a lot of these old-timers who would do the real deal—very humble people."

Traditionally, the Sun Dance begins at the time of the summer solstice. It lasts for the rest of June, and all of July and August. "The Sun Dance occurs when the sun is at its hottest, and when the berries and choke cherries are ripe. Most of the imagery has to do with hunting and gathering," explains an Oglala Lakota activist in Los Angeles.

"A lot of it relates to star-knowledge and Lakota cosmology," adds a community leader in the Minnesota community. Petitionary prayer is a part of the ceremony, he explains. "Traditionally, we Lakota were never agriculturalists, so prayer for rain and a good harvest is not a traditional purpose of the ceremony. However, an individual dancer might bring that concern to the ceremony. He might make that petition on someone else's behalf while he danced. That would be up to him."

A Detroit resident is preparing for his third Sun Dance this summer. "Once you start Sun Dancing, it's a four-year commitment," he says. "After that, whether you go again depends on what Creator wants you to do. I know old men that have been dancing for some twenty odd years." "True," says a Lakota leader. "In fact, the Sun Dance it is really a lifetime commitment. Most men, once they start, they keep doing it for life."

A participant in the Sun Dance is required to undergo eight days of purification. "Once you arrive at the site," says one experienced dancer, "your spend four days in purification in anticipation of joining the dance. You work on the camp and prepare for the ceremony. The other four days are the actual Sun Dance itself. Dancers pledge to go out and dance for four days and four nights, with no food and no water. You walk in faith."

Male Sun Dancers pledge to have their flesh pierced on either side of the sternum. "There is a tree that represents God, Creator. A rope is attached to that tree and is passed through your chest by a skewer type of thing. Walking from that tree to the buffalo robe where you lie down and get pierced will be the longest walk you will ever take in your life—let alone being without food or water for four days. It's a ceremony where you go in humble or you'll come out humble. Sun Dancers lean back, let the rope tug against their skin, and give it all to Creator because that's when you realize your own command, your own mortality, is bigger than you. You're here to do a job and you also get prayers and blessings."

Women may participate in all aspects of the Sun Dance, but they don't get pierced. "The explanation I was given," says a young New Yorker who has participated twice herself, "is that women are life-givers and are cleansed monthly—they are already connected to the Creator. For women, piercing would be redundant." However, women who are menstruating stay away from the ceremony. "This is not because we are 'dirty,'" one explains; "it is because that is when we are most powerful."

In a nutshell, says one young man, "through the Sun Dance you're creating a mini-universe where you're asking the Creator to come into that ceremony. You are giving of yourself—through song, through dancing, through piercing, through prayers—by your suffering and humility." A Lakota community leader concurs: "What happens in the Sun Dance is similar to the Passion of Jesus the Christ." The dance is a testimony of faith, "and it is always done for others," says another community leader. "You never do it for yourself."

People who know authentic Sun Dancers often remark about their humility. They are not likely to talk about the dance, and they do not show off their scars. "It's not a bravery thing," says a Sun Dancer from Detroit. "It's about your prayer, your responsibility. You don't focus on pain. You are asking for all creation to join you there. It's like being attached to the Creator by an umbilical cord through that tall tree." The tree he mentions is at the center of the sacred circle, a Lakota leader explains. "The tree represents a sacred altar." Participants sing as they dance. "One round of singing will last for six hours," a young man explains. "And then you take a break, and then you sing for another six hours. You face a certain direction and you pray to the Creator. Once you get past your fear (which is not of Creator), then it's so simple."

"The Sun Dance is about prayer," says an Oglala Lakota community leader, "but it is also a connection—connection to Great Spirit. The spiritual can overcome anything. The power, the sacredness, the sacred power—through that, anything is possible."

When it comes to Native occasional celebrations, two more terms come to mind: *potlatch* and *powwow.* The potlatch, associated with the Northwest coastal peoples, is a grand occasion for feasting to celebrate occasions like the birth of a child or a rite of passage. The festivities include lots of traditional singing, dancing, and food. For certain Northwest peoples, the dancing makes use of large, elaborate masks. At a potlatch, every guest receives a gift from the host. In former times, gifts might have been as lavish as a canoe, silver jewelry, or a handmade blanket. Now, they are likely to be simpler handmade items, or T-shirts or mugs, or food staples. Even still, assembling all the gifts can take a year of preparation in itself.

The powwow is similar in many ways. It may have originated with the Plains Indians, but now many First Nations have adopted it, and pan-Indian powwows have become commonplace. The Oglala Lakota call this kind of celebration *wacipi* (pronounced "wah-chee-pee"). It can be a family social event, says a Los Angeles resident. "When I was growing up on the reservation, *wacipi* were summer events—a time to gather, to see family, to have fun, and to have Give-Aways." What kinds of things are given away? "You know, whatever people want to give away—material possessions." Handmade things? "Not necessarily," he says. "No, it's anything—horses, guns, all sorts of things. The Give-Away always occurs at the first anniversary of the death of a loved one, and the *wacipi* is an opportune time for this, because so many people are gathered anyway."

When Native Peoples gather for a powwow or any kind of ceremony, prayer often takes the form of song. "My uncle was a singer," says a youth leader. "Everyone in my family was a singer. They knew all the songs, and they would compose songs for any occasion. They were always in the Lakota language. You know, when I go to a pan-Indian powwow, sometimes I'll hear someone singing a Lakota tune, like an honoring song, but he won't be saying any words! It'll be 'Hey yah, hey yah yah, hey yah'—that kind of thing. No words. And I'm thinking, 'What happened to the words? You've got to have the words!"

Powwows may also be huge social events which include dance competitions. A drum is an essential accompaniment, and is to be treated respectfully. Dakota powwows feature the

Grass Dance and the highly athletic Fancy Dance by the men, and the Jingle Dance and Shawl Dance by the women.

The Citizen Potawatomi Nation (which has territorial jurisdiction over a portion of central Oklahoma) has sponsored an annual powwow since 1972. In the early decades, these were intertribal gatherings in late June. When the competitions at this event grew to be too commercialized and too "professional," the community reined it in. For several years, it was held as a reunion festival for Potawatomi only. All attendees were encouraged to join the dance circle, and the organizers provided the required shawls and sashes to anyone who arrived without. One very positive result has been a renewal of interest in the community at large to learn how to dance properly. In October 2003, the Nation reestablished its annual intertribal competition powwow, but with limits on the prize money and incentives for Potawatomi dancers and drummers—even beginners—to participate.

The Potawatomi community's dismay at the commercialization of its ceremonies and its search for a solution points to general Native American distress at the exploitation of sacred rituals and objects. "Our prayers and the prayer songs originate from a divine source," says one Oglala Lakota leader. "Things become desecrated once they are commercialized." Some Native groups and individuals have published their deep anger at non-Indian people who hold imitation sweat lodge ceremonies, Sun Dances, or Vision Quests for monetary gain; at the sale of ritual objects (real or imitation) at flea markets and retail shops; at the sensationalizing of Native rituals by the television and film industries; and more. "Unfortunately," he continues, "some Native Americans do this, too." These activities have provoked lively discussion. Certainly, there is no overarching consensus on the extent to which non-Indian people may participate in Native ceremonies. What is clear is that many Native persons are willing to share their wisdom and their ways. In return, they wish that non-Indians would be careful how they use what they learn.

## Reflections

In America, the academic, business, and civil calendars privilege Christian and, in some places, Jewish observances to an extent. How do the residents of America's multi-religious neighborhood maintain the integrity of their own religious calendar in spite of this? The marketing frenzy in the United States which leads up to the celebration of Christmas on December 25 has been a topic of amusement (and bemusement) in inter-religious dialogue circles for some time—especially given that so much of what takes place in the name of Christmas has so little to do with Christianity! How do members of other faiths in the neighborhood accommodate this national public-religion ritual? What do they say to their children about it?

"When my sister Isha and I were going to public school in Michigan, we sang Christmas songs," Raman Singh recalls. This was not a bad thing for Sikh children to do, she adds, but she also is glad the public schools have become more sensitive to religious differences among students. "They are realizing that everybody is not Christian, that not everybody has a Christmas tree." Trilochan, their father, grins: "We *had* a Christmas tree!" "A couple of times we did," Isha concedes. "Because we asked for it," Raman nods. Trilochan continues, "They were young kids then. Then, as they grew up, we started to not have it."

"You have to realize," Raman explains, "we are a minority community even in India. Sikhs are used to accommodating (and even celebrating) other people's holidays. All the Sikhs in India celebrate *Diwali*, and that's not a Sikh festival! But they're all into it: new presents and new clothes—just like here for Christmas! It's the same idea. But now, my husband and I have started to do more with our kids around our own holidays. Thankfully, we live in a heavily Jewish neighborhood and our

Jewish neighbors don't want to be doing those Christmas things in December either."

"I decorate my house with 'Christmas lights'," Isha chimes in, "but I put them up for *Diwali.* I turn them on again at Guru Nanak's birthday, and then for Guru Gobind Singh's birthday, and then for *Wesak.* So, my lights go up in November, and stay up till April! They may not be on continuously, but I do turn on lights for all of those occasions. And I turn them on during the Christmas holidays too."

"When we were growing up," says Raman, "sometimes we would say things like, 'Why do they have to close the post office for Christmas?' Our dad would say, 'You know, you live here, where the vast majority of people are Christian. It's a cultural thing. Just chill! You're lucky to be able to go to *gurdwara;* you're lucky to *have* a *gurdwara,* you know. We're able to celebrate everything we want to, you know.' I think that really impressed us."

The busy mother of two elementary school students says she has no problem with her children participating in Christian holidays, but she makes sure they are well aware of their own. *Pongal,* a very special harvest festival for Hindus, falls in mid-January. Her children do not get the day off from public school, of course, but she does special things with them at home, and also sends things to school which are symbolic of the holiday. "This year, I sent *Pongal* cookies to my daughter's class. This kind of cookie is very bitter, and I thought the children might not even touch it. But, believe you me, children are very unpredictable. All of them liked those bitter cookies, and they even wanted the recipe!" She wrestles daily with the fact that her children—the only Hindus in their school—do not like standing out in a crowd, and sometimes find "being different" very embarrassing. When the children at the local public school receive *Pongal* treats with enthusiasm, and say, "Oh, I hope you bring those again," it validates the treat, and it validates her children as well.

"When you're a minority," says a rabbi in Lexington, Kentucky, "it's difficult. Last year someone called me up, trying to figure out how best to apologize for scheduling something on *Yom Kippur.* It was big, downtown event, and when the conflict was pointed out, the organizers did look into rescheduling. They couldn't, though, because of deposit money involved. The fact that she called was really a nice gesture. It showed that she recognized that *Yom Kippur* is one of the holiest days of the year for us, and she really was sorry for not factoring it into the planning. It was commendable that someone realized how important our calendar is to us."

People know that civil society is accommodating their religion's needs when their city suspends parking regulations on their holidays, or when they get an official United States Postal Service holiday postage stamp! The first postage stamp ever to commemorate Muslim holidays was designed by Virginia calligrapher Mohamed Zakariya, and was released on September 1, 2001. It has a deep blue background on which gold calligraphy says, *Eid Greetings* and *Eid Mubarak* (Blessed Festival)—suitable for both major Islamic holidays, *Eid al-Fitr* and *Eid al-Adha.*

Because the Muslim lunar calendar never is adjusted to the agricultural seasons, Ramadan can fall during the school year, so it presents slightly different issues each time. "I think that in some ways, having the fast occur during the school year was not really something that I ever felt was a big deal," says the mother of an eleven-year-old. "In the winter, it's just like not eating lunch. It's much harder in the summertime because the days are longer, and you don't drink water the whole day, but the kids are not in school then. When I was a kid in school, fasting wasn't a time where I felt like I wanted extra attention. I think it's enough for my child's teachers just to acknowledge that it's a special time."

In general, that's what our neighbors, our students, and our co-workers hope for.

CHAPTER FIVE

# Observance

THE FACT IS, in many of the religions now practiced in the American neighborhood, ritual life is bigger than prayer life. There are so many devotional acts that do not have the "look" of prayer. A traditional Chinese family might embrace the Confucian notion of the Five Relationships (some of which are familial; others, civic), and with them the notion that tolerance is virtuous, that propriety and ritual "glue" a society together, and that morality is cultivated by disciplining the body daily through such "arts" as calligraphy, music, mathematics, horsemanship, and marksmanship. Sikhs and Zoroastrians may wear special garments. One Hindu mother takes time each morning to make elaborate designs on her New York doorstep—drawing by letting rice flour slip from the ends of her fingers. Her neighbor, an observant Muslim, takes care to follow *halal* food rules, dress modestly, and give to charity. None of this is "prayer" exactly, which is why it sometimes makes more sense to speak of someone as "observant" rather than as "devout." But doing each of these things is indeed a habit of faith—faith that these customs have tremendous value, or are at least worth preserving.

In this chapter, we will look at a few of the shapes these observances take. We will conclude with pilgrimage—a ritual of faith which carries its practitioners out of the neighborhood quite deliberately, and brings them back transformed in some way.

## Fulfilling Commandments

Traditional Jews point not only to the Ten Commandments, but to 613 commandments received by Moses from God on Mount Sinai. The Hebrew word for commandment is *mitzvah* (plural, *mitzvot)* which for some Jews also conveys the sense of "blessing." In addition to formal prayer rituals three times a day, spontaneous dialogue with God, and other ways to pray which traditional Judaism mandates or encourages, there are other *mitzvot* to observe throughout the day—and many Jews incorporate them into their daily lives. As one Orthodox woman puts it, "I pretty much do all the standard, daily rituals. I think we can say of any part of the day, if there are Jewish things to do, I'll be trying to do them. There is a whole layer of customs as part of Jewish ritual life that is just fascinating. It is good to consider what is your personal balance between joy and awe, and how you translate that into your ritual practice. Ritual is there both to create joy and to address the really hard times."

One *mitzvah* is to affix a *mezuzah* to the doorposts of one's home. "It means 'doorpost,'" says a young rabbi, "and it comes from Deuteronomy 11:19–20, where it says that we should teach God's commandments to our children, and that we write them on the doorposts of our house and on our gates. It's also a reference back to the Exodus, when God commanded the Israelites to put a marker of blood on their door." A *mezuzah* is a little box made of almost any material and design. It contains a tiny kosher parchment scroll on which portions of Deuteronomy have been inscribed by a *sofer* (someone specially trained to copy Torah): the *Sh'ma* (the testimony that God is One), and the passage where the word *mezuzah* occurs. It is attached to the door's upright at an angle—at about eye-level. "Many times, a *mezuzah* will have a Hebrew letter on the outside—a *shin*, which stands for Shaddai (Almighty), which is one of God's names," she explains. "It signifies that 'this is a Jewish house' on the cultural level, irrespective of one's level of commitment to other practices."

"And a *mezuzah* doesn't belong just on your gates," she continues. "It belongs on any doorway of your home, except for bathrooms and closets—any place where someone could sleep. So it is not just an external reminder that this is a Jewish house, but an internal reminder that each room belongs to God. Sometimes you'll see a *mezuzah* on a place of business. It doesn't mean necessarily that it's a kosher place, or that it is not open on Shabbat; it means it's Jewish!" Some Jews touch the *mezuzah* as they pass it. "I don't," she says. "It's not my custom. Some people do; not everyone. It varies."

"The Reform movement believes that Jewish life and its daily rhythm should be mindful of, and attentive to, the values that are expressed in the traditional laws, rather than the details of observance," one graduate student explains. "My own personal religious life is more about being intentional about and attentive to these values, and less about counting the number of commanded acts I do in the course of the day. My point is that the most meaningful religious obligations are indeed obligations to be 'interhuman.' *Tzedakah* (charity) is not discretionary. The lesson that Jewish ritual life in all of its multiple facets is designed to reinforce, express, inculcate is the sense that caring behavior is not optional: it's obligatory. Jewish ritual life is a kind of pedagogy of obligation, in the hope that this will create heightened awareness of one's obligation to respond to the needs of others. I have discretion with the details. So if I let go of the details, I hope I retain enough of them to feel the pull of obligation."

## God-Consciousness

"My devotional life includes integrating God's will in my life as much as possible," says a young Turkish-American mother in Alabama. Muslims place much emphasis on developing *taqwa* (God-consciousness), a highly prized human attribute, according to the Qur'an. *Taqwa* has to do with righteousness, dutifulness, and piety. "In the choices I make," she explains, "in choosing the clothes I wear and the places I go, in deciding what to eat and where not to look, I try to stay within the limits of my religion. I am aware that I am not always choosing the ideal option, but at least I struggle to do so. Besides such choices, I try to integrate my knowledge of God's Names in my life. I try to associate the Names of God with God's actions. For example, when I am taking aspirin for my headache, I remind myself to expect the cure itself from God. When I focus on my love for my husband and my husband's love for me, I find myself thanking God for giving that love between us. In other words, I try for *taqwa.* I try to be as aware as possible of the existence and actions of God around us, and to be thankful. This awareness leads me to integrate God's will in my choices."

"There's good and bad music," asserts a member of the Muslim Student Association at a Michigan university as she reflects on the relationship between *taqwa* and pop culture. "The only problem is that in order to discover what's good and what's bad, you have to listen to the bad stuff." Her classmate concurs. "I think the issue of listening to rock music also fits into a larger Islamic mandate: Be productive, be efficient with your time. Whether it's listening to music, or sitting on your porch smoking a cigar—whatever it is, if you can legitimately deem it a waste of time, it is something you should stay away from," he asserts. "There is so much popular music that is disgustingly provocative and demeaning. That alone removes it

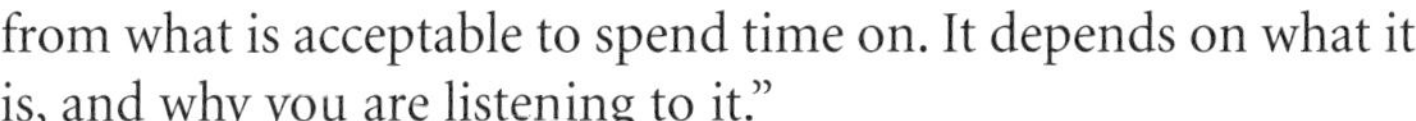

from what is acceptable to spend time on. It depends on what it is, and why you are listening to it."

## Holy Cooking

Food preparation is a devotional ritual for many people. One Hindu woman says she times her cooking by singing certain prayers. "When I begin stirring, I begin singing. When the prayer is done, the food is cooked." One Ojibway's method is similar. "You put your love and your light, your goodness into whatever you're doing," she explains. "I just use cooking as an example. People are happy to make good food, eh? For Native Peoples, everything we take from this earth that's given to us by the Creator—it's always an act of thanksgiving. So, while my mother prepared that tea, she asked for good health and happiness for anybody who would drink this tea. That makes a difference. If you don't pray over your food now, try it, and you'll see how different it is when you pray for blessings of that food."

Hare Krishna monks live together in an *ashram* (which can be a townhouse in the city, or a farmhouse in the country), cooking and eating their meals communally. "We offer all food (whatever we are preparing) to the Lord first," one monk explains, pointing to a shrine near the door. "*Prasadam* means 'mercy of the Lord,' and everything we eat is *prasadam:* it has been offered to the Lord formally before we eat it." Literally, everything is placed on the shrine for a time before it is taken to the table. "Our founder, Prabhupada, taught us how to cook. The consciousness of the cook goes into the food. We don't cook for our own enjoyment, but out of love for the Lord who supplied the ingredients. Everything we eat is sanctified."

## Improving the World

Practitioners of Afro-Caribbean religions might have a home-shrine in a corner—a canopied, multilevel structure filled collage-like with natural objects, icons, and candles. The Lùkùmì call them *tronos* (thrones), and characteristically, the objects they put on them include ceramic statues which look for all intents like Catholic saints (and may even be labeled as such), but their purposes will be different. There may be gifts and prayers to be left for the *orisha* (or for the *lwa,* in Vodou). There may be taboos to observe. "Sometimes, there are things you should not consume, because they are too close to your spiritual guardian; or colors you should avoid," explains one practitioner of Vodou. "Whatever constraints the spirits put on you, they're there to teach you something about how you are to move in the world." But, explains *manbo asogwe* Dowoti Désir, "Vodou is very much about ritual, about performance. *Manbo* means 'keeper of the medicine packet.' Our priestly titles, *manbo* (for women) and *houngan* (for men) reference our ability to contain a certain type of energy—positive, enriching energy—to help heal physically and to mend social ruptures as well." By using a "spiritually charged object," Vodou priests perform the task of "reassembling the fractured shards of people's lives."

In Vodou, worship makes use of a variety of objects and images, but *dwapo* are particularly characteristic. *Dwapo* are "flags" adorned with appliquéd, sequined, beaded depictions of any of the *lwa* and their character traits, and are used with the intention of pleasing the *lwa.* Dowoti Désir has a dozen or more adorning the walls of her home, which also serves as a counseling center for members of her "family" (the community of believers she has initiated). Her practice could be daily, but it isn't, she admits—at least, not in the ritualized or conventional sense. "Maybe I'm a bad priest because I don't sit down in my own shrine and pray every day, and I hope the *lwa* will forgive me for that. On the other hand, I am out there every single day, doing something to better my community, to improve the world I'm in. It that way, I am the embodiment of my prayers."

## Turning Back

Jain daily observance is characterized by practices that do not quite fit the categories of prayer or *puja* or meditation, but are at least as definitive. It begins with daily radical observance of *ahimsa* (the Jain doctrine of non-harming), and with it, the principles of *aparigraha* (non-greed, non-attachment, non-possessiveness) and *anekantwad* (non-absolutism; awareness that in every situation there is more than one way of seeing things).

These principles undergird the lay Jain practice of taking on more and more of a list of disciplines which are somewhat parallel to the ascetic practices of Jains monks and nuns—such as restraint in diet, clothing, and travel; meditating; fasting; various degrees of abstinence from sexual activity; abandonment of all household activity; and detachment from possessions and family. The purpose of taking on such increasingly rigorous discipline is rebirth as someone who will take the vows of an ascetic, and thereby will be able to achieve *moksha* (liberation). *Pratikraman* (literally, turning back) is a form of meditation during which devotees reflect on their spiritual journey, renew their faith, and ask for forgiveness for all mistakes and non-meritorious activities.

For people who have made vows, *pratikraman* is a formal chance to review how they have lived up to those vows in their ongoing effort to move to a higher level. For people who have not taken vows, *pratikraman* is an occasion to contemplate the day when they might be ready to take that step. "Many of us like to end the day with this ritual," says a nurse in the Long Island

Jain community. "We ask for forgiveness from any soul or anyone we may have hurt knowingly or unknowingly," a social worker explains. "When you wake up tomorrow morning, you don't want to have left anything unsettled."

As a formal means for daily repentance, *pratikraman* may well be the most important Jain ritual. It includes the *Navkar Maha Mantra* (Jainism's most important formula) and its traditional form takes three hours to complete, but a condensed version in English has been developed so that today's Jain laypersons will be more likely to hold onto this custom. Devout Jains perform it every morning and evening. However, some teachers say, if you can't manage that, do it once a day. And if that is too much, then do it once a month—or once a year!

## Making Merit

In its traditional environment, Theravada Buddhist observance involves daily ritual interplay between the laity and the *bhikkhus* (which we will call "monks" here, even though it is not the best translation) in which each group has its distinct role. The purpose of this interplay is *dana* (giving)—making merit. Devotees cannot get to Nirvana without it. This daily routine of exchange has been modified during the several decades since Theravada monastic life was planted in the United States. Back in Sri Lanka, there would be lay villagers or lay temple attendants to prepare breakfast and lunch for the monks. Most monks would spend some portion of each morning in walking meditation, standing with their "begging bowl" at house after house. Laypersons would place food in the monks' bowls; the monks would simply be present to the laypersons.

The American context has modified this custom, says one monk, but not the need for merit-making. "Sometimes people bring us lunch, or come from outside to prepare it here, or invite the monks to their home for lunch." This reciprocity of "caring for" and "being cared for" is *dana*—which takes many forms, says the abbot. "Answering the phone and giving information is also a certain *dana*—knowledge *dana*."

In Asia, late summer is monsoon season, so the monks stay in the *vihara* (monastery) but are available to give instruction. This retreat ends with a festival in the fall, at which the monks receive replacement robes from the laity. In the American adaptation of this custom, various families sign up to sponsor a day or a week of the retreat, a special "robe fund" collection box is stationed in one corner of the meditation hall, and the monastery kitchen is a busier place at lunchtime than is typical during the rest of the year.

## Journaling

For Won Buddhist ministers, says the Rev. Chung Ok Lee, daily practice includes the keeping of journals. "We have two different kinds of journals. One is what we call our *dharma* record—how we have mindfully changed our bad habits or practice meditation during the day. In the earlier days, women didn't know how to read or write. So our founder gave us black and white beans to put in our pocket. If you were mindful to select Right Mindfulness, Right Concentration, Right Thoughts, Right Conduct, Right Understanding, Right Speech, Right Action, Right Livelihood—the Eightfold Path—then you would put in a white bean. If you were not mindful, and you were angry at somebody, or reactive, or responding negatively, you would put in a black bean. You would do this all day, and in the evening, you would count the beans and see how you had lived your life. It was very practical. Even nowadays we keep track of our meditation and practice meditation-in-action in this way."

So that is the dharma journal. "The other one is our spiritual journal," she continues, "keeping a journal of your new awakenings, your impressions, and how you practice Won Buddhist teachings in your daily life. We record whether we are practicing or not, and whether our practice gave us a new awakening, a new way of seeing things."

## Pilgrimage

As we reflect on what we have learned in this book about private, congregational, and annual devotions, we may have noticed how often faith-rituals involve more than one of our senses—and sometimes, all five. We might recall the various uses and meanings made of such common life-sustaining elements as fire and water; the role of music; and the notion of holy space. The notion of holy space brings us to the practice of pilgrimage—a ritual of faith based on notions of sacred geography and sacred sites.

*Judaism*

Interestingly, three of Judaism's holidays are called pilgrimage festivals *(Pesach, Shavuot,* and *Sukkot)*. The Hebrew word for pilgrimage festival is *Hag.* It is related linguistically to the Arabic word *Hajj.* In ancient times, when the temple in Jerusalem was still standing, *Pesach, Shavuot,* and *Sukkot* were occasions for coming to Jerusalem to offer sacrifices. However, with the destruction of the temple by the Romans in 70 C.E., the practice had to be discontinued.

"Pilgrimage as a concept is no longer significant for modern Jewry," a Conservative rabbi asserts. "Since the reunification of Jerusalem after the Six Day War of 1963, some Jews have made an effort to visit Jerusalem and to pray at the Western Wall (the remnant of the ancient temple). But it's not like Islam, where going to a special city is a part of your obligation and completing your religious life. There is a longing to go to Jerusalem, and people make an effort to get there at some time in their lives, but it is not formal, and it's not called *Hag.*" A Reform rabbi concurs: "Going to Jerusalem doesn't have the quality of obligation I associate with 'pilgrimage,' and not all that many Jews go. You could be a perfectly adequate Jew and never go to Israel. Menachem Schneerson, the famous Lubavitcher Rebbe, never went to Israel!"

*Islam*

In other religions, however, pilgrimage is highly desirable, even mandatory. "I made *Hajj* twice in three years," says a Muslim chaplain. *Hajj* is one of the Five Pillars of Islam—one of its five normative practices. All Muslims are expected to make the journey to Mecca during the annual pilgrimage season at least once—health and means permitting. All of their debts should be paid, and they should have asked forgiveness of anyone they may have offended. The liturgy of the *Hajj* begins in the airport, with chants of readiness for the experience which lies ahead. Once in Mecca, everyone is dressed in white: men wrapped in two seamless lengths of cloth; women, similarly. A specific route is to be traveled, and specific actions are to be performed.

The *Hajj* is the world's largest annual gathering of humanity. "When I went on *Hajj*, there were four million people present," the chaplain recalls. "What sticks out in my mind? I suppose it was the impact of humanity in a sacred context—how an enormous gathering united both the highest and the lowest of human nature. We all had a single focus. And at the same time, all the complications and logistics of being a biological entity became enormously complicated: sanitation, food, sleep, moving from one place to another, sweat. The business of being a physical being is very much brought forward in the process of making *Hajj*. It was the juxtaposition of the two extremes that was so striking."

"At the same time," she continues, "I was overwhelmed by the breadth of human variety there. At the center of the *Hajj* experience, everybody is dressed more or less alike. But with that sameness were all kinds of tattoos and extraordinary facial features that don't resemble anything that we see in the States, even with all our diversity. There was all this difference, yet everybody dressed the same! Here again is a union of opposites. We were symbolizing our unity at the same time our difference was so prevalent. It's a very striking thing."

For the trip to Mecca to count as *Hajj*—as fulfillment of one of the pillars of practice—it must take place during *Dhu'l-Hijjah* (the final month of the Islamic calendar). However, Muslims may go to Mecca at other times of the year—and many do. This is called making *'Umrah*—making the lesser pilgrimage. The liturgy is similar, but a little less complex, and of course there are fewer people present. It may still, however, be a deeply emotional experience. "I was just eighteen years old," a fashion executive explains. "The opportunity to go to Mecca had arisen rather suddenly, so I can't say that I really prepared for it spiritually. But when I got close enough to the Ka'aba to see the famous black stone near the doorway, I was completely overcome. I sobbed and sobbed."

### *Bahá'í Faith*

"I made our Bahá'í pilgrimage to Haifa, Israel, last December," a classroom assistant explains. Why Haifa? "You see," she explains, "Bahá'ulláh was born and raised in Iran—as was the Báb. But he was imprisoned because he was spreading this new message. He was exiled, first to Iraq, then Turkey, then to what is now Israel—where he died. That is why the Bahá'í pilgrimage sites are in Israel. Bahá'ulláh's declaration of his mission was made in Baghdad. That is also a pilgrimage place, if it ever becomes safe." Different from Muslims, Bahá'ís have no special pilgrimage ritual to perform, "but we are encouraged to pray at the shrines," she says. "We go to the shrine of the Báb, the shrine of Bahá'ulláh, then we are taken on a tour of the various places where they lived."

"I was on my pilgrimage in March of last year," says a photographer. "There I was, in the holiest spot in the world for Bahá'ís, and I wasn't achieving what I had hoped to achieve. Of course, that is a sign of my own immaturity, but I was having a difficult time feeling connected to God. We can only stay in Haifa a total of ten days. We have to be out by sunset of the tenth day, if we're a pilgrim. That's out of respect for the Israeli government. So, I was very lucky when I got out of the bus on the morning of the tenth day. The other people in my group took off for the reception center immediately, but I went straight to the Shrine of Bahá'ulláh. And there was nobody else in there! I had it all to myself for fifteen minutes—which is very unusual. And during the quiet, it hit me—such a pure feeling, very mystical and powerful. Only once in my life have I ever felt that close to God. That feeling is so pure, and powerful, and wonderful."

Bahá'í pilgrimages take place almost continuously the year around. (The pilgrimage site administrators have an annual break for a month.) "We have to apply," the photographer explains, "and we can go more than once. I think if I were to apply today to go again, I'd have to wait about six years." This process is necessary, he explains, "because we're sending Bahá'ís from all over the world, and the sites can only take two hundred pilgrims each time."

"I put my name on the waiting list soon after I became a Bahá'í," says a medical student, "and it's been four years and I haven't heard yet." "I went in 1991," says a businesswoman, "and I applied again in 2000. I checked my status the other day, and probably I'll come to the top of the list sometime in June of this year. That means I may get to go sometime next year."

"My mother applied for pilgrimage when she became a Bahá'í—around 1979," says a teenager. "But it takes at least five years. So, in 1983, her time came up. By then, she was getting married to my father. He's Jamaican and she's American, and because of visa issues, she didn't go. She never applied again because of money and circumstances. Last December, she reapplied, thinking, 'Hmm, five years from now, we'll have the money; we'll be able to go!' But then in February, they sent her a message back which said that, because she didn't go the first time her name came up, they are still honoring that request. She got bumped up near the head of the list! And so, we're going *next* year—we just received our paperwork!"

### *Jainism and Hinduism*

The entire continent of India is dotted with pilgrimage sites for Hindus, Jains, Buddhists, and Sikhs. Devotees have their favorites. For American Jains and Hindus who are able to go back to India regularly, pilgrimage is part of the reason they make that trip.

In India, Jains have access to temples, holy sites, and *sadhus* (holy people) in a way that will never be possible in America. Since most Jain ascetics take a vow never to ride in vehicles again, the only way to spend time in their presence is to go to them. For this reason, the president of one midwestern Jain society spends a month in India several times a year. Jains engage in *vandanna*—the practice of prostrating before monks and nuns to express deep respect for them as spiritual guides. Jains who cannot get to India to honor them in person can accomplish *vandanna* by prostrating in the direction of India, where the *sadhus* are. There is also a category of Jain renunciate who is allowed to travel in vehicles. Occasionally, one of them will make a sort of pilgrimage to America in order to be present near the Jain community here, as did Acharya Shri Atmanandji during the summer of 2004. The word is spread, and Jains gather. This too is pilgrimage in a sense—albeit to Kings Park, New York.

"I go to the Seven Hills," says one Hindu temple administrator. "I do it every year." His destination is the sacred temple of Sri Venkateswara—also called the Balaji Temple—located north of the city of Chennai (formerly known as Madras). Sri Venkateswara means Lord of the Venkata Hill, and is a name of Vishnu. "Hindus go there even to get a glimpse of him! It is a big blessing, you know. It is for us like the Vatican for Catholics. You can get there by bus, train—even helicopter. (They have a heli-pad now.) I go by bus or train, but mostly I trek: I go by foot. We take a vow. It is enjoyable. It takes about four or four-and-a-half hours. People walk there by the thousands. When you get to the temple, you must wait for hours to get in. But the reward is that you can have a view of Sri Venkateswara."

To accommodate the constant crush of fifty thousand pilgrims a day, the shine is open eighteen to twenty hours at a time. The temple complex is huge, but since everyone's goal is to get inside the main shrine, the administration has devised a system. Pilgrims pick up a token upon arrival, and then they are free to wander the grounds and enjoy the spiritual benefits of the other shrines while they wait their turn for *darshan* (seeing and being seen by the *murti* of Vishnu).

Members of the BAPS movement are expected to make pilgrimage to Swaminarayan's birthplace in northern India, plus the six temples he established. "These are choice locations for reminding yourself of God," says one midwestern engineer. Members of this movement believe that Lord Swaminarayan was an *avatar* of Vishnu—that he was God incarnate. This means, the engineer explains, "we think that God was there at those temples. So you go and remind yourself: these are locations where God appeared. We try to go once a lifetime. You have to make the circuit of all the sites."

The circuit actually includes ten holy places, and visiting them all requires at least a week. "You have to go to all ten," the engineer explains. "I have done part of it. Our temple's priest has done all of it. I am honest. I will have to start over. You can't pick up where you left off! There is a sequence of temples. When they complete this, most people feel relieved, very spiritual. A lot of people feel that before their death they have to go on this pilgrimage." Most devotees plan on walking at least some of the distance. "You have to go through some difficulties," the engineer continues. "You can't just go in an air-conditioned bus. Then it is not personal. Pilgrimages should involve giving up something."

The Ganges River is a pilgrimage site in itself. It has been described in many ways in Hindu holy writings—as the sacred daughter of the Himalayas, as Shiva's hair, as Ganga-Ma (the Divine Mother). Devotees will try to bring back some of the water for use by the worshiping community until the next devotee can make the journey. "We use Ganges water for *puja*," one explains, "and to purify our ritual objects." A young professional adds, "When people go on pilgrimage to the Ganges, they'll mix some of the water they bring back into a larger pool of water, and consider that water to be 'Ganga-fied'! Other people believe that all water is ultimately Ganga water. I've done that. Last December, I was at a place right on the Pacific Ocean. I went down to do *puja* by the water. I thought of the water as Ganga. After all, the Ganges River dumps into the ocean, and eventually that water reaches California. You could make any water a Hindu pilgrimage site. I do that. Water *is* a pilgrimage site. Whenever I go to the Atlantic or Pacific Ocean, I take the water and apply it to my forehead as if it were Ganga. I think I have always done that. That's how I conceive of it. Ironically, if I went to the Ganga itself, I'd be less likely to scoop up the water and touch it to my forehead, because I'd be afraid of the pollution!"

One extraordinary pilgrimage takes place every three years. Called the *Kumbh Mela* (Nectar Fair), it rotates between four cities near the confluence of the Ganges and Yamuna Rivers (where the mythical Saraswati River is said to flow in as well). Any *Kumbh Mela* is an auspicious occasion. However, every twelve years, it is especially so—it is a *Maha Kumbh Mela* (Great Nectar Fair). And, every *twelfth* twelve-year fair is exponentially beneficial to attend. The most recent one, in 2001, was such an occasion—a Twelfth *Maha Kumbh Mela.* More than seventy million people attended over the course of forty-four days, making it arguably the largest ever ingathering of humanity for a specific purpose.

This holy bathing ritual is said to be at least two thousand years old. The idea is that bathing in the rivers—particularly at certain times during the festival—will enable the devotee to break free of *samsara* (the cycle of rebirth) and achieve *moksha* (liberation) upon death. The festival is also an opportunity for *darshan* with any of hundreds of *sadhus* (holy people) and *sannyasin* (renunciates), and to visit the local temples—some of which are exquisite.

All of this said, there are ways to go on Hindu pilgrimage without leaving America. In fact, says a retired diplomat, "going to any temple is a pilgrimage," and America has an increasing number of beautiful ones to visit. Providing for an American Hindu pilgrimage site was the reason behind the founding of the Divya Dham (Divine Place of Pilgrimage), a temple in Woodside, New York, which is housed in a rehabilitated warehouse. Its interior space includes an attempt to recreate Indian sacred geography on American soil.

Inside this temple, you first make your way past 1008 representations of Shiva. Then you come to fifty-one *murtis* of the divine feminine—various portrayals of the Goddess Sati (Shiva's consort). Further inside, you can circumambulate an enormous diorama of the Himalayas—an indoor replica of the very center of the universe, from one Hindu perspective. The temple founder's purpose in installing all this was, in part, educational. The diorama calls to the devotee's mind the many sacred narratives in which these mountains figure. Beyond this, however, he hoped that visiting this temple would have the same kind of physical, mental, and spiritual benefit a pilgrim would gain from a trip to India itself.

## Reflections

As we bring our survey of pilgrimage possibilities and other faith-filled observances to a close, there comes to mind an ancient Christian motto: *lex orandi, lex credendi* (the law of praying is the law of believing; praying shapes believing). It makes us puzzle: Does the way we worship (or practice or observe or reflect) indeed build up belief? "Praying shapes believing" suggests that our rituals of faith bring us into contact with the ineffable, which, because it is now real to us, leads us to faith. If it is true for Christians, might it also be the case for our neighbors? How do our neighbors' rituals of faith—the devotional habits they maintain day by day, week by week, and year by year—embody what they believe? How do ours? Or, should the motto be the other way around? Do our beliefs build up our worship? Does believing shape praying, or practicing, or observing, or reflecting? How do our non-Christian neighbors feel about this? These are interesting questions to raise with them.

And it is worthwhile to ask questions, rather than to jump to conclusions about our neighbors' rituals of faith. There is a broad range of those rituals—both in their engagement with the daily, regular, annual, and occasional devotional habits we have highlighted in this book, and in the meaning made of them. Suffice it to say that, while Orthodox, Reform, and Conservative are Jewish denominators, most of the religions we have encountered also have their traditionalists, their reformers, and their conservators—people who wish to remain faithful to traditional forms, but who wish at the same time to do some redefining at some level.

And speaking of forms, it is important to remember that a form may remain consistent outwardly, but carry very different meaning from one occasion to the next. We see that with the Zoroastrian *Jashan,* which looks the same whether it be held for a celebration or a funeral. We see it with Hindu *puja,* which looks the same whether the *murti* represents God-Above-All, or a sub-deity. We see it with Jain *puja,* which looks very much like Hindu practice; but Jains differ sharply from Hindus in their understanding of what the statue represents, and what kind of transaction the ritual accomplishes.

"Whenever I teach a group of students who come from many different Christian denominations," one professor points out, "no matter how I explain what happens in Christian worship, someone is bound to interject, 'But in my church, we don't do it that way.'" We will find great variety of practice, understanding, and explanation among our neighbors of other faiths. We will also find people whose practices derive from one of the religions we have discussed here, but who do not fit neatly into any of the categories we have used. That is to be expected. Multireligious America is full of people who stand ready to remind us, as did the Keetoowah woman who spoke about her pan-Indian prayer circle, "Our tradition is not frozen in time. It is living. It is organic."

# Endnotes

1. H. Byron Earhart, ed., *Religious Traditions of the World* (San Francisco: HarperSanFrancisco, 1993), 7.
2. See Exodus 3:14. For the entire story, see Exodus, chapters 3 and 4.
3. This comes from the teaching of the theologian Mardanfarrokh (ninth century C.E.).
4. These didactic descriptions can be very colorful. For examples, see: http://www.zarathushtra.com/z/article/fravahar.htm, or http://www-leland.stanford.edu/group/zoroastrians/faravahar.shtml.
5. Note the spelling: *Brahma* and *Brahmin* are terms with a similar look and sound, but they mean other things. A *Brahmin* is a member of the priestly caste, albeit not necessarily a priest *per se,* while *Brahma* is the Creator.
6. *Rig Veda* 1.164.46.
7. U. S. Government documents refer to the Anishinabe as "Chippewa." Some Anishinabe refer to themselves as Ojibway (often spelled Ojibwe).
8. The *adhan* is always delivered in Arabic. It may be translated as follows: "God is greater [than anything]" (4x); "I bear witness that there is no god but God" (2x); "I bear witness that Muhammad is the messenger of God" (2x); "Come to prayer" (2x); "Come to success" (2x); "God is most great" (2x); "There is no god but God." This is the Sunni version; the Shi'ah version has an additional phrase or two; and, for the dawn prayer, the Sunni call includes the line, "Prayer is better than sleep!"

9. *Jaap Sahib,* verses 84 and 159. Translated by Harjett Singh Gill (New Delhi: Gobind Sadan Institute for Advanced Studies in Comparative Religion).
10. A Madhva Brahmin is a member of the priestly class who follows Dvaita Vedanta (dualistic philosophy; the belief in the essential distinction between God and everything else, particularly between God and the human self).
11. "O Absolute, Ultimate Source of the Three Dimensions [earth, atmosphere, heaven]: we contemplate your light—the universal source of wisdom; may Divine Grace illuminate our intellect." *Aum Bhoor Bhuwah Swaha Tat Savitur Varenyam Bhargo Devasaya Dheemahi Dhiyo Yo Naha Prachodayat.*
12. The language of this mantra is Sanskrit and the transliteration here is a fairly standard one, but the Tibetan pronunciation is closer to *Om mani peme hung.*
13. *Baruch atah adonai eloheinu melech ha'olam shecheyanu v'kiy'-manu v'higyanu lazman hazeh.*
14. Qur'an 2:255, Abdel Haleem translation.
15. Ali is remembered by Sunni Muslims as the Fourth Rightly Guided Caliph (fourth successor of the Prophet in leadership of the Muslim community), and by Shi'ah Muslims as their First Imam (divinely inspired leader).
16. The Turkish spelling of this prayer's name is *Cevsenü'l-Kebîr;* the pronunciation remains the same.
17. *Al-Sahifat al-Kamilat al-Sajjadiya* (The book of one who constantly makes prostration).
18. *Venkateshwara* is a form sometimes taken by Vishnu in the *Puranas.* The *Puranas* are later Hindu scriptures which aim to clarify the teachings of the Vedas by means of stories.
19. Jeff Covey maintains the website of the Buddhist Network of Greater Baltimore, which is quoted with his permission. http://www.bngb.org/. Last accessed: February 22, 2005.
20. In explanations about Zoroastrianism, *Naw-Rúz* is sometimes spelled *Now-Rúz, Nau-Rúz,* or *Norooz.*
21. Technically, the Bahá'í calendar is called the *Badi* Calendar. The literal meaning of *Badi* is ambiguous: possibilities are "Wonderful" or "Beginning."
22. Dale Lehman's remarks are adapted from the "Planet Bahá'í" website, and are used with his kind permission. See http://www.planetbahai.org. Last accessed: February 21, 2005.

# Resources

## QUICK INFORMATION GUIDE TO RELIGIONS

The descriptions below are meant to give the reader with little or no background knowledge of the world's religions a *very* rudimentary orientation to the origins, beliefs, and practices of the religions discussed in *Faith in the Neighborhood.*

## Afro-Caribbean Religion

Afro-Caribbean religion is an umbrella term for adaptations of African traditional religion brought to the Western hemisphere during the Middle Passage (the era of slave-trading) include Vodou (Afro-Haitian religion) and Lùkùmì (Afro-Cuban religion, also called Santería). Sacred knowledge is conveyed by means of storytelling and sung narratives, which may exist in written form but not in the sense of a "holy book" equivalent to the Bible for Christians. Believers seek divine guidance from many sources.

*Beliefs:* The One Supreme God is believed to be manifested through spirits (called *lwa* in Vodou, or *orisha* in Lùkùmì) and ancestors. Sacred energies reaffirm each individual's ties to the spiritual realm, to ancestors, and to the community.

*Practices:* Autonomous practice-groups (called families) are formed through initiation. The initiates of a particular priest are his or her "children." Priests (women or men) perform rituals and healing exercises.

*To dig deeper:* Fernandez-Olmos, Margarite, and Lizabeth Paravisini-Gebert. *Creole Religions of the Caribbean: An Introduction from Vodou and Santeria to Obeah and Espiritismo.* New York: New York University Press, 2003.

## Bahá'í

The Bahá'í Faith was founded in mid-nineteenth-century Iran by Mírzá Husayn-'Alí Núrí, called Bahá'u'lláh by followers. Shoghi Effendi Rabbání (Bahá'u'lláh's grandson) established the Bahá'í administrative order and supervised the faith's spread worldwide. The writings of Bahá'u'lláh (more than one hundred volumes) form the core of Bahá'í scripture. The writings of Abdu'l Bahá (Bahá'u'lláh's son and interpreter) and Shoghi Effendi (his grandson) also have special status. Bahá'ís revere and use the sacred texts of the world's other religions as well.

*Beliefs:* According to its doctrine of progressive revelation, the Bahá'í Faith is the fulfillment of all prior religions, and provides divine guidance for this age. Bahá'u'lláh and his herald, the Báb (Sayyid 'Ali Muhammad), are revered as the Twin Manifestations of God who proclaimed God's message for the present age: the oneness of God, the oneness of religion, and the oneness of humankind. The Bahá'í Faith champions racial and gender equality, economic justice, universal education, ecological sensitivity, the essential harmony of science and religion, and the establishment of a universal language and a world federal system.

*Practices:* The Bahá'í Faith has clearly defined local, national, and international administrative principles, with all decision-making by consultation and consensus. A local assembly requires a quorum of nine members. There are no ordained clergy, and little in the way of prescribed rituals. Members are encouraged to pray, meditate, and read from the Bahá'í writings daily. They are obligated to practice chastity and monogamy, and to abstain from alcohol and drugs. They meet regularly in a home or community center for worship, consultation, and fellowship at the beginning of each of the nineteen months of the Bahá'í calendar. A fast is observed annually from March 2 to March 20.

*To dig deeper:* Momen, Moojan. *The Bahá'í Faith: A Short Introduction.* Oxford: Oneworld, 1997.

## Buddhism

Buddhism is a Western term for the many expressions of the teachings of the Buddha, Siddhartha Gautama (c. 563–483 B.C.E.), who rejected the extremes of excessive self-indulgence and rigorous asceticism for a Middle Way of morality, concentration, and wisdom. Theravada (Way of the Elders), the southern branch, is dominant in Sri Lanka and most of mainland Southeast Asia. Mahayana (Great Vehicle), the northern branch, took root in China, Tibet, Viet Nam, Korea, and Japan, and includes schools such as Pure Land, Nichiren, and Zen. Vajrayana (Diamond Vehicle), which emphasizes compassionate action and special practices under the guidance of a teacher, is considered a form of Mahayana by some scholars, and a distinct western branch by others. It is associated primarily (although not exclusively) with Tibet, but not all Tibetan Buddhists practice Vajrayana. All of the above are present in the United States, and a distinct and eclectic American Buddhism is emerging as well. A vast body of ancient authoritative literature is believed to be definitive records of the teachings of the Buddha himself, but no single collection of writings is revered by all Buddhists. Individual sects have generated authoritative literature in their own right up to the present time. Most American temples and practice-groups are autonomous.

*Beliefs:* The Buddha taught Four Noble Truths: that life inevitably involves suffering; that the origin of suffering is desire; that suffering will end when desire is extinguished; and, that desire is extinguished by following the Noble Eightfold Path (right understanding, thought, speech, action, livelihood, effort, mindfulness, and meditation). This will lead to achievement of Nirvana (cessation of participation in *samsara,* the endless cycle of birth, death, and rebirth). The Mahayana ideal is the Bodhisattva—one who attains Nirvana but refuses it, remaining in *samsara* in order to bring others to enlightenment. Traditionally, Buddhists "take refuge" in the Buddha, the *Dharma* (teachings), and the *Sangha* (community), but may differ in their interpretation of these terms.

*Practice:* All forms of Buddhism emphasize mindfulness—being fully present in whatever one is doing. Monasticism has a significant place in most forms of Buddhism, but lay and monastic roles are less differentiated in Mahayana. Daily devotional practice varies from branch to branch, but may include meditation, selfless service, paying respect to others, study, or chanting.

*To dig deeper:* Snelling, John. *The Buddhist Handbook: A Complete Guide to Buddhist Schools, Teaching, Practice, and History,* revised and updated. Rochester, Vermont: Inner Traditions International, 1999.

## Confucianism

Confucianism refers to beliefs and practices based on the socio-political teachings of K'ung Fu-tse (Master Kung). He lived in China, 551–479 B.C.E., and promulgated *Ju-Chiao* (the teachings of the scholars). Major texts are the *Analects* of K'ung Fu-tse, the *Doctrine of the Mean,* the *Great Learning,* and the writing of Mencius. Confucianism was the state religion of during several eras of China's history.

*Beliefs:* Confucianism seeks to create true spiritual nobility by developing the virtues. Its core concept is the importance of harmony in the family, the community, and the state. In Confucian understanding, the Tao is the way human beings should follow. "Heaven" is an ethical principle of orderliness.

*Practice:* Veneration of ancestors and deities, worship of Heaven, development of the virtues, and maintenance of essential societal relationships are to be done with attention to propriety and detail. Festivals are celebrated according to a lunar calendar, adjusted periodically to the solar agricultural seasons. Confucianism has long been practiced in conjunction with Taoism and Mahayana Buddhism as the Three Teachings.

*To dig deeper:* Jochim, Christian. *Chinese Religions: A Cultural Perspective.* Englewood Cliffs, N.J.: Prentice-Hall, 1986.

# Hinduism

Hinduism is Western label for *Sanatana Dharma* (Eternal Law), and is an umbrella term for a number of streams of beliefs and practices with roots in the Indian sub-continent. It has a vast heritage of sacred texts, including the Vedas, the *Upanishads,* and epics like the *Ramayana* and *Mahabharata.* However, no specific ones are authoritative for all Hindus everywhere. The *Bhagavad-Gita* (Song of God) is a well known portion of the *Mahabharata.* In addition to the ancient classic literature, some congregations give particular priority to the writings of their own current or founding spiritual leader.

*Beliefs:* In general, Hindus believe in Brahman: one Ultimate Reality—both ever-present and beyond time and space. Brahman is both impersonal and personal. Some understand Brahman-as-Personal is Vishnu; for others, it is Shiva. For still others, it is the Divine Mother (the Parashakti, called by various names such as Durga or Kali or Parvati). Others understand all of Hinduism's many deities as pointers to particular aspects, powers, and functions of the one Ultimate Reality. Hinduism teaches of *samsara,* an endless cycle of birth, death, and rebirth that causes each soul to transmigrate from one earthly existence to another and to progress toward maturity and achievement of *moksha* (release and return to Ultimate Reality). Hindus believe in *karma*—the moral and physical law of cause and effect. Following *Dharma* (divine law) brings one into harmony with Ultimate Reality. Some streams of Hinduism are monistic, teaching that the Ultimate Creator and all creatures are of the same substance.

*Practice:* Some Hindus are devotees of a particular deity and may consider themselves to belong to one of the three main sub-traditions of Hinduism: Shaivites (devotees of Shiva), Vaishnavites (devotees of Vishnu), and Shaktas (devotees the Divine Mother). Devotees of a particular guru (teacher and spiritual leader) may be identified by the name of the movement he or she founded. Hindu yoga (spiritual discipline) takes many forms: *karma yoga,* the path of selfless action; *raja yoga,* meditation or psychological exercises; *hatha yoga,* postures and breathing exercises; and *jnana yoga,* study. *Bhakti yoga* (devotional activities performed at a home or community shrine) includes *darshan* (seeing and being seen by holy images or people), *puja* (ritual offering to the deity), *abhishekam* (bathing a sacred image), *yajna* (fire sacrifice), or pilgrimage. Holidays are observed by *puja,* festivals, fasts, dance, chant, and readings or dramatizations of sacred texts.

*To dig deeper:* Eck, Diana. *Encountering God: A Spiritual Journey from Bozeman to Banaras.* Boston: Beacon Press, 1993.

## Islam

Islam is based on divine revelations received by the Prophet Muhammad (570–632 C.E.) in the Arabia peninsula, 610–632 C.E. For Muslims, the Qur'an, Islam's holy book, contains the very words of God, summarizing and superceding previous scriptures. Second in authority is the Prophet's *Sunnah* (his example—his own sayings and deeds), authenticated and compiled as the huge body of literature called the *Hadith* (report, tradition). Islam also has a vast legacy of literature on Islamic law, philosophy, theology, and mysticism. Islam's two major branches, Sunni and Shi'ah, agree on most matters of doctrine and practice, but differ on issues of authority. Sufism, whose adherents may come from either branch, denotes a broad range of belief and practice focusing on Islam's mystical dimension. Since the mid-1960s, most African American Muslims have been Sunni Muslims, but a few are Shi'ah, and others belong to movements such as the Nation of Islam that differ sharply from the mainstream in belief and practice.

*Beliefs:* Muslims believe that there is but One God, whom they call by the Arabic word Allah. God is unique and incomparable, but can be described in terms of attributes, such as "the Merciful" and "the Compassionate." God has created all that is, and has complete authority over human destiny. On the Day of Judgment everyone will be called to account. Spiritual heritage is traced to Abraham through his son Ishmael. The Ka'aba (the ancient shrine toward which all Muslim prayer is oriented) is said to have been erected by Adam and restored by Abraham, Islam's spiritual ancestor. Muslims believe God has sent many prophets, including Abraham, Moses, and Jesus, but that Muhammad is the "Seal," the last in this chain.

*Practices:* Islam has Five Pillars of obligatory practice: ritual testimony to God's oneness and Muhammad's messengerhood, ritual prayer five times a day, annual return of a percentage of one's wealth to the community, fasting during the month of Ramadan; and pilgrimage to the holy city of Mecca (health and means permitting). *Jum'ah* (congregational worship) is held on Fridays in the early afternoon. The Islamic calendar is lunar, and holidays shift through the solar seasons.

All Muslims believe in *Shari'ah* (divine law), the primary sources for which are the Qur'an and the Prophet's *Sunnah.* The sciences of Qur'an commentary and Islamic jurisprudence *(fiqh)*—of which there have always been multiple schools of interpretation—are the means by which divine revelation is applied to daily life. Islamic legal reasoning defines what Islam considers *halal* (permissible) and *haram* (prohibited) in all aspects of life.

*To dig deeper:* Elias, Jamal J. *Islam.* Upper Saddle River, N.J.: Prentice-Hall, 1999.

## Jainism

Jainism (from the Sanskrit *jina*—"conqueror" of one's inner passions) is an ancient Indian religion based on the notion that the cosmos goes through unceasing six-hundred-million-year cycles of integration and disintegration. With each eon of disintegration comes a series of twenty-four *tirthankaras* (crossing-makers)—great spiritual leaders who attain infinite knowledge, revive the Jain way of life, establish a monastic order, and assist in the liberation of countless other human beings. Mahavira (599–527 B.C.E.) was the twenty-fourth and last *tirthankara* for the current eon. His sermons provide the core of Jain scriptures, the *Agam Sutras,* but Jainism's two branches differ over the exact contents. Each branch also supplements this with scholarly works dating from the first ten centuries of the common era.

*Beliefs:* Jains believe that the universe is beginningless and endless. Nothing is ever created or destroyed. Everything undergoes continuous self-modification, without a divine manager. Jainism teaches that *perfect being*—pure consciousness with no *karma* attached to it—is attainable by all. Human beings who have rid themselves of all *karmas* break free of the wheel of *samsara* (worldly concerns) and become liberated, omniscient, omnipotent souls.

*Practices:* Jainism promotes religious tolerance, ethical purity, environmental harmony, and spiritual contentment. Its core principles are *ahimsa* (non-harming), *anekantwad* (non-onesidedness), and *aparigraha* (non-attachment). It advocates a life directed by right knowledge, right faith, and right conduct. Dedicated Jains take five vows: non-violence, truthfulness, non-stealing, celibacy, and non-attachment. Asceticism is the ideal. Jain monks or nuns take rigorous vows, and some laypersons take on an eleven-stage discipline of increasing renunciation. Jains practice strict vegetarianism, and many maintain a rhythm of regular fasting. Many (but not all) Jains employ images of one or more of the *tirthankaras* in their devotional practice.

*To dig deeper:* Tobias, Michael. *Life Force: The World of Jainism.* Fremont, Calif.: Jain Publishing, 1991.

## Judaism

Judaism is founded on the ancient Middle Eastern monotheistic religion of the people of Israel and their ritual practice which came to be centered in the temple in Jerusalem. Traditionally, Jews are defined as a people in relationship with the one and only Creator who established a covenant relationship with the patriarch Abraham, who spoke to humanity through Moses on Mount Sinai, and who gave a series of commandments by which this covenant people is to live. Judaism now refers to the system of beliefs and practices developed after the destruction of the temple by the Romans in 70 C.E. In place of temple sacrifice, Jews now are to engage in prayer, repentance, and *tzedakah* (giving of charity and striving for justice). Present-day Jews share a sense of peoplehood—a sense of history which includes exodus from slavery, receipt of a homeland designated by God, destruction of the homeland, diaspora, Holocaust, and return to the homeland by establishment of the modern state of Israel.

*Beliefs and Practices:* The home is central to practice. While the synagogue (from the Greek for "a gathering") is central to community life, some Jews choose to join a *chavurah* (friendship group), a *minyan* (prayer quorum), or a Jewish philanthropic or advocacy organization instead of—or in addition to—synagogue membership. During the twentieth century, American Judaism diverged into various philosophical and liturgical movements differing on interpretation of Torah and Talmud, thus in degree and style of practice—especially regarding rules of eating, dress, and Sabbath observance.

*Orthodox* refers to various current expressions (ranging from ultra-traditional to Hassidic to modern) of pre-Enlightenment traditional Judaism, all of which accept the divine authorship of the Torah, and the divine, binding, unchangeable nature of *Halakhah* (Jewish law). *Reform* sees the Torah and Talmud as divinely inspired, but humanly recorded. Observance is a matter of informed individual choice. Greater emphasis is put on ethics and social action than on ritual. Modernization of Jewish rituals and practices and broad use of the vernacular is encouraged. *Conservative,* a middle path between Orthodox and Reform, accepts the binding nature of *Halakhah* but interprets it more liberally than Orthodox Judaism. It returned the use of Hebrew in worship (although not exclusively), a move echoed by late twentieth-century Reform Judaism. *Reconstructionist* sees Judaism as an evolving civilization. It has always retained more traditional ritual and practice than the Reform movement, but with deep reinterpretation. It rejects explicitly the traditional Jewish notion of "chosenness." *Humanistic* combines non-theistic philosophy and humanistic values with celebration of Jewish identity and culture, and recasts liturgies and celebrations accordingly. *Jewish Renewal* is a transdenominational movement rooted in Jewish mysticism.

*To dig deeper:* Kushner, Harold. *To Life! A Celebration of Jewish Being and Thinking.* Boston: Little, Brown and Company, 1993.

## Native American Religion

This umbrella term for the beliefs, practices, and institutions of some five hundred fifty indigenous American societies with diverse languages, customs, and concepts of the divine includes the religions of particular nations such as Navajo, Keetoowah (Cherokee), or Lakota that have been reclaimed and continue to evolve. It also includes pan-Indian movements and associations that combine practices of many tribes and nations, and new religious movements such as the Native American Church. There is a rich oral tradition of sacred narratives and prayers, some of which are now in written form.

*Beliefs:* Broad generalities are difficult, but commonalities include a belief that everything has life, that all life has a spirit, and that all life is interconnected—which leads to a profound respect for the earth, plants, and animals. Most would affirm an essential monotheism with multiple realms of spiritual beings, and a certainty of life after death.

*Practices:* These may include agricultural and hunting rituals, ceremonies to honor passage from one stage of life to the next, use of totems, *shamanism* (use of spiritual specialists), and holistic approaches to health care.

*To dig deeper:* Martin, Joel W. *The Land Looks After Us: A History of Native American Religion.* New York: Oxford University Press, 2001.

## Shinto

The original name for Japan's ancient indigenous natural religion is *kami-no-michi.* The name Shinto—from the Chinese *Shen-tao*—dates from the sixth century C.E. Both mean "the way of the gods." Shinto has no canon of scriptures, but a colorful body of folk literature conveys basic beliefs, and several ancient collections of writings are deemed important.

*Beliefs:* Shinto-followers seek harmony with the *kami* (deities or spirits), manifest in natural phenomena, clan ancestors, and spirits of deceased emperors, saints, and heroes. Shinto maintains a positive attitude toward nature and life, but gives high priority to ritual purity. Pollution is believed to be caused by decay or bodily discharges (not moral guilt), and must be cleansed ritually. Human character and relationships must be kept healthy and pure. Shinto's esteem for nature speaks to today's ecological concerns.

*Practices:* Shinto practice includes worship at a public or home shrine, observing purification customs and the annual cycle of festivals. Some thirteen sects, dating from the nineteenth century, have their own characteristic practice style, and process for certifying priests.

*To dig deeper:* Ellwood, Robert S. and Richard Pilgrim. *Japanese Religion: A Cultural Perspective.* Englewood Cliffs, N.J.: Prentice-Hall, 1992.

## Sikhism

Sikhism was founded by Guru Nanak (1469–1539) in Punjab, India. After his death, the community was led by a series of nine Gurus, the last of whom died in 1708. The fourth Guru founded the Golden Temple, Sikhism's holiest site, in the city of Amritsar (from which the Sikh Code of Conduct is set and administered). The fifth Guru organized Sikhism's holy book, the *Guru Granth Sahib,* which contains hymns and writings of the first five Gurus, along with hymns and writings of Hindu and Muslim saints. The tenth Guru established the *Khalsa* (Community of the Pure) and the ritual of initiation. All Sikhs are followers of the Sikh *Panth* (Way); all initiated Sikhs (women and men) are members of the *Khalsa,* and some define the term more broadly. Sikhism has no clergy; anyone may lead worship. In the United States, local *gurdwaras* (houses of worship) are autonomous institutions, but some networking has been developed. The vast majority of Sikhs are part of the religion's mainline. Members of the movement founded by Yogi Bhajan (Harbhajan Singh, 1929–2004), the primary vehicle of conversion to Sikhism in the United States, speak of themselves as followers of Sikh Dharma, a term not generally used by other Sikhs.

*Beliefs:* For Sikhs, God is One, personal, omnipotent, the immortal creator of all. Sikhism teaches the brotherhood of humanity, rejection of caste, and futility of idol-worship. The goal is *moksha* (liberation): release into God's love, thus into everlasting bliss. Sikhs believe that, shortly before his death, Guru Gobind Singh (the tenth Guru) declared that ultimate authority would henceforth reside in Sikhism's holy book, rather than in a human guru. The *Guru Granth Sahib* is therefore regarded as a living teacher and object of highest sanctity.

*Practice:* Sikhs are to worship God, earn an honest living, and serve humanity. Communal worship features congregational prayer-singing and takes place in a *gurdwara* (Door of the Guru), which can be any room or building in which the holy book is the central object and treated with reverence. Individual worship includes daily ritual prayers and remembrance of God's holy name. The Sikh Dharma movement adds *kundalini yoga* to traditional Sikh practices. Some Sikhs undergo a ritual initiation called "taking *amrit.*" Sikhs may wear one or more of the Five Ks (five articles of faith): unshorn hair (which men usually cover with a turban), comb, underwear, a ceremonial dagger, and a steel bracelet. Initiated Sikhs must wear these articles, and are to abstain from alcohol and tobacco. They add Singh (Lion) if male, and Kaur (Princess) if female, to their name.

*To dig deeper:* Singh, Jasprit. *Style of the Lion: The Sikhs.* Ann Arbor, Mich.: Akal Publications, 1998.

## Taoism

The name "Taoism" arose to differentiate this ancient tradition from Confucianism. As an umbrella term, it holds together various longevity practices, a literary-philosophical tradition, and a plethora of sects which draw upon both. The *Tao-te Ching* (The Book of the Way and its Virtue) articulates Taoism's philosophical basis. Sectarian Taoism, dating from the second century C.E., has a priesthood and ordained ascetics. It exists in the United States, but practice-groups are more common, and participants may not necessarily consider themselves "Taoists." Taoism has long been practiced in conjunction with Confucianism and Mahayana Buddhism as the Three Teachings.

*Beliefs:* Tao is the unnamed first-cause of the universe, a force that flows through all life. The goal is to become one with the Tao through *wu-wei* (actionless action)—that is, allowing nature to take its course. The *yin-yang* symbol, an important concept in Confucianism as well, expresses the core principle of "balance out of chaos." It represents the complementarity of opposites, and the virtue of holding opposites in balance.

*Practice:* Emphasis is on maintaining the harmony of the family. In order to align oneself with the *Tao,* one may practice *Tai Ch'i,* the cultivation of *ch'i* (inner energy) by means of system of exercises, or *Ch'i-kung,* which promotes longevity and well-being by means of dynamic and static meditation postures. Folk Taoism involves many domestic rituals. Taoist practice may include ceremonial worship of deities (from the Jade Emperor to the Kitchen God), herbal medicine, *Feng Shui,* and more.

*To dig deeper:* Jochim, Christian. *Chinese Religions: A Cultural Perspective.* Englewood Cliffs, N.J.: Prentice-Hall, 1986.

## Zoroastrianism

Also called Zarathustrianism, Zoroastrianism is the western name for "The Good Religion." It is based on the teachings of the Prophet Zarathustra ("Zoroaster" in Greek), who lived sometime between 1200 and 550 B.C.E., in what is now Iran. Zoroastrianism was the state religion during three eras of Persian/Iranian history. It has been a significant presence in India since the ninth century, where adherents are known as Parsis. The religion's conservative wing insists on the authority of the entire *Avesta* (collection of sacred texts). For "progressive" or "liberal" Zoroastrians, only the *Gathas* (hymns arguably dating from Zarathustra himself) have authority. American Zoroastrians divide on these theological-philosophical grounds, the two streams differing significantly in belief and practice. Additionally, they may fall informally into denominations according to which of several calendars govern their annual observances. American worship centers are autonomous, but some networking has been established.

*Beliefs:* Zoroastrians worship Ahura Mazda (Wise Lord), the one God. Ahura Mazda is the uncreated, immanent, and transcendent source of all that is good, true, and beautiful, for whom fire is the only appropriate symbol. Fire may also symbolize the divine spark within every person. The *Amesha Spentas* (Bountiful Immortals)—Discerning Mind, Righteousness, Benevolence, Good Power, Perfection, and Immortality—are divine attributes which are to be emulated by humanity in order to bring about the perfection of creation, which is the ultimate goal. For traditionalists, the twin Spirits, Spenta Mainyu and Angra Mainyu, represent the good force and the destructive force. They are in constant battle, but ultimately, good will triumph by Ahura Mazda's power. Humanity has innate freedom of will, and when all human will is in harmony with God's will, Angra Mainya will be conquered. Assistance in choosing the good comes from angelic beings (the *Yazatas)* and one's guardian spirit (one's *Fravashi).*

*Practices:* Zoroastrians are to think good thoughts, speak good words, and do good deeds. The *Navjote* (the initiation rite) is the same for girls as for boys. Observant Zoroastrians pray five times daily in the presence of "clean" fire (symbol of God and of righteousness). The Zoroastrian priesthood is hereditary, and priests are necessary for the performance of the *Jashan* (the fire ceremony commemorating any important event).

*To dig deeper:* Boyce, Mary. *Zoroastrians: Their Religious Beliefs and Practices.* New York: Routledge, 2001.

## For General Reading

Eck, Diana. *A New Religious America: How a "Christian Country" Has Become the World's Most Religiously Diverse Nation.* San Francisco: HarperSanFrancisco, 2001.

Fisher, Mary Pat. *Living Religions,* sixth edition. Upper Saddle River, N.J.: Prentice-Hall, 2005.

Matlins, Stuart M., and Arthur J. Magida, eds. *How to Be a Perfect Stranger: The Essential Religious Etiquette Handbook,* third edition. Woodstock, Vermont: Skylight Paths Publishing, 2002.

Neusner, Jacob. *World Religions in America: An Introduction,* third edition. Louisville, Ky.: Westminster/John Knox, 2003.

# Glossary

*Abhishekam* (Hinduism): literally, to make wet all around, to bathe; the devotional act of pouring water, milk, and other substances over a *murti* (a statue of a deity).

*Acharya* (Hinduism, Jainism, Buddhism): in Hinduism, the teacher who presents the Sacred Thread and teaches the sacred doctrine and texts to a student; in Jainism, an ascetic teacher but not necessarily a fully ordained monk; in Buddhism, a teacher of *dhamma.*

*Adhan* (Islam): the call to prayer.

*Advaita* (Hinduism): non-dualism; the notion that the human self and Ultimate Reality actually are of the same essence; there is no real distinction between them, and any difference we *perceive* is due to ignorance.

*Ahimsa* (Jainism): non-harm; doctrine of non-violence.

*Ahura Mazda* (Zoroastrianism): literally, Wise Lord; the most common name for God.

*Aikido* (Shinto): Japanese program of martial arts, meditation, and development of personal and interpersonal awareness.

*Aleinu* (Judaism): Prayer of Adoration recited at the conclusion of prayer book services.

*Allahu akbar* (Islam): literally, God is greater; opening declaration of the *adhan* (call to prayer).

*Amaterasu-omikami* (Shinto): the Sun Goddess; the supreme deity.

*Ambika* (Hinduism): literally, Mother; the Ultimate-as-Feminine-Personal in gentle form; also, Amba.

*Amesha Spentas* (Zoroastrianism): Bountiful Immortals; interpreted either as six archangels, or as six attributes of God.

*Amidah* (Judaism): Standing Prayer; a long series of blessings, thanksgivings, and petitions in the Morning and Evening Prayer liturgies.

*Amitabha* (Buddhism): the Buddha of Boundless Light; also, Amida Buddha.

*Amrit* (Sikhism): nectar; sweetened water used for initiation; *Amrit Sanskar* (Sikhism): initiation rite; *amritdhari*, an initiated Sikh.

*Anekantwad* (Jainism): non-one-sidedness; the principle of respect for multiplicity of viewpoints.

*Angra Mainyu* (Zoroastrianism): the uncreated Destructive Spirit, source of evil.

*Aparigraha* (Jainism): the principle of non-attachment.

*Arahant* (Buddhism): a perfected being who has listened to and practiced the Buddha's teachings; also, *lo-han.*

*Ardas* (Sikhism): petition; lengthy concluding prayer for congregational worship, also part of the individual daily evening prayer rites.

*Arti* (Hinduism, Jainism): ritual offering of light.

*Ashram* (Hinduism): center for study and meditation, (often) the home of renunciates and their students.

*Ashura* (Islam): Arabic for "tenth"; Shi'ah commemoration of the martyrdom of al-Husayn (grandson of the Prophet) on the tenth of *Muharram* (the first month of the Islamic lunar calendar).

*Asogwe* (Afro-Caribbean): Vodou priest.

*Ason* (Afro-Caribbean): gourd rattle, Vodou symbol of priestly authority.

*Atahuna* (Native American): Keetoowah (Cherokee) festival of reconciliation and forgiveness.

*Atman* (Hinduism, Sikhism): the true Self underlying outward human appearance.

*AUM* (Hinduism; Jainism): the Primal Sound from which the universe evolved; also, OM.

*Avalokitesvara* (Buddhism): literally, the Lord Who Looks In Every Direction; the Bodhisattva of boundless compassion.

*Avatar* (Hinduism): the earthly manifestation of a deity.

*Avesta* (Zoroastrianism): holy book, including liturgical and legal material. *Avestan:* the ancient language in which the Zoroastrian holy books are written.

*Baisakhi* (Hinduism, Sikhism): for Hindus, Spring Festival; for Sikhs, a celebration recalling the establishment of the *Khalsa* (Community of Pure Ones) and the rite of initiation in 1699 by Guru Gobind Singh. Also, *Vaisakhi.*

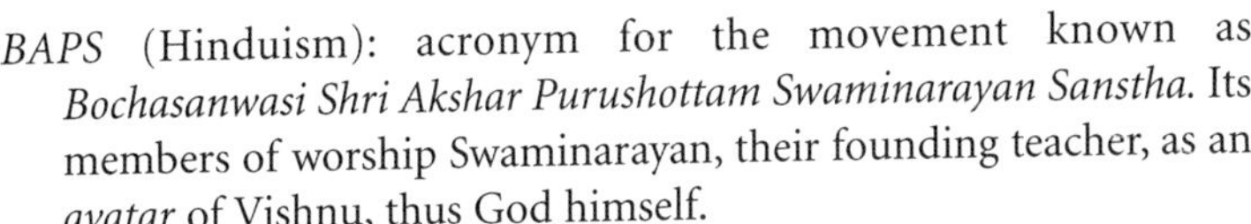

*BAPS* (Hinduism): acronym for the movement known as *Bochasanwasi Shri Akshar Purushottam Swaminarayan Sanstha.* Its members of worship Swaminarayan, their founding teacher, as an *avatar* of Vishnu, thus God himself.

*Bar Mitzvah* (Judaism): Son of the Commandment, a Jewish boy who has attained the age of thirteen and is now ready to be counted as an adult in the quorum necessary for communal prayer; the ceremony acknowledging attainment of this status.

*Bat Mitzvah* (Judaism): Daughter of the Commandment, a Jewish girl who has attained the age of twelve; the ceremony acknowledging attainment of this status.

*Berakhot* (Judaism): literally, blessings; formulas beginning "Blessed be God" to be recited on particular occasions, such as before and after meals.

*Bhagavad-Gita* (Hinduism): sixth book of the *Mahabharata* (a Hindu epic), in which Krishna teaches the path of spiritual progress.

*Bhagavan* (Hinduism, Jainism): One Who Has All Fortunes; in Hinduism, an epithet for Brahman as that which possesses wealth, knowledge, overlordship, valor, dispassionateness, and fame; in Jainism, an honorific for a *tirthankara;* in both, an honorific for a respected individual. Also, *Bhagawan.*

*Bhajan* (Hinduism, Jainism, Sikhism): chant, song of praise.

*Bhakti yoga* (Hindu): path of devotion.

*Bhavana* (Jainism): literally, to nurture or develop; exercises in contemplation and reflection.

*Bimah* (Judaism): platform in a synagogue from which the Torah is read, the *shofar* is blown, and the sermon may be preached.

*Bodhisattva* (Buddhism): one who achieves Nirvana, but refuses it in order to bring more beings to Enlightenment; the goal of Mahayana.

*Bon Dieu* (Afro-Caribbean): Afro-Haitian (Vodou) name for God; in Kreyòl (the language of Haiti), Bondjé.

*Brahma* (Hinduism): the personal Creator principle of the universe.

*Brahman* (Hinduism): Ultimate Reality, the impersonal ultimate principle.

*Brahmin* (Hinduism): priestly class, the highest of the four traditional castes.

*Busk* (Native American): Keetoowah (Cherokee) festival of purification.

*Ch'eng Huang* (Taoism): God of the City Wall and Moat.

*Ch'i* (Taoism): air, breath, strength; vital energy in living things; *Ch'i-kung:* breathing exercises, for the purpose of harnessing inner energies to develop spiritual awareness.

*Chado* (Shinto): the Way of Tea; tea ceremony.

*Chanukah* (Judaism): Festival of Lights; also, *Hanukkah.*

*Chaughadiya* (Jainism): segment; a ninety-minute period, one of sixteen in a twenty-four-hour day.

*Dambala* (Afro-Caribbean): the Great Serpent with its tail in its mouth, thus a Vodou cosmological symbol depicting the circle of life and death.

*Dana* (Buddhism): giving; merit-making.

*Darshan* (Hinduism): auspicious sight; seeing and being seen by the divine through an image or holy person or holy site. In Jainism, being in the presence of an image of the *tirthankaras* or a renunciate. Also, *darsan.*

*Das Lakshan Parva* (Jainism): Ten Virtues Festival; Digambara name for a ten-day observance of rigorous fasting, review of Jain principles, formal forgiveness-asking, spiritual review, and renewal of faith; also, *Das Lakshana Parva.* See also, *Paryushan Parva.*

*Days of Awe* (Judaism): ten-day period of reverence stretching from *Rosh ha-Shanah* to *Yom Kippur.*

*Devi* (Hinduism): Brahman as feminine; the Divine Mother as ultimate source; (for some), the feminine counterpart of a male deity.

*Dharma* (Hinduism, Buddhism, Jainism): literally, upholding. For Hindus, moral order, righteousness, religion. For Buddhists, the teaching of Buddha, and correct conduct for one's level of spiritual awareness. Theravada Buddhists may use the Pali *dhamma.* For Jains, the teaching of the *tirthankaras;* also, that which makes or encourages motion. Followers of Yogi Bhajan call Sikhism "Sikh Dharma."

*Dhikr* (Islam): acts of devotion involving repetition of the Names of God, praise formulas, or litanies, sometimes in conjunction with physical and breathing exercises; sometimes spelled *zikr.*

*Digambara* (Jainism): literally, one whose clothes are the sky; Jain branch characterized by ascetics who renounce clothing, and by the use of unadorned *tirthankara murtis* in temples and home shrines.

*Diné* (Native American): Navajo.

*Diwali* (Hinduism): Festival of Lights.

*Du'a'* (Islam): supplication.

*Durga* (Hinduism): one of the names for the divine feminine; Shiva's consort in her fiercely protective aspect.

*Dussehra* (Hinduism): Goddess Festival, also called *Navaratri.*

*Dvaita* (Hinduism): dualism; the notions that all things are different from one another in essence, and the most difference is between God and the individual self.

*Dwapo* (Afro-Caribbean): ritual flags with appliquéd, sequined, and beaded depictions of any of the *lwa* (spiritual entities) and their character traits. Also, *drapo.*

*Eid al-Adha; Eid al-Fitr* (Islam): see *Id al-Adha; Id al-Fitr.*

*Ekadashi* (Hinduism): the eleventh day after a new or full moon, to be marked by fasting and meditation featuring the chanting of the name of God.

*Elul* (Judaism): fourth month of the Jewish calendar, the month immediately preceding *Rosh ha-Shanah.*

*Fatihah, al-* (Islam): literally, The Opener; the first chapter of the Qur'an, which is also a key component of the obligatory prayer rite (see *salat*).

*Feng Shui* (Taoism): the practice of determining the most harmonious position for a building.

*Five Pillars* (Islam): the five normative practices— *shahadah* (testimony to God's Oneness and Muhammad's prophethood), *salat* (ritual prayer five times a day), *zakat* (return of a percentage of one's wealth to the community), *Hajj* (pilgrimage to Mecca at least once during the annual pilgrimage season, health and resources permitting), and *sawm* (fasting during the month of Ramadan).

*Five Precepts* (Buddhism): the five promises made by devout Buddhists—to avoid killing, stealing, lying, unchastity, and taking of intoxicants.

*Four Noble Truths* (Buddhism): the Buddha's essential teaching, that suffering (unsatisfactoriness) is the result of desire, and can be extinguished by following the Noble Eightfold Path.

*Four Stages of Life* (Hinduism, Jainism): Student, Householder, Retiree, Renunciate.

*Fravahar* (Zoroastrianism): ancient figure who looks like a bearded man astride widespread wings; his "saddle" is an unbroken ring, and below that extend tail-feathers and two long threads, each with a curl at the end. As an Avestan term, its meaning has been interpreted as "forward-pulling force" and as a form of the verb "to choose"; thus it may signify the *Fravashi* (guardian spirit) Ahura Mazda provides for each person, or the option to follow the tenets of the religion.

*Fravarti* (Zoroastrianism): Zoroastrian confession of faith; also, *Fravarane.*

*Fravashi* (Zoroastrianism): guardian spirit; pure, incorruptible spiritual idea of each and every entity created by Ahura Mazda.

*Fulu* (Taoism): power-filled line-drawing.

*Ganapati* (Hinduism): see *Ganesha.*

*Ganesha* (Hinduism): also, Ganesh; elephant-headed deity of wisdom and good fortune, the Remover of Obstacles, son of Parvati and Shiva. Sometimes called Ganapati.

*Gathas* (Zoroastrianism): hymns of Zarathustra; earliest Zoroastrian sacred texts.

*Gautama* (Buddhism): the Buddha's family name.

*Gayatri Mantra* (Hinduism): a prayer sometimes called the Mother of the Vedas (because some see it as a summary of the teachings of this early sacred literature), to be said as part of morning and evening devotions by "twice-born" Hindus (members of the upper three castes).

*Geh* (Zoroastrianism): watch; one of the five periods into which a twenty-four-hour period is divided.

*Gishiki* (Shinto): ceremony.

*Gi'-tchi Man-i-to'* (Native American): in the Algonquian language, Great Spirit, Life-Giver.

*Granthi* (Sikhism): the devotee whose duty it is to tend the *Guru Granth Sahib* (Holy Book) during worship.

*Gur Mantra* (Sikhism): the Punjabi phrase *Waheguru,* which means, literally, "praise to the Guru."

*Gurdwara* (Sikhism): Sikh house of congregational worship in which the Sikh holy book is installed.

*Guru* (Hinduism, Sikhism): for Hindus, a teacher, usually a renunciate; for Sikhs, one of the ten historic inspired leaders of the community.

*Guru Granth Sahib* (Sikhism): the Sikh holy book.

*Gzhemnido* (Native American): in the Algonquian language, Creator; a name of God.

*Hadith* (Islam): literally, tradition, report; an authoritative, authenticated account of something the Prophet Muhammad said or did; the body of such literature.

*Haftarah* (Judaism): literally, conclusion; a reading from the Prophets assigned as a companion to the Torah portion for the week or festival.

*Haggadah* (Judaism): Passover seder order of service, often with elaborations and commentary.

*Hajj* (Islam): pilgrimage to Mecca which is to be made during a specific period of the Islamic year, and which involves particular details of preparation and performance.

*Halakhah* (Judaism): Jewish legal system, or a particular part of it, derived from the Torah plus other scriptural and traditional material.

*Halal* (Islam): permissible, according to Islamic law.

*Haraigushi* (Shinto): ceremonial wand.

*Haram* (Islam): prohibited, according to Islamic law.

*Hatha yoga* (Hinduism): literally, sun-moon path to God; the ritual discipline of breathing exercises and postures.

*Hiddur Mitzvah* (Judaism): literally, beautification of the commandment; the making of beautiful ritual objects, or beautifying a ritual itself.

*Holi* (Hinduism): festival of colors.

*Holla Mohalla* (Sikhism): annual celebration inaugurated in 1680 C.E. by Guru Gobind Singh (1666–1708), featuring Sikh martial arts demonstrations and competitions.

*Homa* (Hinduism): fire sacrifice; synonymous with *yajna.*

*Ho-tei* (Buddhism): also, Mi-Lo-Fwo; the Happy Buddha, a popular depiction of the Buddha as benevolent.

*Hounfó* (Afro-Caribbean): Vodou ritual space—the temple and its grounds; also, *hounfor.*

*Houngan* (Afro-Caribbean): Vodou male priest.

*Hukam* (Sikhism): God's divine agency; also, the daily practice of opening the scriptures at random and reading a passage as God's directive for the day.

*Id al-Adha* (Islam): celebration feast ending the annual pilgrimage season; also, *Eid al-Adha* or *Idu'l-Adha.*

*Id al-Fitr (Islam):* celebration feast ending Ramadan; also, *Eid al-Fitr* or *Idu'l-Fitr.*

*Ik Ongkar* (Sikhism): Punjabi for "The Only One" or "There is Only One," thus a name of God, or the opening statement in the creedal prayer, the *Mool Mantra;* as calligraphy, a Sikh symbol used on the Sikh flag; sometimes, *Ek Ongkar.*

*Imam* (Islam): leader, particularly of communal prayer; in Shi'ah Islam, one of a series of authoritative and divinely-guided leaders of the entire community.

*Jaap Sahib* (Sikhism): 199-verse hymn taken from the Sikh scriptures, one of the five texts recited daily by initiated Sikhs.

*Jade Emperor* (Taoism): deity who is creator of earth and heaven, and determines all that happens in both; also, Yu-huang.

*Japji* (Sikhism): a thirty-eight-stanza hymn composed by Guru Nanak which stands at the beginning of the *Guru Granth Sahib,* and itself begins with the *Mool Mantra;* one of the five hymns initiated Sikhs recite daily.

*Jashan* (Zoroastrianism): an important occasion or an important event; and, the communal ceremony commemorating or celebrating it, performed by a priest and making use of a fire-urn.

*Jawshan al-Kabir* (Islam): literally, the Great Armor; a one-hundred-stanza supplication reflecting on God's attributes; also, *Cevsenü'l-Kebîr* (Turkish spelling).

*Jina* (Jainism): literally, "conqueror"; one who conquers one's passions and need for attachment.

*Jinn* (Islam): in Islamic cosmology, beings created out of fire, but sharing some qualities with humans, and ranking below them and the angels.

*Jnana yoga* (Hinduism): the path to God through study.

*Ju-Chia* or *Ju-Chiao* (Confucianism): literally, School of Scholars; the original Chinese label for what K'ung Fu-tse taught.

*Jum'ah* (Islam): literally, assembly; the weekly congregational prayer, held at midday on Fridays.

*K'ung Fu-tse* (Confucianism): Confucius (c. 552 B.C.E.).

*Ka'aba* (Islam): literally, cube; the building in the center of the great mosque in Mecca, toward which Islamic prayer is oriented.

*Kaddish* (Judaism): holy, in Aramaic; doxology ending the individual sections of Jewish liturgy; *mourners' kaddish:* prayer said at the end of each service by close relatives of the deceased during the year following his or her death, and on the anniversary of the death.

*Kali* (Hinduism): literally, black; the divine feminine in ferocious or terrifying form; the terrifying aspect of the divine Creator; the Hindu Goddess of Life and Death, or Transformation and Power, or Enlightenment and Liberation.

*Kaliyuga* (Hinduism): in Hindu cosmology, an "age of strife" equivalent to 4,320,000 solar (or lunar) years, the last of four increasingly disorderly "great ages"; the world is said to be in the midst of a *kaliyuga* which began in 3102 B.C.E.

*Kami* (Shinto) (plural or collective as well as singular): the extraordinary, the sacred, but also individual deities or spirits.

*Kamidana* (Shinto): deity-residence; a home shrine (often a high shelf).

*Kannushi* (Shinto): priest

*Karah prashad* (Sikhism): pudding distributed at the end of the prayer service to all in attendance at Sikh communal worship.

*Karma* (Hinduism, Buddhism, Jainism): for Hindus and Buddhists, moral law of cause and effect; for Jains, particle residue on one's soul from all of one's actions, both positive and negative.

*Karma yoga* (Hinduism): the path to God through action; the spiritual discipline of selfless service.

*Karttikeya* (Hinduism): a son of Shiva; deity of war and pestilence; also, Skanda, Kumara, or Muruga.

*Kashrut* (Judaism): fitness; food acceptable for consumption, according to Jewish dietary laws.

*Kayotsarga* (Jainism): meditation method based on renunciation of physical comfort and bodily motion.

*Keetoowah* (Native American): Cherokee.

*Khalsa* (Sikhism): literally, Pure; the community of initiated Sikhs.

*Khutbah* (Islam): sermon (particularly for Friday midday prayer).

*Ki* (Shinto): power from Divine Nature

*Kiddush* (Judaism): sanctification; *kiddush* cup: cup used in Sabbath dinner ritual.

*Kirpan* (Sikhism): dagger, sword; one of the Five Ks.

*Kirtan* (Hinduism; Sikhism): devotional hymn-singing, often with instrumental accompaniment.

*Kosher* (Judaism): see *kashrut.*

*Koshinsatsu Takeagehiki* (Shinto): annual festival of purification by burning, featuring destruction and replacement of spent ritual objects.

*Kreyòl* (Afro-Caribbean): the language of Haiti, and the spelling preferred by Vodouisants; also, Creole.

*Krishna* (Hinduism): an *avatar* of Vishnu.

*Kshatriya* (Hinduism): warrior class, the second of the traditional "twice-born" castes in the traditional Hindu system.

*Kuan-Yin* (Buddhism): the one who hears the sound of the world; the Bodhisattva of Compassion as feminine.

*Kumara* (Hinduism): a son of Shiva; see *Karttikeya.*

*Kundalini yoga* (Hinduism, Sikh Dharma movement): the Path to God through creating and sustaining the power of the whole body by means of an integrated system of exercise, breath control, and meditation.

*Kushti* (Zoroastrianism): sacred cord worn wrapped several times around the waist by initiated Zoroastrians, which is untied and retied during ritual daily prayer.

*Lakshmi* (Hinduism): Goddess of Wealth; Consort of Vishnu.

*Lama* (Buddhism): literally, Higher One; a Tibetan Buddhism monk, particularly recognized to be the reincarnation of a great spiritual teacher.

*Langar* (Sikhism): a free communal vegetarian meal at a *gurdwara,* served and eaten in a way which demonstrates the abolition of caste.

*Lo-han* (Buddhism): see *arahant.*

*Lùkùmì* (Afro-Caribbean): Afro-Cuban religion.

*Lwa* (Afro-Caribbean): in Vodou, spiritual entities, similar to *orisha* in other Afro-Caribbean religions.

*Maha Mantra* (ISKCON): defining chant of the Krishna Consciousness movement.

*Mahabharata* (Hinduism): The Great Story of the Bharat Family (or, The Great Story of India); an epic which includes the *Bhagavad-Gita.*

*Mahayana* (Buddhism): literally, Great Vehicle; the northern stream of Buddhism.

*Mahayuga* (Hinduism): in Hindu cosmology, a "great age," said to be equivalent to 4,320,000 solar or lunar years.

*Maheshvara* (Hinduism): literally, Great Lord; personification of Shiva's veiling aspect or function.

*Maitreya* (Buddhism): literally, "the Friendly and Benevolent One" or "One Who Possesses Loving-kindness"; a ninth-stage Bodhisattva, one step away from being a fully enlightened Buddha.

*Mala* (Hinduism): prayer beads.

*Manbo asogwe* (Afro-Caribbean): a female Vodou priest; a male priest is *houngan asogwe.*

*Mandir* (Hinduism): temple.

*Mantra* (Hinduism, Jainism, Buddhism, Sikhism): literally, an instrument of thought; a sound, word, or phrase (sometimes thought to be of divine origin) chanted to evoke the vibration of an aspect of creation, to focus meditation, or as an act of praise.

*Matsuri* (Shinto): festival.

*Megillah* (Judaism): literally, scroll; most often refers to a scroll containing the story of Esther.

*Menorah* (Judaism): candelabra; seven-branched candlestick, the earliest symbol of Judaism.

*Mezuzah* (Judaism): literally, doorpost; a small box containing passages from Deuteronomy, placed on the right-hand doorposts into and within Jewish homes and businesses.

*Middle Passage* (Afro-Caribbean religion): the longest, most horrific part of the journey of slave ships from West Africa during the period of trans-Atlantic slave trade.

*Midrash* (Judaism): literally, interpretation; a kind of literature which engages in the interpretation of the Jewish scriptures.

*Mikvah* (Judaism): Jewish ritual bath.

*Minchah* (Judaism): afternoon prayer service.

*Minyan* (Judaism): quorum of ten adults (men, for Orthodox Jews) necessary for Jewish communal worship.

*Mishnah* (Judaism): the first compilation of the Oral Law; a compendium of legal opinion dating from approximately 200 B.C.E. to 200 C.E., organized under six broad headings (agriculture and tithing, Sabbath and holidays, family law—including marriage issues, civil and criminal law, rules concerning Temple sacrifice, and ritual purity laws); the sages cited are called the *Tannaim* (the Teachers), but are sometimes also referred to as "the Rabbis."

*Misogi* (Shinto): purification ritual in water (under a waterfall, in the sea, or in a river).

*Mitzvah* (Judaism): commandment.

*Mobed* (Zoroastrianism): priest—an hereditary office; *ervad* and *dastoor (dastur)* may also be used; men not of the priestly class who have been trained and authorized to perform certain duties and ceremonies are called *mobedyar.*

*Moksha* (Hinduism, Jainism): release, liberation (that is, from *samsara*—the cycle of rebirth); sometimes, *moksh.*

*Mool Mantra* (Sikhism): Punjabi for "basic sacred formula"; affirmation of faith, one of the first compositions of Guru Nanak, and the first entry in the *Guru Granth Sahib* (Sikh holy book).

*Muharram* (Islam): first month of the Islamic lunar calendar, the first ten days of which are observed as a period of mourning for the death of al-Husayn (a grandson of the Prophet) by Shi'ah Muslims.

*Murti* (Hinduism, Jainism, Buddhism): literally, form or embodiment; usually, a statue used for devotional purposes.

*Muruga* (Hinduism): see *Karttikeya.*

*Nam* (Sikhism): Punjabi for "name"; a designator for "God."

*Nagoshi-no-Oharai* (Shinto): day of Great Purification in the annual cycle during which stagnant *ki* (natural energy) from the first half of the year is purified and replaced.

*Namaste* (Hinduism): literally, I bow to you; traditional Indian greeting, often interpreted as "the divine in me greets the divine in you."

*Nandi* (Hinduism): the bull, Shiva's vehicle.

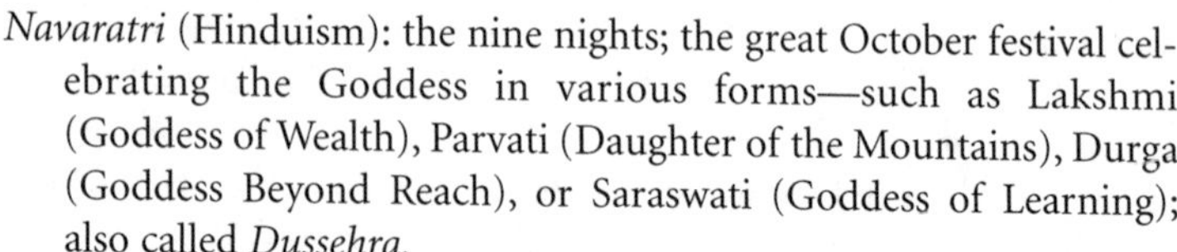

*Navaratri* (Hinduism): the nine nights; the great October festival celebrating the Goddess in various forms—such as Lakshmi (Goddess of Wealth), Parvati (Daughter of the Mountains), Durga (Goddess Beyond Reach), or Saraswati (Goddess of Learning); also called *Dussehra.*

*Navjote* (Zoroastrianism): literally, New Birth or New Worshiper; ancient rite of initiation.

*Navkar Maha Mantra* (Jainism): the Great Salutation Formula; Jainism's most important formula, also known as the *Pancha Namaskara* (the fivefold salutation) because it pays homage to the five categories of spiritual beings: the *arahants,* the *siddhas;* the living spiritual leaders; the teachers of the scriptures; and all renunciates.

*Naw-Rúz* (Bahá'í, Zoroastrianism): in Farsi, New Day; ancient Persian New Year observance incorporated into Bahá'í and Zoroastrian practice because of the Iranian roots of these religions; other spellings include *Now-Rúz, Nau-Rúz,* and *Norooz.*

*Nembutsu* (Buddhism): Japanese for "mindfulness of the Buddha"; the Pure Land Buddhist practice of chanting the phrase, "I take refuge in the Amida Buddha."

*Ner tamid* (Judaism): Eternal Light; a light kept burning over the ark (a synagogue's storage place for Torah scrolls).

*Nichiren* (Buddhism): a Japanese Buddhist reform movement named for a monk who lived 1222 to 1282, and which considers the Lotus Sutra to be the most genuine embodiment of the Buddha's teachings.

*Nien-fwo* (Buddhism): Chinese for "mindfulness of the Buddha"; see *nembutsu.*

*Nirvana* (Buddhism): cessation of participation in *samsara,* the endless cycle of birth, death, and rebirth.

*Nishan Sahib* (Sikhism): Punjabi for "respected flag," the triangular flag flown over *gurdwaras.*

*Noble Eightfold Path:* as taught by the Buddha in his inaugural sermon, the way to earn release from suffering (thus rebirth)—right (or perfect, or complete) understanding, motives, speech, action, livelihood, effort, mindfulness, and meditation.

*Non-kesadhari* (Sikhism): a Sikh who has cut his or her hair.

*Obon* (Buddhism): Japanese Buddhist Hungry Ghost Festival; a season celebrated by drumming, singing, and dancing. It includes the Floating Lantern Ceremony in memory of those who have died; in other cultures a similar festival may be called *Ullabana* (hanging down).

*Oceti Sakowin Oyate* (Native American): the Seven Campfires Nation, for whom Lakota is one of the historic languages.

*Odaimoku* (Buddhism): literally, Sacred Title; the mantra of Nichiren Buddhists: *Namu Myoho Renge Kyo* (I take refuge in the sublime Lotus Sutra).

*Ogun* (Afro-Caribbean): Yoruba for Lord of Iron, sometimes represented with St. George statuary.

*Olodumare* (Afro-Caribbean): Yoruba for "Entity"—thus God as First Cause, self-existent, self-born, and self-sustaining; the omnipresent, immutable, reliable, source of all wisdom.

*Olorun* (Afro-Caribbean): Yoruba for Sky-Resident, thus God as transcendent.

*Orisha* (Afro-Caribbean): Yoruba for a deity; sometimes used to mean West African traditional religion in general.

*Oriyoki* (Buddhism): literally, taking just enough; the monastic practice of eating mindfully.

*Oshogatsu* (Shinto): Japanese New Year (January 1).

*Pali* (Buddhism): the Indian dialect in which the Buddha's teachings were first recorded.

*Pancha Namskara* (Jainism): see *Navkar Maha Mantra.*

*Panj Pyarey* (Sikhism): the Five Beloved; the five men who came forward when Guru Gobind Singh asked who would give his or her life for the faith, an act which led to the founding of the *Khalsa* and the rite of initiation; or, five initiated Sikhs who conduct a rite of initiation.

*Panth* (Sikhism): Way; the whole Sikh community.

*Parashakti* (Hinduism): Eternal Divine Mother; the feminine aspect of the Supreme; Brahman as feminine.

*Parsi* (Zoroastrianism): a member or descendent of the community of Zoroastrians in residence in India since the eighth century C.E.; also, Parsee.

*Parvati* (Hinduism): literally, Daughter of the Mountain (Himalaya); a name of the feminine aspect of Ultimate Reality; consort of Shiva; mother of Ganesha.

*Paryushan Parva* (Jainism): Coming Together Festival; Swetambara name for an eight-day period of rigorous fasting, review of Jain principles, formal forgiveness-asking, spiritual review, and renewal of faith; also, *Paryushana Parva.* See also *Das Lakshan Parva.*

*Péristyle* (Afro-Caribbean): in Vodou, a temple's interior space which is open to the public and distinguished by having a large tree which acts as a centerpost.

*Pesach* (Judaism): Passover; the Feast of Unleavened Bread—an eight-day recollection of escape from slavery into freedom through divine intervention.

*Phylacteries* (Judaism): see *tefillin.*

*Pongal* (Hinduism): harvest festival in mid-January.

*Potlatch* (Native American): ceremonial feast which includes gift-giving.

*Poto mitan* (Afro-Caribbean): centerpost of a Vodou temple.

*Powwow* (Native American): family or community social event including such activities as dance competitions; sometimes an occasion for marking the anniversary of the death of a relative.

*Prasadam* (Hinduism, Jainism, Buddhism, Sikhism): blessed food; also, *prashad* or *prasad.*

*Pratikraman* (Jainism): literally, returning from violations; formal review of any vows, repentance, and forgiveness-asking.

*Pratima* (Hinduism, Jainism): literally, a reflected image; a deity-statue; see *murti.*

*Puja* (Hinduism, Buddhism, Jainism): literally, respect, homage; rituals of offering in which an image (of a deity, or the Buddha, or a *tirthankara*) is treated as an honored guest.

*Pujari* (Hinduism, Jainism): usually, a temple staff-member with special training for performing the daily rituals of offering and respect-paying.

*Punjabi* (Sikhism): the language of the region of northern India in which Sikhism emerged; people, things, customs from that region.

*Punya* (Hinduism): acquisition of good *karma,* or merit.

*Purim* (Judaism): holiday commemorating the heroism of Queen Esther on behalf of the Jewish people.

*Rabbi* (Judaism): teacher; synagogue leader. "The Rabbis" refers to the ancient sages whose opinions are cited in the Talmud, and/or who helped to codify Jewish scriptures.

*Raja yoga* (Hinduism): royal yoga, which features eight "limbs" or steps: restraint (abstinences), discipline (observances, such as austerity and devotion), postures, breath-control, sense-withdrawal, concentration, meditation, and *samadhi* (super-conscious state of union with the divine through total self-surrender).

*Rama* (Hinduism): *avatar* of Vishnu.

*Ramadan* (Islam): the month of the annual daybreak-to-sunset fast.

*Ramayana* (Hinduism): The Rama Vehicle; with the *Mahabharata,* one of the two major Hindu epics.

*Ridván* (Bahá'í): a twelve-day spring festival commemorating Bahá'í founder Bahá'u'lláh's declaration of his mission in 1863.

*Rosh ha-Shanah* (Judaism): New Year.

*Rúz* (Bahá'í, Zoroastrianism): literally, day; also, *ros, roz.*

*Sacred Thread* (Hinduism): a knotted cord worn over one shoulder by "twice-born" Hindu boys and men (and some upper-caste girls and women) who have gone through a ceremony marking their transition to the Student Stage of Life.

*Sadashiva* (Hinduism): Shiva as Revealer, one of his five functions or aspects.

*Sadhu* (Hinduism, Jainism): renunciate.

*Sake* (Shinto): rice wine.

*Sakoiatisan* (Native American): in the Haudenosaunee (Iroquois) language, the Ultimate Great Mysterious Force.

*Salat* (Islam): the obligatory prayer rite.

*Salawat* (Islam): supplication requesting God's blessing on the Prophet.

*Samayik* (Hinduism; Jainism): the meditation practice of "staying in equanimity" by giving up attention to worldly affairs, attachment, aversion, passions, or desires.

*Samsara* (Hinduism, Jainism, Sikhism, Buddhism): the cycle of life, death, and rebirth.

*Sanatana Dharma* (Hinduism): Eternal Law or Eternal Teaching; umbrella term for a cluster of modern expressions of ancient Indian religious tradition; Hinduism itself.

*San-chiao* (Buddhism, Confucianism, Taoism): the Three Teachings; the symbiotic relationship between Chinese Buddhism, Confucianism, and Taoism.

*Sangat* (Sikhism): group or association, especially a congregation gathered to praise God in the presence of the *Guru Granth Sahib* (holy book), where everyone, Sikh or not, is treated equally.

*Sangha* (Hinduism, Jainism, Buddhism): the community, including monks, nuns, lay men and women; in Theravada Buddhism, the community of monks, and in some countries, nuns; in Mahayana Buddhism, all Buddhists, lay and ordained.

*Sannyasin* (Hinduism): one who has entered the classic Fourth Stage of Life by formal renunciation of all ties to family, name, caste, and property, and thus is believed destined for *moksha* (liberation from *samsara*) upon dying.

*Sanskrit* (Hinduism): the classical language of Hindu scriptures.

*Santería* (Afro-Caribbean): literally, "saint worship," Afro-Cuban religion.

*Saraswati Puja* (Hinduism): ritual performed on last night of *Navaratri.*

*Satsang* (Hinduism): devotional gathering.

*Sensei* (Buddhism, Shinto): Japanese for "teacher," a term of respect. for martial arts instructors, Pure Land priests, and Zen priests below the rank of Roshi.

*Setsubun* (Shinto): New Year according to old Japanese lunar calendar.

*Shabbat* (Judaism): seventh day of the Jewish week, observed from sundown Friday until an hour past sundown on Saturday, by worship and abstinence from work.

*Shahadah* (Islam): testimony, specifically the formula, "I bear witness that there is no god but God; Muhammad is the Messenger of God."

*Shaivite* (Hinduism): those for whom Shiva is Brahman-as-Personal; also, Shaiva.

*Shakti* (Hinduism): divine creative power as feminine, consort of Shiva; *Shakta*—one who worships Brahman-as-Personal as the Eternal Mother (often in the form of Kali or Durga).

*Shakyamuni* (Buddhism): alternate name for Siddhartha Gautama (the Buddha), which refers to his membership in the Shakya tribe.

*Shari'ah* (Islam): literally, "the broad path that leads to water"; Divine Law.

*Shavuot* (Judaism): Feast of Weeks; also called Pentecost.

*Shaykh* (Islam): elder; learned spiritual leader, often of a Sufi circle.

*Shehecheyanu* (Judaism): blessing said in thanksgiving for a new or unusual experience or long-awaited occasion.

*Shi'ah* (Islam): branch of Islam whose members assert that Ali (the Prophet's son-in-law) should have succeeded Muhammad as leader of the Muslim community upon his death. It differs somewhat from Sunni Islam on certain matters, including which collections of *Hadith* are considered authoritative, and in certain details of practice.

*Shiva* (Hinduism): for some Hindus, Ultimate Reality itself; for others, the Personal Cosmic Destroyer aspect of God; sometimes, the third deity of the Trimurti (with Brahma and Vishnu); also, Siva.

*Sh'ma* (Judaism): creedal statement beginning "Hear, O Israel: The Lord your God, the Lord is One...."

*Shofar* (Judaism): ram's horn blown on *Rosh ha-Shanah.*

*Siddha* (Jainism); a perfected soul.

*Siddhartha* (Buddhism): the Buddha's given name; also, Siddhartha Gautama.

*Siddur* (Judaism): prayer book; specifically, a book of liturgies for Jewish services.

*Simchat Torah* (Judaism): literally, Joy of Torah; a celebration of the completion of the annual Torah lectionary.

*Skanda* (Hinduism): see *Karttikeya.*

*Smudging* (Native American): the burning of herbs for purposes of purification; *smudge:* the smoldering herbs.

*Sofer* (Judaism): someone specially trained to copy Torah by hand.

*Soto* (Buddhism): one of the two major schools of Zen.

*Spenta Mainyu* (Zoroastrianism): the Holy Spirit of Zoroastrian cosmology.

*Subha* (Islam): prayer beads; also, *tasbih.*

*Subramanya* (Hinduism): see *Karttikeya.*

*Sudreh* (Zoroastrianism): undergarment worn by initiated Zoroastrians.

*Sufi* (Islam): a Muslim mystic who has placed himself or herself under the guidance of a *shaykh,* and has been initiated into a *tariqah* (practice-circle, or Order).

*Sukkot* (Judaism): Feast of Booths, or Tabernacles.

*Sunnah* (Islam): example; usually, that of the Prophet Muhammad.

*Sunni* (Islam): follower of the Prophet's example; mainstream Islam.

*Sutra* (Buddhism): literally, thread; a collection of the Buddha's teachings.

*Swetambara* (Jainism): literally, white-clad; the branch of Jainism in which male and female renunciates wear white garments.

*T'ai-chi ch'üan* (Taoism): a method of physical and mental discipline consisting of slow, graceful movements.

*Taiowa* (Native American): in Hopi language, the Ultimate Great Mysterious Force.

*Tallit* (Judaism): rectangular prayer shawl with tassels on each corner; *tallit katan:* a rectangular undergarment with tassels on each corner

*Talmud* (Judaism): the authoritative compendium of rabbinical commentary on the Mishnah, including legal, ritual, theological, and ethical material.

*Tao,* the (daw) (Taoism, Confucianism): the Way, the Path; for Taoism, the "unnamable," thus the metaphysical absolute, the way of passive acceptance and mystical contemplation; for Confucianism, the right way within the human world.

*Taqwa* (Islam): God-consciousness, leading to righteousness, dutifulness, and piety.

*Tasbih* (Islam): prayer beads; also, *subha.*

*Tawhid* (Islam): assertion of God's absolute Oneness; acceptance of all that the fact of God's Oneness implies.

*Techina* (Judaism); plural, *techinot:* a genre of women's supplication literature.

*Tefillat ha-Derekh* (Judaism): Prayer for Traveling.

*Tefillin* (Judaism): black leather boxes worn on the head and left arm by observant adult male Jews during the weekday morning prayer ritual; also called *phylacteries.*

*Tetragrammaton* (Judaism): YHWH; God's unpronounceable name.

*Theravada* (Buddhism): literally, the Way of the Elders; the surviving expression of the earliest schools of Buddhism; sometimes called Hinayana (Lesser Vehicle).

*Three Baskets* (Buddhism): the *Tipitaka* (Pali) or *Tripitaka* (Sanskrit), the vast collection of the Buddha's teachings and rules for the monastic life which is authoritative for Theravada Buddhists.

*Three Teachings* (Chinese religion): see *San-chiao.*

*T'ien* (Taoism, Confucianism): Heaven; the timeless, omniscient, omnipresent, impersonal governing power.

*Tilak* (Hinduism): a dot of red powder applied between one's eyes as a devotional act; *tilak chandlo:* the dot plus a U of yellow sandalwood paste applied to their foreheads by members of the BAPS movement as part of their morning devotions.

*Tirthankara* (Jainism): ford-maker, crossing-maker; someone capable of guiding others out of the endless cycle of worldly affairs; one of the twenty-four inspired teachers who appear during each eon to perform this function for humanity, Mahavira being the most recent.

*Torah* (Judaism): the Five Books of Moses; the Pentateuch; more broadly, the entirety of Jewish sacred texts.

*Trimurti* (Hinduism): Sanskrit for "three-formed", thus the three interrelated manifestations of Ultimate Reality as creator, sustainer, and destroyer.

*Triple Jewel* (Buddhism): in Pali, *Tiratana;* in Sanskrit, *Triratna;* the formula affirmation of faith, by which one "takes refuge" in the Buddha, the *Dharma,* and the *Sangha;* also, Triple Gem, or Triple Refuge, or Threefold Refuge.

*Trono* (Afro-Caribbean): in Afro-Cuban religion, canopied, multilevel structures used as shrines for the *orisha.*

*Tsao Chün* (Taoism): Lord of the Stove; the Kitchen God.

*Tunka'sila* (Native American): in the Lakota language, "grandfather," a name of God.

*T'u-ti Kung* (Taoism): Earth God.

*Twice-born* (Hinduism): the upper three levels of traditional Hindu society—*Brahmin* (priestly), *Kshatriya* (warrior), and *Vaishya* (merchant).

*Tzedakah* (Judaism): justice, righteousness; thus, the duty of giving to those in need.

*Uku* (Native American): Keetoowah (Cherokee) Priest's Festival.

*Upanishads* (Hinduism): a body of literature that completes the Vedas, and lay out key doctrines such as *karma, samsara,* and reincarnation.

*Vahid* (Bahá'í): in Bahá'í cosmology, a nineteen-year unit; in the Farsi language, "one" or "unity."

*Vaishnava* (Hinduism): one for whom Brahman-as-Personal is Vishnu; also, *Vaishnavite.*

*Vaishya* (Hinduism): third of the four "twice-born" castes; traditionally, the caste of merchants, businessmen, and farmers.

*Vajrayana* (Buddhism): Diamond Vehicle; a sub-branch of Mahayana Buddhism that emphasizes compassionate action and special practices under the guidance of a teacher.

*Vandanna* (Jainism): the practice of prostrating before monks and nuns to express deep respect for them as spiritual guides for the present.

*Vedanta Society* (Hinduism-based, though members do not usually call themselves "Hindu"): an ethical-spiritual movement based on the *Upanishads,* established by Swami Vivekananda in New York in 1896, essentially a Western branch of the Ramakrishna movement in India.

*Vedas* (Hinduism): knowledge; ancient scriptures forming the basis of Hindu belief and practice; the *Rig Veda* is the oldest of these collections.

*Vihara* (Buddhism): monastery (Sri Lankan Theravada term).

*Vipasanna* (Buddhism): literally, to see particularly; the practice known as insight meditation.

*Vishnu* (Hinduism): for some Hindus, Ultimate Reality itself, incarnating repeatedly for the sake of the material world; for others, the Personal Sustainer aspect of Ultimate Reality, thus preserver of the universe; sometimes, the second deity of the Trimurti (with Brahma and Shiva).

*Vivekananda, Swami* (Hinduism): charismatic teacher, 1863–1902; a disciple of Ramakrishna who, by attending the Parliament of the World's Religions (Chicago, 1893), broadened awareness of Hinduism in the United States.

*Vodouisant* (Afro-Caribbean): an adherent of Vodou (Afro-Haitian religion); in Kreyòl, *Vodouwizan.*

*Wacipi* (Native American): among the Oceti Sakowin Oyate, the name for the kind of celebration often called powwow.

*Waheguru* (Sikhism): the Almighty; God.

*Wakan Tanka* (Native American): Lakota name for the Ultimate Great Mysterious Force.

*Wei-to* (Buddhism): the Protector.

*Wesak* (Buddhism): festival commemorating the Buddha's birth, enlightenment, and departure into Nirvana; also, *Vesak.*

*Worldview* (All): the doctrine or philosophy, narratives, rituals or practices, experiences, ethical or legal understandings, and institutions by which one makes sense of the world, and answers questions such as "Why are we here?" and "What happens when we die?"

*Wudu'* (Islam): washing ritual to be performed in preparation for obligatory prayers.

*Wu-wei* (Taoism): actionless action; non-action, non-striving.

*Yajna* (Hinduism): fire sacrifice.

*Yaum* (Islam): day (twenty-four-hour period), or, occasion; *Yaumu'l-Jum'ah:* Day of Gathering, Friday, on which Muslims are expected to gather in a mosque to perform the midday obligatory prayer and to hear a *khutbah* (sermon).

*Yazatas* (Zoroastrianism): divine beings much like archangels.

*Yin-yang* (Taoism, Confucianism): balance out of chaos; the complementarity and necessity of opposites.

*Yoga* (Hinduism): path or ancient method for attaining release from *samsara.*

*Yom Kippur* (Judaism): Day of Atonement; highpoint of the Jewish year, observed with a twenty-five-hour fast and seeking forgiveness from one's neighbors and associates.

*Yoruba* (Afro-Caribbean): referring to the religion of people of this language-group from Western Africa (particularly Nigeria).

*Zazen* (Buddhism): sitting meditation; the primary practice of Zen Buddhism.